Advancements in Cyber Crime Investigations and Modern Data Analytics

This book presents a fresh perspective on combating cyber crime, showcasing innovative solutions from experts across various fields. With the integration of artificial intelligence (AI), contemporary challenges are addressed with state-of-the-art strategies. The book discusses a wide range of timely issues within the domain of cyber crime and investigation, emphasizing AI-driven solutions and future multidisciplinary perspectives. As data becomes central to all digital interactions, it also becomes increasingly vulnerable, making it a prime target for adversaries. This comprehensive volume compiles technical approaches to counter, investigate, and manage these complex avenues of misconduct under the umbrella of "Cyber Crime."

Key Topics:

- LLMs as a Solution for SARs Triaging
- Technical Capacities to Counter CSAM
- A Journey of Mobile Forensic Investigation
- Digital Forensics Solving Financial Crimes
- Deepfake-Driven Financial Crimes and Countermeasures

This book offers a thorough examination of the current landscape of cyber crime, the capabilities available to combat it, and the advanced measures required to stay ahead. A detailed roadmap of digital forensics, the science of decrypting cyber crime, is a key highlight, alongside an exploration of the rising capabilities of AI. We extend our gratitude to all the contributors and hope this book answers many questions while igniting curiosity and providing a stimulating intellectual experience.

Abhishek Pradhan
Nextechno Gen Pvt. Ltd., Delhi, India

Mukund Purohit
National Forensic Sciences University, Gandhinagar, India

Phil Legg
School of Computing and Creative Technologies, University of the West of England, UK

Nicholas Ryder
School of Law and Politics, Cardiff University, UK

Shishir Kumar Shandilya
School of Data Science and Forecasting, Devi Ahilya Vishwavidyalaya, Indore, India

Devangana Sujay
SECURE – Centre of Excellence in Cyber Security, VIT Bhopal University, Bhopal, India

Reuben Walker
Synalogik Innovations Limited, UK

Contributors

Haresh Barot
National Forensic Sciences University, Gandhinagar, India

Samantha Bourton
Bristol Law School, University of the West of England, UK

Luca Cadonici
European Forensics Institute

Chitrak Chakraborty
VIT Bhopal University, India

Agni Datta
SECURE – Centre of Excellence in Cyber Security, VIT Bhopal University, Bhopal, India

Bhag Dei
Bahra University, Waknaghat, Solan, India

Diana Johnson
Bristol Law School, University of the West of England, UK

Vineet Kapoor
Madhya Pradesh Police, Bhopal, India

Beemamol M
Pondichery University, India

Sakalya Mitra
VIT Bhopal University, India

V.B. Gupta is a Professor and Head of the School of Data Science and Forecasting at Devi Ahilya Vishwavidyalaya (DAVV) in Indore, India. He has a Ph.D. from the Indian Institute of Technology, Delhi, and has over 30 years of experience in teaching and research. His areas of specialization include data science, mathematical modeling, simulation, environmental management, technology diffusion and systems engineering. Dr. Gupta has published over 70 research papers in national and international journals and conferences. He is a member of the System Dynamics Society of India and has reviewed several research papers submitted in national and international journals. He has served as member of several academic committees of University Grants Commission, New Delhi. He developed several P.G. programs. Dr. Gupta is a passionate advocate for the use of mathematical modeling and simulation to solve real-world problems. He is a strong believer in the power of education to transform lives and societies.

About the Editors

Shishir Kumar Shandilya is an Associate Professor in the School of Data Science and Forecasting at Devi Ahilya University in India. He is also a Visiting Professor at Liverpool Hope University in the United Kingdom. He is a Cambridge University-certified professional teacher and trainer, a TEDx speaker, an ACM Distinguished Speaker, and a senior member of IEEE. Shandilya is a NASSCOM-certified master trainer for security analysts in SOC (SSC/Q0909: 7 NVEQF Level 7). He has received the IDA Teaching Excellence Award for distinctive use of technology in teaching by the Indian Didactics Association in Bangalore (2016), and the Young Scientist Award for two consecutive years, 2005 and 2006, by the MP Science Congress and MP Council of Science and Technology. He is a highly regarded author with published research works in reputable academic publishers such as Springer, IGI-USA, River Denmark, and Prentice Hall of India. Dr. Shandilya also has international and national patents and copyrights granted for adaptive cyber defense methods. His research interest includes adaptive defense, advanced digital investigation and forensic methods, explainable artificial intelligence, privacy-preserving computing, nature-inspired cryptography (NIC), and Nature-inspired cyber security (NICS).

Devangana Sujay is an independent researcher in the field of digital forensics. Her research topics range from admissibility of digital evidence to child sexual abuse material and privacy preservation. Her core competencies relate to digital forensics, cyber security, and cyber law. She works at SECURE – Centre of Excellence in Cybersecurity as a coordinator and has done studies in the area of digital forensics. She has also had the experience of working with the Data Security Council of India as Technology Policy Intern. Her other affiliations include being an active member of WiCyS-Women in Cybersecurity and BBWIC-Breaking Barriers Women in Cybersecurity.

Contents

Designed cover image: © Shutterstock

First edition published 2025
by CRC Press
2385 NW Executive Center Drive, Suite 320, Boca Raton FL 33431

and by CRC Press
4 Park Square, Milton Park, Abingdon, Oxon, OX14 4RN

CRC Press is an imprint of Taylor & Francis Group, LLC

ISBN: 9781032742700 (hbk)
ISBN: 9781032748276 (pbk)
ISBN: 9781003471103 (ebk)

DOI: 10.1201/9781003471103

Typeset in Sabon
by Newgen Publishing UK

Advancements in Cyber Crime Investigations and Modern Data Analytics

Edited by

Shishir Kumar Shandilya, Devangana Sujay, and V.B. Gupta

CRC Press
Taylor & Francis Group
Boca Raton London New York

CRC Press is an imprint of the
Taylor & Francis Group, an informa business

Acknowledgements

We unequivocally believe in being thankful in action not by just saying "thank you" or just acknowledging them to show our gratitude for someone's assistance. We are fortunate that our journey in digital forensics and cyber crime started way back, but over the period of time it got concrete and was sculpted by Dr Shishir Kumar Shandilya, our co-author and mentor. His mentorship has been a guiding light throughout the entire process of writing this book. We would like to extend special thanks to Dr. V.B. Gupta, Professor and Head SDSF at Devi Ahilya Vishwavidyalaya, Indore. His guidance, support, and profound knowledge have been invaluable during the process of editing this book. We would like to express our deepest gratitude to all the contributors of this book for their unique insights and diligent research that have played an integral role in the creation of this comprehensive work. Their expertise and dedication have made this book a valuable resource in the field of cyber crime investigation.

All our beloved authors have reflected high levels of research capabilities, and we thank them for their dedication to the community of cyber security, cyber crimes, and research and for bringing forward their valuable insights into combating today's battle.

We would also like to extend our sincere thanks to our families, friends, and colleagues for their support and encouragement throughout the process of editing this book. We are grateful to our publishers, CRC Press – Taylor and Francis, especially Radhika and her team, for their commitment, and attention to each detail that has been instrumental in bringing this book to fruition.

Lastly, but by no means least, we would like to acknowledge our readers. We hope that this book will serve as a useful tool in your journey to understand and combat cyber crime, and we look forward to your feedback and engagement.

DAVV, Indore, India – **Dr Shishir Kumar Shandilya**
VIT Bhopal, India – **Devangana Sujay**
DAVV, Indore, India – **Dr V.B. Gupta**

Chapter 1

Introduction to Cyber Crime Investigation

A Modern Approach

Agni Datta, Devangana Sujay, and Shishir Kumar Shandilya

1.1 INTRODUCTION

Today, investigators face increasingly daunting challenges in their investigation of truth. The surge in data volumes, diverse data types, and a proliferation of distributed data sources are rendering traditional investigative methods increasingly inadequate. The stakes are higher than ever. *Have you ever considered the precise role of the forensic scientist who arrives at a crime scene?* Forensic science refers to the scientific analysis of evidence gathered at crime scenes. Someone astutely observed, "*When the wrong people use something new, it can achieve greater success than its creators.*" Ironically, this observation rings true with ever-expanding technology. Blockchain and artificial intelligence (AI) are prime examples; their initial buzz mirrored a similar pattern. Despite predating modern law enforcement, forensic science has a rich history and has emerged as an indispensable tool for law enforcement agencies (LEAs) in the modern era.

Forensic science aids law enforcement by furnishing precise and impartial analyses of crime scene evidence, facilitating suspect identification, timeline verification, and comprehension of the crime's circumstances. Where once much of the observational evidence at crime scenes relied solely on the human eye, current best practices incorporate advanced techniques like fingerprinting, DNA testing, and chemical analysis. These advanced forensic methods hold promise for resolving previously unsolvable cold cases, fostering enhanced accuracy and equity in the judicial process. While cautious adoption of new technologies is essential to mitigating unintended negative repercussions, the potential upsides are undeniable. The field's evolution over the next few decades promises to be captivating.

It's crucial to underscore that forensic science supplements rather than supplants traditional investigative methods. Law enforcement agencies meld conventional investigative approaches – such as interviews and surveillance – with forensic science to ensure a comprehensive, accurate investigative outcome. Forensic science shines brightest when it corroborates and substantiates conclusions drawn from witness testimony and other evidence.

DOI: 10.1201/9781003471103-1

Now, digital forensics, an emerging subfield, will assume increasing importance as more information migrates to electronic devices, paralleled by a rise in digital crimes. We anticipate that innovative developments will bolster forensic capabilities, yielding faster, more precise, and adaptable investigations. The era of forensics heralds a new paradigm in cyber crime investigation, with a focus on mobile, cloud, and network forensics, particularly Internet of Things (IoT) and drone forensics. The identification and collection of potential evidence vary significantly depending on the state of its parent device; for example, collecting evidence from a functional phone differs markedly from gathering it from a powered-off device. The acquisition process, tools, and techniques used entail extensive procedures with significant practical implications.

1.2 CYBER CRIME

Here, we present a comprehensive and technologically adept guide for tackling different instances of cyber crime. This entails transitioning from security breaches to incidents and from incidents to investigations, particularly through the complex process of digital forensics. Cyber crime encompasses a wide array of criminal activities executed via digital devices and/or networks. These offenses involve utilizing technology to commit fraud, identity theft, data breaches, computer viruses, scams, and other malicious actions. Cybercriminals exploit vulnerabilities in computer systems and networks to gain unauthorized access, steal sensitive information, disrupt services, and inflict financial or reputational harm on individuals, organizations, and governments.

In 2000, the tenth United Nations Congress on the Prevention of Crime and the Treatment of Offenders classified cyber crimes into five groups: unauthorized access, damage to computer data or programs, sabotage to impede the functioning of a computer system or network, unauthorized interception of data within a system or network, and computer espionage. Both state and non-state actors globally engage in cyber crimes, including espionage, financial theft, and other transnational offenses. Cyberwarfare involves cyber crimes that surpass international borders and involve the actions of at least one nation-state. Throughout history, a timeline of cyber crime assaults and assailants has been documented. One consistent factor in this chronology is the evolution of technology, serving as both a tool for malicious attackers and a defense mechanism for safeguarding cyberspace. From the Morris worm and Melissa virus to more recent threats like Androxgh0st and Akira, the world has faced a plethora of cyber threats, though the ultimate objectives of these malicious actors remain elusive. Taxonomizing categories of cyber crime is challenging, as it's difficult to create an all-encompassing list of types. Regardless, we can provide a succinct list highlighting major categories:

- **Computer Fraud:** Manipulative practices targeting computer systems for financial gain or malicious purposes.
- **Cyberterrorism:** Targeting critical infrastructure, government systems, or civilian populations to cause fear, disruption, or harm.
- **Cyberextortion:** Using digital threats to coerce individuals or organizations into paying a ransom.
- **Ransomware:** Encrypting files on a victim's computer, demanding ransom for decryption.
- **Cybersex Trafficking:** Exploiting vulnerable individuals for sexual purposes.
- **Cyberwarfare:** Nations engaging in cyberattacks to exert influence or gain strategic advantage.
- **Computers as a Tool:** Used for illicit activities such as money laundering and intellectual property theft.
- **Obscene or Offensive Content:** Anonymity of the Internet enabling dissemination of harmful content.
- **Ad-Fraud:** Manipulating online advertising systems for financial gain.
- **Online Harassment:** Anonymity emboldening abusive behavior online.
- **Drug Trafficking:** Dark web facilitating drug trafficking using cryptocurrencies and encryption. Further examination reveals additional categories, such as data theft, cyberterrorism, child pornography, and violations of intellectual property rights.

Distinguishing between cyber crime and cyberattack involves navigating fine lines, as while security has legal counterparts, attacks and their tools serve as vectors for perpetrating crimes. From a technical perspective, attacks can use a multitude of methodologies.

1.3 DIGITAL VIOLENCE AND CYBER CRIME

In organizations, cyberbullying involves using technology such as social media, email, instant messaging, or other digital platforms to harass, intimidate, or humiliate someone in the workplace. This behavior can have a profound impact on both individuals and the organization, leading to decreased morale, increased turnover, reduced productivity, and higher absenteeism. Moreover, cyberbullying can result in legal and financial repercussions for both the victim and the organization. To combat and prevent cyberbullying, organizations can implement clear policies and procedures for online behavior, offer training on appropriate digital communication, and respond swiftly and effectively to reports of cyberbullying. By promoting a culture of respect and accountability, organizations can work to prevent cyberbullying and ensure a safe and supportive workplace for all employees.

The concept of cyberbullying is particularly thought-provoking given our current world, characterized by digital violence in which cyber attackers now outnumber serial killers. Digital violence entails the misuse of digital technologies and tools, such as computers, smartphones, and Internet of Things devices, to inflict harm. Generally, professionals use "digital violence" as an umbrella term to encompass various forms of abuse and harassment. Digital violence can occur concurrently with physical violence and often intersects with offline violence. Both strangers and acquaintances can perpetrate it, and it can take place publicly on digital platforms, privately on personal devices, or in other digital spaces such as virtual reality or the blockchain. Intuitively, we can say that digital violence is deeply rooted in systems of oppression, including cis-heteropatriarchy, white supremacy, homophobia, transphobia, and misogyny. The groups most vulnerable to violence in real life are also the most vulnerable to online abuse and harassment. Although survivors often bear the burden of implementing prevention strategies, they can never fully prevent abuse, and it is never their fault.

Digital violence covers a wide range of criminal acts committed over the Internet, often through channels like email or text messages. The integration of smartphones and computers into our daily lives has transformed and accelerated many aspects of our existence, a trend that will continue with ongoing technological advancements. While the Internet offers many benefits, it also has significant drawbacks. Topics that influence people in real life can quickly go viral on the web. Current world events, wars, societal tensions, and the increasing brutalization of society are just a few examples. The Internet has become a major platform for fraud, violence, hatred, and hate speech.

Social networks, in particular, often feature harsh and rude language. Derogatory and inhumane content typically targets vulnerable individuals and minorities, including women, homosexuals, and migrants. It also affects public figures, public service providers, and celebrities. The correlation between words and actions is significant; digital violence can transform into physical violence and vice versa, often occurring simultaneously. In the field of digital forensics, scientific investigation seeks to understand digital violence, which is also understood to be a part of "cyber crime." This involves tracing the origin of incidents to determine what went wrong, how it went wrong, and how to prevent it, ultimately uncovering the motives behind such acts. The effort and expertise required in digital forensics are crucial to addressing and preventing digital violence.

1.4 PRIVACY AND SECURITY

While solving cyber crime is crucial, it doesn't automatically lead to privacy violations, making privacy protection a major focus in all areas, whether securing an entity or investigating it. What underlined the shift from a physical human society to a virtual one was the emergence of a vast ocean of assets that required security: data. This suggests that if something went wrong, the first place to check was the data. However, this approach only leads the investigator to aim for a specific piece of evidence. Technologically tested and proven data-driven forensics is the way to go in the case of deciphering attacks and, thus, the crime itself.

Living creatures often tend to seize what they consider precious through various actions: Bees collect nectar and accumulate it in a beehive, ants take shelter in colonies, and humans lock it up with a handy pair of locks and keys. Unbeknownst to us, the invasion would infiltrate these comfortable cocoons, bringing with it the loss of privacy, the breach of confidentiality, and the unending variations and escalation of these threats. Something worth noting is that there is undoubtedly a lot to learn from these "*born-with*" or natural characteristics. Researchers closely study these natural activities and occurrences, transferring ideas from them to cybersecurity, resulting in the emergence of a new domain known as "Nature-inspired Cyber Security (NICS)." For a variety of reasons, privacy is critical to digital investigations and evidence. It safeguards the rights of individuals who might face a digital investigation.

Emails, texts, and photos are examples of digital evidence that may be very private and sensitive, and improper treatment of this data may have detrimental effects on an individual's reputation and right to privacy. Confidentiality is also required to ensure the investigation's validity. Digital evidence may be contested in court and may not be allowed to be used as evidence if it was collected in a way that violated someone's privacy. This could potentially undermine the suspect's case, leading to the dismissal of the charges. Preserving privacy further helps to protect companies' reputations. For instance, improper handling of sensitive material about a company during an inquiry may result in a loss of confidence from clients and business partners, as well as financial damages. Digital forensics raises serious privacy issues, such as data centralization. Forensic methods typically see all of the digital data on a computer or device, tempting investigators to violate user privacy because they may find other interesting things not originally sought or authorized during their searches.

To put it succinctly, police in the United States (U.S.) have similar restrictions on what they can search for during situations such as traffic stops. Forensic investigators frequently misjudge data due to their limited understanding of the variety of data they encounter, and they may be overly suspicious of innocent data. For instance, it may be difficult to tell if people in a photograph are at least 18 years of age if an email-documented meeting between suspects is part of a conspiracy or a social event, or which financial transaction documents indicate an alleged Ponzi scheme. Investigators may open a large number of files because they do not understand what they are looking at and may see things outside the bounds of their authorization.

Additionally, unwarranted reporting of forensic findings is a significant risk. Because of the difficulty of judging data, investigators may cause harm by reporting incorrect results. For instance, child abuse is often difficult to ascertain in photographs. Nevertheless, in the U.S., reporting suspected child abuse by a forensic investigator can lead to serious consequences, including legal proceedings and parental access restrictions, regardless of the subsequent proof of child abuse. Investigating shared resources, such as server computers, cloud sites, or family computers, may violate the privacy of third parties not subject to the investigation. For instance, it is unjustified for governments to search all the data on cloud servers for terrorism clues since terrorists are very rare, and the benefits of searching are likely small compared to the privacy risks.

Another key issue with digital forensics is the possibility of surreptitious searches, where the data owner may not be aware of the search. In contrast to physical object searches in the United States, which require the owner's presence and warrant service, investigators can seize and remotely investigate a drive using the appropriate protocols. Even if the owner of the drive is present during an investigation, they might not comprehend the proceedings and may not be able to discern any violation of their privacy. There is also the risk of selling private forensic data. Since private user data has monetary value, unscrupulous investigators could sell it to Internet brokers of user information, like the customers of Google and Microsoft. This could significantly expand the scope of a privacy violation. Governments are unlikely to take this action, but businesses and individuals, such as computer repair personnel, might. Moreover, the criminal use of digital forensics is a significant concern. Digital forensics can leverage Internet-of-Things (IoT) systems, such as home-monitoring systems, to reveal to thieves the presence or absence of individuals at a specific location. Unscrupulous investigators could use private data they find for personal gains, such as bank card numbers they find to steal from bank accounts, passwords they find to break into systems or embarrassing private information they find for blackmail.

The Chinese and Russian governments, as reported, seem to engage in extensive digital forensics to pilfer technology secrets from different countries' corporate computer systems, and these same methods could potentially target individuals. Assessing the damage to privacy is challenging since it is difficult to assign monetary damages to privacy violations in general. Often, the damage is non-financial and difficult to measure. However, in cases of large breaches, class-action lawsuits may serve as a deterrent against abuses. Another issue is the lack of support for privacy management by forensic tool vendors. Currently, the major forensic software tools provide little support for tracking privacy issues during a forensic investigation.

1.5 FINANCIAL CRIMES

Undoubtedly, the expansion of financial crime in modern society necessitates advanced data analytics techniques for detection and prevention. Forensic accounting, particularly in cases of money laundering, significantly benefits from modern data analytics, enhancing the ability to track money trails. The scientific community is paying considerable attention to these advancements, powered by increasingly intelligent algorithms. Among the most ruthless forms of financial fraud are Ponzi schemes, lottery scams, and money laundering. Besides, the modern world is rife with cryptocurrency-related crimes. The two main components of money laundering through cryptocurrencies are privacy coins and mixers, both emphasizing untraceability. Cryptocurrencies operate on blockchain technology, which has revolutionized security through decentralization, with anonymity being a major selling point. Although intended to protect privacy, this anonymity has also provided a haven for criminals. This has led to the rise of ransomware attacks, where perpetrators demand payments in bitcoin to unlock data encrypted by complex cryptographic keys.

> Before moving forward, consider a theoretical scenario illustrating the importance of digital forensics in the financial sector: A customer reports to a financial institution that they have withdrawn a substantial amount of money from their account without their knowledge or consent. Although the bank's internal monitoring system flagged the transaction as suspicious, the funds had already left the account. In this case, digital forensics can be employed to: preserve digital evidence, such as transaction logs, server records, and access logs, ensuring it remains intact for examination; investigate the preserved evidence to trace the origin of the unauthorised transaction, identify any vulnerabilities or security breaches, and determine how the cybercriminal gained access to the account; identify the individuals or groups responsible for the unauthorised fund transfer; mitigate the impact by freezing affected accounts, securing compromised systems, and enhancing security measures; and potentially use the gathered evidence in legal proceedings to prosecute cybercriminals.

Digital forensics offers several significant advantages to financial firms, setting them apart from other sectors in terms of cyber risk management. Financial institutions handle sensitive customer data and financial assets, making them prime targets for cyberattacks. Digital forensics helps safeguard this data by quickly identifying and mitigating breaches. Speed is crucial in cybersecurity incidents, and digital forensics allows financial firms to respond rapidly to breaches, minimizing damage and potential financial losses. Strict regulatory frameworks govern the financial sector, and digital forensics ensures compliance by thoroughly investigating and reporting all cybersecurity incidents as mandated by law. Maintaining customer trust is critical, and the swift, transparent resolution of cybersecurity incidents, facilitated by digital forensics, helps to preserve customer confidence. Financial firms can enhance cybersecurity measures with insights from digital forensics to stay ahead of evolving threats. If a business becomes a victim of cyber crime, immediate steps include isolating affected systems to prevent further compromise and preserving digital evidence in a forensically sound manner.

In addition, engaging a qualified digital forensics team with expertise in cybersecurity investigations is crucial to guiding the investigation and ensuring best practices. Conducting an initial analysis to identify indicators of compromise (IoCs), such as IP addresses, domain names, and malware hashes, is followed by a thorough analysis of compromised systems, examining memory dumps, network traffic, and system logs to trace the attacker's actions. Attribution of the attack to a specific individual, group, or nation-state involves analyzing the tactics, techniques, and infrastructure used. Legal counsel should be involved to ensure the investigation adheres to legal requirements, and legal and regulatory requirements for notifying affected parties should be followed if sensitive customer data is compromised. Detailed incident reports should be prepared for internal review and regulatory reporting if necessary. Digital forensics allows financial firms to reconstruct the sequence of events leading up to a fraudulent incident by analyzing digital artifacts such as log files, timestamps, and system records, helping to identify processes and procedures to prevent future crimes. It aids in identifying the origin of fraudulent activities by tracing the digital footprints left by attackers, and sharing this information helps other organizations understand potential risks. Identifying vulnerabilities in the organization's infrastructure through investigation allows for the necessary fixes to prevent further attacks. Understanding how fraud was perpetrated is crucial for prevention, and digital forensics provides insights into the techniques, tactics, and procedures used by attackers, enabling institutions to strengthen their defenses.

1.6 CHILD PROTECTION AND VIRTUAL SAFETY

Next, we'll talk about one of the most severe and hardest pains for countries and law enforcement: child exploitation. Child pornography, a common term for images depicting sexual abuse against children, is a distinct category of content that cannot be considered a form of expression or opinion. To address this issue, it is imperative to restrict the dissemination of such material, making it challenging or impossible for offenders to upload it onto the public Internet. Therefore, we need to take proactive measures to eliminate this content and capture those responsible for its creation, distribution, or consumption. However, it is worth acknowledging that removing child pornography at its source is often unfeasible when the original materials are located outside the jurisdiction. More importantly, it can prolong the process of removing such materials from foreign jurisdictions.

To effectively combat child pornography circulation, countries must establish a unified mechanism to prevent access to websites hosting or distributing such material. Collaboration among public authorities is essential to efficiently remove and block such content, ensuring alignment with legal and judicial procedures while respecting the rights of end-users. Law enforcement agencies tasked with investigating child sexual abuse, including cyber crime, should have access to robust investigative tools such as interception, covert surveillance, electronic monitoring, and financial investigation methods tailored to the severity and nature of the offenses under scrutiny. Authorities should also have the legal authority to operate under covert online identities. Various social and technological factors contribute to the prevalence of child sexual abuse, which operates at global, macro, and individual levels. The evolution and widespread accessibility of Internet technologies play a pivotal role in facilitating sexual violence against children online. Children's eagerness to adopt new technologies and the allure of the virtual world further exacerbate this issue, especially considering the inadequate regulation of pornographic material on the Internet.

The environmental context has a significant influence on child exploitation. Urban environments, characterized by advanced communication infrastructure and anonymity, provide fertile ground for the increase of deviant behavior, including online exploitation. On the contrary, rural settings offer a sense of safety and proximity to nature, fostering healthy physical and emotional development. However, challenges such as underdeveloped utilities and economic instability can exacerbate vulnerabilities in rural communities, leading to issues like substance abuse and crime. The convergence of urban and rural environments through interconnected communication systems, such as the Internet and social networks, has blurred traditional boundaries and escalated the prevalence of violence, necessitating enhanced measures to protect children. Recent incidents, such as attacks on users in virtual environments, underscore the urgency for innovative approaches to ensure the safety of all individuals, particularly vulnerable populations.

Without a shadow of a doubt, digital forensics and modern investigative methods are crucial in combating child exploitation and enhancing virtual safety. Evidence often includes images, videos, chat logs, and metadata, which can help identify perpetrators, victims, and their interactions. Besides, techniques like geolocation analysis and data correlation enable investigators to track the movement of offenders and their online activities, aiding in the identification of trafficking networks and the rescue of victims. Moreover, advancements in machine learning and artificial intelligence have facilitated the development of tools for automated detection of illicit content, allowing for swift identification and removal of harmful material from online platforms. These methods, coupled with international cooperation and legislative measures, form a comprehensive approach to combating child exploitation and promoting virtual safety.

1.7 FUTURE OF CYBER CRIME AND AI

As previously noted, humans' attempt to clone themselves into a digital yet intelligent counterpart has taken inspiration from nature, resulting in novel pathways. At its core, the concept aims to replicate human intelligence by focusing on the brain, leading to the emergence of deep learning. Formally defined, deep learning involves teaching machines to analyze data akin to the human brain's processes. Another avenue, machine learning, seeks to equip machines with the ability to mimic human-like cognition. Both branches fall under the broader umbrella of artificial intelligence, with the common goal of comprehending complexities while harnessing the potential of these advancing paradigms. The intersection of artificial intelligence and forensic science has significant implications. AI's role in data analysis, particularly in forensic contexts, is poised to revolutionize investigative methodologies in unforeseen ways. For example, current applications include using AI to sift through vast volumes of video and audio data for criminal activity identification and suspect apprehension using facial recognition algorithms. This marks a departure from traditional pattern-based crime detection methods, ushering in an era where AI could potentially play a major role in criminal activities.

The emerging field of AI regulation reflects society's growing awareness of the need for ethical and legal frameworks to govern AI's deployment. Initiatives such as the EU AI Act exemplify efforts to establish guidelines for the responsible use of AI technologies. These regulations are essential as AI's capabilities, whether beneficial or detrimental, increasingly intersect with legal and ethical considerations. The fusion of AI with forensic analysis tools holds promise for enhancing investigative outcomes within shorter timeframes. Applications range from multimedia artifact categorization to cyber crime detection, where machine learning algorithms are instrumental. However, challenges persist, including the lack of transparency in AI decision-making processes. Explainable AI (XAI) offers a potential solution by enhancing the interpretability of AI models, thereby fostering trust and collaboration between human analysts and AI systems.

Future research efforts could explore the integration of large language models (LLMs) into cyber crime investigations, facilitating more effective data analysis by law enforcement agencies. This integration holds the potential to bolster AI-based cybersecurity measures, enabling proactive responses to evolving cyber threats. An illustrative example of this integration is the essential role of suspicious activity reports (SARs) in investigative workflows, particularly in combating financial crimes like money laundering. Technologies such as Natural Language Processing (NLP) and LLMs aid in SAR triage, with privacy concerns often favoring offline models. Additionally, the rise of synthetic media, facilitated by AI capabilities, presents challenges in distinguishing between authentic and manipulated content. Financial frauds perpetrated using deepfakes underscore the importance of robust categorization mechanisms to prevent evidence mishandling. The convergence of AI and forensic science holds immense potential but also poses significant challenges. Establishing regulatory frameworks, enhancing transparency in AI decision-making, and integrating emerging technologies into investigative workflows are critical steps toward leveraging AI's transformative potential responsibly.

1.8 CHALLENGES IN EMERGING FIELDS

In digital forensics, criminal methods and technology constantly change, making cyber threat investigation and mitigation difficult. Digital landscapes with encrypted data, dispersed systems, and anonymization provide forensic analysts with several challenges. Anti-forensic measures, which hide culprits' tracks, make evidence retrieval difficult. Blockchain technology, bitcoin transactions, and anonymization technologies make the attribution of illegal activity difficult. Artificial intelligence helps cybercriminals exploit loopholes and hide their digital trail. Cloud computing poses jurisdictional and access issues, while mobile devices and IoT networks provide massive, complicated data sources for analysis. Criminals use crime-as-a-service and ransomware-as-a-service platforms, democratizing cyber crime and challenging forensic methods. Memory forensics, blockchain analysis, and social engineering scrutiny are essential for managing new cyber dangers. Digital forensic investigations in this dynamic environment depend on a detailed awareness of new difficulties and the skillful use of cutting-edge technology. Consider Table 1.1 for a further study.

As unconventional ideas become mainstream, it's natural for skepticism to arise. Especially as these innovations become integrated into our daily lives, promising efficiency gains while also raising significant security concerns, including privacy. Addressing these issues is as complex as the innovations themselves. New fields like cloud forensics, metaverse forensics, and drone forensics present both fresh challenges and opportunities. As our digital world transcends physical boundaries, synthetic media such as deepfakes pose substantial hurdles for cyber crime investigations. Similarly, the rise of cyberattacks on smart mobility systems underscores the growing importance of automobile forensics.

In this ongoing tug-of-war between malicious actors and investigators, modern cyber crime investigation techniques and advances in data analytics hold promise for thwarting, detecting, and countering cyber threats.

Table 1.1 Modern Challenges in Digital Forensics

Challenge	*Description*
Anti-forensic Techniques	Perpetrators often use anti-forensic techniques to cover their tracks, making it difficult for forensic analysts to retrieve evidence. These techniques include data obfuscation, file hiding, data destruction, and tampering with file metadata.
Anonymization Techniques	Criminals utilize various anonymization techniques to conceal their identities and activities online. These techniques include TOR (The Onion Router), VPNs (Virtual Private Networks), proxy servers, and anonymizing cryptocurrencies like Monero.
Artificial Intelligence	The use of AI in cyberattacks introduces challenges in detecting and attributing malicious activities, as attackers leverage AI to evade detection. AI-powered attacks can include adversarial machine learning, AI-driven phishing, and automated malware generation.
Blockchain Analysis	While blockchain technology provides pseudonymity for users, forensic analysts can use blockchain analysis techniques to trace transactions and identify individuals involved in illicit activities. These techniques include address clustering, transaction graph analysis, and deanonymization methods.
Cloud Forensics	Investigating data stored in cloud environments presents challenges due to the distributed nature of cloud computing. Cloud forensic techniques include data acquisition from cloud service providers, analyzing cloud logs, and identifying shared resources among multiple users.
Cryptocurrency Forensics	Analyzing cryptocurrency transactions requires specialized tools and techniques to trace funds and identify cryptocurrency addresses associated with criminal activities. Cryptocurrency forensic techniques include blockchain analysis, transaction flow analysis, and wallet tracing.
Crime-as-a-Service (CaaS)	Criminals can now purchase cyber crime tools and services on the dark web, facilitating a broader range of cyberattacks and making attribution more difficult. Crime-as-a-service platforms offer services such as DDoS (Distributed Denial of Service) attacks, exploit kits, and malware distribution.
Data Encryption	With the widespread use of encryption technologies, accessing encrypted data poses a significant challenge in digital forensics investigations. Forensic analysts utilize techniques such as cryptographic key recovery, brute-force attacks, and memory analysis to decrypt encrypted data.
Fileless Malware	Fileless malware operates entirely in memory, leaving no traces on disk, posing challenges for traditional disk-based forensic techniques. Memory forensics techniques are essential for detecting and analyzing fileless malware, including memory dump analysis, process memory analysis, and memory forensics tools.

Table 1.1 (Cont.)

Challenge	*Description*
Memory Forensics	Analyzing volatile memory for evidence of malicious activities presents challenges due to its transient nature and complexity. Memory forensics techniques involve extracting and analyzing data from RAM (Random Access Memory), identifying process artifacts, and detecting malware in memory.
Mobile Forensics	With the prevalence of smartphones and mobile devices, extracting and analyzing data from these devices poses unique challenges in digital forensics. Mobile forensic techniques include logical and physical acquisition of mobile devices, parsing mobile app data, and recovering deleted data.
Network Forensics	Investigating cyber crimes often involves analyzing network traffic and logs to trace malicious activities, requiring specialized expertise and tools. Network forensic techniques include packet capture and analysis, network flow analysis, and intrusion detection system (IDS) logs analysis.
Ransomware	Ransomware attacks encrypt data and demand payment for decryption, posing challenges in data recovery and attribution for forensic analysts. Ransomware forensic techniques involve ransomware analysis, identifying ransomware variants, and decrypting files using ransomware decryption tools or backup data.
Ransomware-as-a-Service (RaaS)	The emergence of ransomware-as-a-Service platform allows cybercriminals to launch ransomware attacks without requiring technical expertise, increasing the prevalence of such attacks. RaaS platforms offer ransomware distribution services, infrastructure, and support for a share of the profits.
Social Engineering	Cybercriminals exploit human psychology to manipulate individuals into disclosing sensitive information or performing actions that compromise security, posing challenges for digital forensics investigations. Social engineering forensic techniques involve analyzing communication logs, identifying phishing attempts, and educating users about social engineering tactics.

Nonetheless, adaptability, innovation, and collaboration are indispensable assets in confronting evolving cyber threats. Legal and privacy concerns also play a pivotal role in digital forensic investigations. As privacy rights and regulations evolve, it's crucial to reckon with their impact on investigations. Novel data sources, acquired with consent or through compliance requests to service providers, offer valuable insights, while compliance sources provide data unaffected by local storage devices.

Recognizing that the aim of data collection in digital forensic investigations is to establish innocence or guilt highlights the importance of amassing comprehensive data. While AI technologies are unlikely to replace human examiners, they optimize the investigative process, especially in data-intensive investigations where vast amounts of information are involved. Several tangible trends are reshaping the future of digital forensics, necessitating preparedness among professionals. Adaptability to evolving data landscapes, convergence with adjacent fields like Digital Forensics and Incident Response (DFIR) and Open Source Intelligence (OSINT), and collaboration across disciplines are vital for comprehensive data analysis.

As the digital forensic landscape evolves, professionals must remain proactive in embracing new technologies and methodologies. Continuous education and collaboration with adjacent fields are critical to tackling the challenges presented by the ever-changing digital terrain. The complexity of modern computer systems and networks poses challenges in collecting and analyzing digital evidence. Cryptographic methods are constantly evolving, proprietary data artifacts are growing, and the mass expansion of devices and systems makes accessing pertinent data difficult. To mitigate these challenges, organizations are increasingly adopting a "triage" approach, focusing on critical data rather than complete images. This pragmatic strategy gains traction as data continues to burgeon across multiple devices. Furthermore, the use of unmanned aerial vehicles (UAVs) has gained significant popularity in non-human-interacted work, showing promising potential to enhance security. Research and implementation efforts in this area are actively ongoing.

In the face of evolving threats, the ability to promptly and meticulously communicate risks is crucial for organizations. Digital resilience has become the holy grail for every organization, requiring adherence to standard procedures to build a strong shield against vulnerabilities. As we embrace digitalization, it's essential to acknowledge that transformation often involves abandoning established practices. Global policies and legal frameworks must optimize the balance between technology and governance to monitor and control technological advancements. In the coming years, the world's goal is to establish legal boundaries to control the power of technological advancements and address cybersecurity threats effectively. It's crucial to recognize that we are in a cold war with destructive technology, whether due to innovation or malicious intent.

1.9 REMARK

This chapter delves into the core tenets of cyber crime investigation, offering a modern lens through which to examine this ever-evolving discipline. Characterized by complex digital footprints and clandestine operations, cyber crime presents unique challenges necessitating a modernized investigative approach. The foundation of cyber crime investigation lies in the very definition of cyber crime itself. In disposition, cyber crime surrounds any unlawful activity involving a computer or network, including a broad range of malicious acts, including hacking, identity theft, fraud, and cyberterrorism. The landscape of cyber crime is fluid, continually shifting in tandem with technological advancements and a growing interconnected world. Hence, traditional investigative methods often fall short in the face of these elusive perpetrators.

A modern approach to cyber crime investigation is therefore paramount. This necessitates the integration of cutting-edge technologies, interdisciplinary expertise, and a complete understanding of digital forensics. This chapter explores the foundational principles of cyber crime investigation, including the criticality of preserving digital evidence, the role of forensic analysis in uncovering digital trails, and the legal frameworks governing investigative procedures. Real-world case studies and concrete examples illuminate the complexities of cyber crime investigation, along with the tactics utilized to identify, apprehend, and prosecute cybercriminals.

Likewise, this chapter scrutinizes inherent challenges and ethical quandaries, including privacy concerns, jurisdictional complexities, and the delicate balance between security and civil liberties. By promoting a holistic understanding of these complexities, this chapter aims to equip both aspiring and seasoned investigators with the requisite knowledge and skills to navigate the dynamic terrain of cyber crime investigation with mastery and ethical integrity. This chapter serves as a gateway to cyber crime investigation, laying the groundwork for a thorough exploration of its nuances and complicatedness.

Chapter 2

Privacy-Based Triage of Suspicious Activity Reports Using Offline Large Language Models

Phil Legg, Nicholas Ryder, Samantha Bourton, Diana Johnson, and Reuben Walker

2.1 INTRODUCTION

In 2021-2022, the UK Financial Intelligence Unit (UKFIU) received 901,255 Suspicious Activity Reports (SARs), observing an increase of 21% from the previous financial year. This represents a staggering growth, in part fueled by technology-enabled criminal activity such as cyber crime and online financial crime, with technology providing a means for perpetrators to scale up criminal behaviors. For entities that are required to report suspicious activity, compiling all the necessary details can be challenging, in part due to missing or unavailable information [1]. Likewise, for the UKFIU, as the volume of reporting increases, the ability to triage and investigate cases has naturally become significantly more complex.

In this work, we investigate how recent developments within Natural Language Processing (NLP), specifically Large Language Models (LLM), can aid triage of reports at scale. The UKFIU published a series of glossary codes that are used to classify a report and are designed to assist with the triage and handling of a SAR. However, there have been cases where glossary codes may not be provided by the reporting entity or may be misclassified by either the reporting entity or the handling analyst, and therefore hindering the investigation process. We therefore consider whether LLMs can be deployed to manage this task, potentially alleviating many hours of effort from analysts and reporting entities. Furthermore, can this performance be achieved whilst maintaining privacy? Since SARs are confidential, sensitive documents, the use of popular online LLMs such as OpenAI's ChatGPT, Microsoft CoPilot and Google Bard would not be appropriate. These models are provided as a service by large technology firms, where the user input is therefore shared with the provider to improve their service, rendering these unsuitable for confidential matters. Less known are a series of offline models, including Mistral, Falcon, and LLaMA. These models are significantly smaller than online service models and, hence, do not have the same extensive knowledge base available. However, they can be downloaded and deployed locally, making them ideal for privacy-preserving applications. If

 DOI: 10.1201/9781003471103-2

being used for a bespoke task such as SARs glossary code triage, can offline models provide both privacy-preservation as well as accurate classification is the question being explored.

The remainder of the paper is as follows: Section 2 provides related works of investigation into SARs and into the use of NLP and machine learning (ML) techniques for text analytics. Section 3 provides the methodology used for our investigation. Section 4 presents the results of our study, showing the performance of both online and offline models for completing the task. Section 5 gives a discussion of the effectiveness of LLMs for SARs triage, whilst Section 6 gives our conclusion.

2.2 RELATED WORKS

For our related works, we study how NLP has been used as part of criminal investigation, and we also explore how different techniques for NLP, including the use of LLM have been applied in similar contexts.

Hughes et al. [2] investigate the use of NLP for tackling child sexual abuse media distribution online, by analyzing the use of language on police chat and social networking communities. Schraagen and Bex [3] consider the challenge of extracting details from user-generated text, using a crime report dataset to understand the semantic relations that characterize the offense. Specifically, they explore how parts of speech can be extracted from the report. They study the design and performance of a Long Short Term Memory network as well as a Support Vector Machine to classify sequential text patterns as parts of speech or partial parts of speech. Dixon and Birks also explore the use of NLP for policing [4], as a means of relating text reports to a problem-based policing framework, that describes a four-stage process of scan, analysis, response and assessment. By utilizing NLP to better map reports to these processes, a more systematic approach to managing investigations could be achieved.

In terms of broader applications of suspicious activity monitoring, Raza and Haider [5] present SARDBN (Suspicious Activity Reporting using Dynamic Bayesian Network) that is intended to identify suspicious financial activities. They use a combination of clustering and dynamic Bayesian network (DBN) to identify anomalies in a sequence of financial transactions. Similarly, Desrousseaux et al. [6] explore the use of Neural Networks for the prediction of financial suspicious activity in the banking sector. Hayble-Gomes also explored the use of AI in SARs, in particular, how AI can help to identify what information should be considered when composing a SAR [7].

More recently, LLMs have captured the attention of both researchers and the public, largely through the public release of OpenAI's ChatGPT in November 2022 [8]. Generative Pre-trained Transformers (GPT) models work on the basis of attention [9], providing a means of maintaining context of a discussion between the end-user, and the system that provides a written response. LLMs have been deployed in a variety of applications, including for topic classification in the domain of public affairs [10] as well as the enforcement of consumer rights in Germany [11]. Whilst they have demonstrated good performance in many text-based tasks, there are some concerns around the increasing scale of LLMs, and whether these models could potentially become too big [12] that may lead to degrading performance. Finally, as new LLMs are developed and hosted online for public use, there is a serious concern about the privacy of data shared with LLMs [13]. For our research, we are interested in studying how the performance of offline models can be compared against online service models for the task of classifying SARs against the relevant glossary codes as given by the UKFIU. Specifically, can offline models achieve a comparable level of performance as larger online service models, whilst offering privacy since the models can be deployed locally is the debate to be resolved. Secondly, answers need to be figured out on the query of whether smaller offline models provide any further benefits for specific task completion, compared to the online service models that are constantly evolving in both complexity and scale.

2.3 METHODOLOGY

Our experimental methodology consists of the following stages:

- We use ChatGPT-3.5 to generate an initial dataset that consists of 60 Suspicious Activity Reports informed by 12 different glossary code classifications.
- We use the same ChatGPT-3.5 session context to assess whether the LLM can classify the generated reports against the initial glossary codes, to acquire a baseline performance where context is maintained.
- We then use the generated dataset with an offline model (Mistral OpenOrca) to assess classification performance where no prior knowledge of the dataset generation conversation is available. In this example, we provide only a single prompt that informs the model of the possible glossary codes available.
- Finally, we perform the same experiment as above but for the online ChatGPT-3.5. This has no prior context of the data generation process, and we provide only a single prompt that informs the model of the possible glossary codes available.

2.3.1 Dataset Generation

Due to the confidential nature of SARs, obtaining real submitted reports is not possible. Therefore, to facilitate this study and to have a scalable approach for generating suitable reports, we employ LLMs for the task of initial data generation.

Table 2.1 SAR glossary codes as defined by UKFIU

Glossary Code	*Description*
XXGVTXX	Requiring a defense under POCA (consent) if the value of the suspected money laundering falls below a value of £3,000
XXTBMLXX	Trade-based money laundering
XXMLTMXX	Money laundering through markets
XXTEUKXX	Tax evasion UK-based
XXF3XX	Corporate tax evasion (tax evasion by businesses, corporations)
XXF5XX	VAT fraud e.g. carousel, Missing Trader Intra-Community (MTIC) fraud
XXD9XX	Bribery and corruption
XXMSHTXX	Modern slavery/human trafficking
XXPROPXX	Purchase, sale and rental of real estate property
XXVAXX	Virtual assets
XXF4XX	Personal tax evasion (tax evasion by individuals e.g. income tax)
XXPRFXX	Professional enablers: persons providing professional services or specialist knowledge that wittingly or unwittingly facilitates money laundering

We use the OpenAI ChatGPT-3.5 platform to curate a set of 60 Suspicious Activity Reports across 12 possible SARs glossary code classifications.

We use the OpenAI ChatGPT-3.5 platform to curate a set of 60 Suspicious Activity Reports across 12 possible SARs glossary code classifications. The 12 glossary code classifications that we use for data generation in this study are given in Table 2.1. For each of the glossary codes that we consider for this study, we use the following user prompts to obtain suitable outputs (as shown for glossary code XXGVTXX):

- **User:** *What is a Suspicious Activity Report?*
- **User:** *What does the statement "XXGVTXX – Requiring a defense under the Proceeds of Crime Act (POCA) (consent) if the value of the suspected money laundering falls below a value of £3,000" mean in relation to Suspicious Activity Reports?*
- **User:** *Can you provide 5 example SARs based on the glossary code XXGVTXX?*

By means of example, the following text provides one example case as generated for the glossary code XXGVTXX: *Description: A series of transactions involving multiple wire transfers totaling £2,700 were conducted by Customer B within a short timeframe. These transfers were sent to various international accounts located in jurisdictions known for their loose financial regulations. Customer B has no apparent legitimate business or personal connections to these accounts. Reason for suspicion: Unusual pattern of wire transfers to high-risk jurisdictions without clear business or personal connections.*

The sequence of prompts used ensures that the LLM context window has knowledge of what a SAR is, along with knowledge of the specific glossary code description, to then facilitate the curation of five new example reports based on the defined glossary code. The full dataset will be available on GitHub from our project repository: https://github.com/pa-legg/sars-nlp.

2.3.2 Glossary Code Classification

Following the creation of the SARs dataset, we conducted the first experimentation against this same LLM context within the OpenAI ChatGPT-3.5 platform. The user prompt is given as follows (where SCENARIO is the exact text for each scenario as generated previously):

- **User:** *Given the following statement, what SARs glossary code would best classify this scenario? SCENARIO*

If the returned prompt correctly states the glossary code used for generating the scenario, then it is considered to have successfully classified the scenario with the appropriate glossary code.

Since the LLM context described here is responsible for both the generation and the classification of each scenario, this can be considered to be a well-informed model that serves as a baseline comparison. Clearly any model being used to classify SARs should not have intrinsic knowledge of the underlying label that is assigned to the particular scenario. We will next explore using a new model that does not have this advantage.

2.3.2.1 Cold Start Classification

Having generated our 60 test cases, we now deploy an online model and an offline model for further testing. Specifically, we use a new OpenAI ChatGPT-3.5 context for further online testing that does not have knowledge of the previous data generation phase. For offline testing, we use the Mistral OpenOrca 7B Q6 K model within the LM Studio software environment. This model consists of seven billion parameters and can be easily deployed on a standard modern laptop. For comparison, it is speculated that ChatGPT-3.5 has 175 billion parameters, however, some details of the OpenAI implementation are not made publicly available. Nevertheless, it is clear to see that the offline model is significantly smaller, which would imply less functionality and capability with general task performance. Our offline LLM maintains a context length of 2024 tokens. OpenAI claims that ChatGPT-3.5 has a maximum context of 4096 tokens, which is approximately about 3000 words. It is less clear how OpenAI maintains context as a conversation extends the context window length since the proprietary system is only accessible as an online service.

User: The following data structure defines the set of glossary codes and descriptions that a SARs can be classified as: ['XXGVTXX Requiring a defence under POCA (consent) if the value of the suspected money laundering falls below a value of £3,000', 'XXPRFXX Professional enablers: persons providing professional services or specialist knowledge that wittingly or unwittingly facilitates money laundering.', 'XXTBMLXX Trade-based money laundering (TBML)', 'XXPROPXX Purchase, sale and rental of real estate property', 'XXVAXX Virtual assets', 'XXMLTMXX Money laundering through markets', 'XXSNEXX Money laundering linked to sanctioned entities', 'XXSATXX HMRC Self-Assessment Tax Refund system', 'XXGPSXX Government Priority Schemes', 'XXTEOSXX Tax evasion offshore', 'XXTEUKXX Tax evasion UK-based', 'XXF1XX - Proceeds from benefit fraud', 'XXF2XX - Excise evasion (duty on alcohol, tobacco, fuel etc.)', 'XXF3XX - Corporate tax evasion (tax evasion by businesses, corporations)', 'XXF4XX - Personal tax evasion (tax evasion by individuals e.g. income tax)', 'XXF5XX - VAT fraud e.g. carousel, Missing Trader Intra-Community (MTIC) fraud', 'XXF9XX - Frauds against private sector', 'XXD9XX - Bribery and corruption', 'XXV2XX – Risk to vulnerable adults', 'XXV3XX – Risk to children particularly including sexual abuse and exploitation', 'XXD9XX – Bribery and corruption', 'XXILTXX – Illegal lotteries', 'XXFIREXX – Firearms', 'XXDRUXX – Illegal supply of drugs', 'XXOICXX – Organised immigration crime', 'XXMSHTXX – Modern slavery/human trafficking', 'XXPCPXX - Counter-proliferation', 'XXVICTXX - Where the purpose of the activity is to return money to a victim of crime']

Figure 2.1 User prompt for cold start.

We initialize both conversations with the prompt: *"What is a Suspicious Activity Report?"*, as we did previously, to ensure that the model has this definition within the current context window. We then provide a statement that defines a data structure that describes the glossary codes and their descriptions, as shown in Figure 2.1. In both online and offline cases, the model provides a response to acknowledge the information provided and reiterates key details to summarize the input. This stage effectively introduces the defined concepts into the LLM context window. Similar techniques have been proposed, including Retrieval Augmented Generation (RAG) [14]; however, RAG is typically used to search a document collection for corresponding information, rather than for defining a set of possible classifications. This is an important distinction to make, since a SAR may not necessarily match the exact definition of a glossary code as provided (like RAG may treat the document collection as a look up functionality), however a classification may be able to be inferred.

As before, we provide each scenario using the format defined previously (*"Given the following statement, what SARs glossary code would best classify this scenario?")*. If the returned prompt correctly states the glossary code used for generating the scenario, then it is considered to have successfully classified the scenario with the appropriate glossary code.

2.4 RESULTS

We present the results for our three test cases in Tables 2.3, 2.4, and 2.5. In each table, we show the expected glossary codes on the left side of the table, and we show the predicted labels as given by the LLM across the top columns of the table, akin to a confusion matrix. Unlike a traditional machine learning classification task however, the set of possible labels that the prediction could be drawn from is not bounded. Hence, each table shows the broader set of predicted glossary codes that we will discuss further. The set of correct classifications is highlighted along the diagonal, where the maximum possible correct classifications would be 5 for each actual label.

In the first experiment, where ChatGPT-3.5 maintains the context from the data generation phase, a total of 48 out of 60 SARs were classified correctly (shown in Table 2.2). Secondly, where our offline model, Mistral OpenOrca, is used with just the simple SARs definition prompt, we find that this model can still classify 41 of 60 cases correctly (shown in Table 2.3). For a model that is deployed offline, and with limited initial context of what makes for a SAR and the set of possible SARs glossary codes available, this result is considered to be very good. Some cases of misclassification occur, for example, three cases of XXTBMLXX (Trade-based Money Laundering) are classified as XXMLTMXX (Money Laundering through markets). Since these two codes are actually quite similar in their underlying meaning, it is not necessarily surprising to see that there may be misclassification that occurs. This is an important observation, since the inherent nature of SARs glossary codes means that some reports may well map to more than a single code. We discuss this observation further later in the paper. Another important observation is where the LLM has predicted glossary codes that are not considered as part of our testing categories, however are valid codes as presented in our original dialogue that we provide to the system. As an example, one case of XXTEUKXX (Tax evasion UK-based) is misclassified as XXTEOSXX (Tax Evasion Offshore). In this particular case, whilst the original SAR was considered to be XXTEUKXX, as classified by the LLM, the report did make mention of offshore accounts, and so again, this case would reasonably be considered to address both glossary codes.

Finally, in our third test we use a clean ChatGPT-3.5 context, providing our initial SARs prompt. As shown in Table 2.4, we find that only 35 of the 60 reports are correctly classified. This performance is actually worse than that of the offline model. Most misclassifications are for other glossary codes that are observed within the dataset, with only a single misclassification that occurs for a glossary code that is considered as valid but not part of our test set, which is a case of XXF4XX (Personal tax evasion) being classified as XXTEOSXX (Tax-evasion offshore).

Table 2.2 ChatGPT-3.5 (with data generation context)

	XXGVTXX	**XXTBMLXX**	**XXMLTMXX**	**XXTEUKXX**	**XXF3XX**	**XXF5XX**	**XXD9XX**	**XXMSHTXX**	**XXPROPXX**	**XXVAXX**	**XXF4XX**	**XXPRFXX**	*XXFIXX*	*XXF2XX*	*XXTEOSXX*	*XXILTXX*	*XXSNEXX*	XXPCPXX	VSOCXX
XXGVTXX	**1**	1	1		1														
XXTBMLXX		**4**				1													
XXMLTMXX			**2**					1	1	1									
XXTEUKXX				**2**	2						1								
XXF3XX					**5**														
XXF5XX						**5**													
XXD9XX							**5**												
XXMSHTXX								**5**											
XXPROPXX									**5**										
XXVAXX										**5**									
XXF4				1							**4**								
XXPRFXX									1			**4**							

Note: Glossary codes in italics are valid codes but not part of our test set. Glossary codes underlined are not valid codes. The diagonal shows 48 correct classifications out of a possible 60.

Table 2.3 Mistral OpenOrca (with no prior context)

	XXGVTXX	XXTBMLXX	XXMLTMXX	XXTEUKXX	XXF3XX	XXF5XX	XXD9XX	XXMSHTXX	XXPROPXX	XXVAXX	XXF4XX	XXPRFXX	*XXFIXX*	*XXF2XX*	*XXTEOSXX*	*XXILTXX*	*XXSNEXX*	XXPCPXX	VSOCXX
XXGVTXX	3											1		1					
XXTBMLXX		2	3																
XXMLTMXX		1	2																
XXTEUKXX				2	1						1				1				
XXF3XX					5														
XXF5XX						5													
XXD9XX							5												
XXMSHTXX								5											
XXPROPXX									3							1	1		
XXVAXX										4							1		
XXF4											4				1				
XXPRFXX									1	2		1			1				

Note: Glossary codes in italics are valid codes but not part of our test set. Glossary codes underlined are not valid codes. The diagonal shows 41 correct classifications out of a possible 60.

Table 2.4 ChatGPT-3.5 (with no prior context)

	XXGVTXX	**XXTBMLXX**	**XXMLTMXX**	**XXTEUKXX**	**XXF3XX**	**XXF5XX**	**XXD9XX**	**XXMSHTXX**	**XXPROPXX**	**XXVAXX**	**XXF4XX**	**XXPRFXX**	*XXFIXX*	*XXF2XX*	*XXTEOSXX*	*XXILTXX*	*XXSNEXX*	XXPCPXX	VSOCXX
XXGVTXX	1	1	1					1				1							
XXTBMLXX		5																	
XXMLTMXX		1							1	1								2	
XXTEUKXX				5															
XXF3XX				5															
XXF5XX						5													
XXD9XX							5												
XXMSHTXX								5											
XXPROPXX								1	4										
XXVAXX										5									
XXF4				4											1				
XXPRFXX			1				1		1	1									1

Note: Glossary codes in italics are valid codes but not part of our test set. Glossary codes underlined are not valid codes. The diagonal shows 35 correct classifications out of a possible 60.

However, what is particularly interesting about these results is that there are two glossary codes that occur within the predicted results, that are not genuine glossary codes and were not part of our original prompt. These codes are XXPCPXX and VSOCXX. The LLM convincingly describes these glossary codes as XXPCPXX - Counter- proliferation and VSSOXX - Shell companies. This reveals yet another crucial aspect of LLMs, since the model is designed to always provide a response, even if it may not necessarily know or have a suitably correct answer.

In three cases, the model has given these codes and convincingly described what would seem to be a glossary code, following the pattern of how actual glossary codes are formed. This demonstrates the concept of hallucinations, where the model will effectively make up information to be able to provide a response where it may not actually have an appropriate answer to give.

2.5 DISCUSSION

We discuss some of the key challenges identified through this work, as guidance for others working in related areas.

Without initial prompting, both the offline and online models perform poorly against the task, since neither model has a clear understanding of what the UKFIU glossary codes are or what format these take. Without the use of the initial prompt, the offline model gives responses such as: *In this scenario, the best SARs glossary code to classify the situation would be "Trade-Based Money Laundering."* (correct response), and: *In this scenario, the best SARs glossary code to classify the situation would be "Unusual Transactions or Behavior"* (incorrect response). Similarly, the online model gives responses such as: *Based on the scenario described, the most appropriate SARs glossary code would likely be "Trade Based Money Laundering - Trade Based Money Laundering"* (correct response), and: *Based on the scenario described, the most appropriate SARs glossary code would likely be "Counterfeit Instruments/Fraudulent Activities - Counterfeit Instruments/Fraudulent Activities"* (incorrect response). In both cases illustrated, neither model is aware of the structure that a glossary code should take, nor are they aware of the precise wording that a glossary code description would have.

LLMs can be fine-tuned for specific tasks, where a user may provide a series of prompts and expected responses, for which the underlying machine learning model can be trained. In both the case of ChatGPT-3.5 and Mistral OpenOrca, this fine-tuning has already been performed for the purposes of having a question-and-answer-based response that can act like a conversation. This process is known as Reinforcement Learning with Human Feedback (RLHF). Where this fine-tuning is not performed, any LLM would effectively return the next likely word in a sequence, given an initial sequence of words (i.e., sentence completion). Whilst it would be feasibly possible to fine-tune a model to specifically handle SARs, this approach would likely not yield significant results without a very large corpus of training examples. As discussed previously, real SARs are not readily available. Furthermore, the variability of SARs content would mean that a fine-tuned model would still struggle to fully conceptualize all possible dialogues that could map to a single glossary code. Instead, we take the approach of informing the model about SARs, and explicitly telling the model about the mapping between glossary codes and their corresponding descriptions. This then allows the model to infer the relationship between a given SARs text, and the possible descriptions as given by the SARs glossary code descriptions, rather than mapping against learned mappings of SARs classifications. We believe this provides a more flexible approach for document classification, where the content of the documents could be largely diverse and varied, and yet still need to be mapped against one or more of the provided glossary codes.

Our results showed two cases where novel glossary codes were generated by the ChatGPT-3.5 LLM: *XXPCPXX - Counter-proliferation* and *VSSOXX - Shell companies*. This was particularly interesting to observe, since the definitions given in their response are convincing, and yet completely false in nature. It is possible that the larger model that ChatGPT-3.5 uses actually gives greater scope for hallucination, compared to the more constrained Mistral model. One of the main benefits of the LLM is to be able to interpret the natural English language, and to some extent it can be argued that both the online and offline models can perform this task well already. The initial prompt we provide then helps to give the model some context and some association between descriptions and their relevant glossary codes. As a result, it is quite possible that this shows where smaller models can be more effective in achieving a precise task, such as report classification, compared to their online counterparts. It is important to recognize that ChatGPT-3.5 is a general-purpose conversational agent, however, this result demonstrates that larger models may not necessarily be the most effective approach where the end user is more concerned with achieving a specific task.

Finally, we acknowledge the challenge of data generation. We mention that the dataset used for this study was generated using ChatGPT-3.5, where we prompted the model to provide five examples for each of the 12 glossary codes under test. In this study, we do not consider any verification of these generated SARs, and we recognize that some of the generated reports may actually introduce some ambiguity in the most appropriate glossary code. A prime example would be the cases where the actual code provided is XXTEUKXX; however, the SAR makes reference to UK-based and offshore tax evasion, and so misclassification as XXTEOSXX is not necessarily incorrect, but is not the label as originally provided. However, the use of ChatGPT-3.5 for the purpose of data generation did mean that we could scale up our dataset quickly and easily. Further work would need to consider a generation of a larger dataset, as well as supporting multiple possible classifications for each SAR, to avoid cases where either an inappropriate label has been provided, or where multiple labels would all be suitably correct.

2.6 CONCLUSION

Our study demonstrates the novel use LLMs for the handling of SARs. Specifically, we are able to demonstrate the effective performance of off-line models compared to online services, meaning that a privacy-preserving approach can be achieved by deploying locally hosted models where information does not need to be shared with a third party. Given the sensitive, confidential nature of SARs, this is a fundamental requirement for any data processing stage of how the reports will be handled by law enforcement. Whilst offline models may be smaller compared to general purpose models that have attracted much public attention, we show that smaller models may in fact be more suitable for specific task deployment, due to their constrained nature that can potentially avoid issues of hallucination, where a LLM may not necessarily be able to provide a correct response, but will nevertheless attempt to do so regardless of whether this is correct or not. As we have demonstrated, we believe that LLMs have a great potential to be integrated with modern criminal investigation and law enforcement process to rapidly combat the growing nature of financial and online crimes. In future work, we hope to explore how LLMs can be integrated further into modern cyber crime investigations and help law enforcement to filter relevant data observations from a wider range of data sources in a timelier manner.

REFERENCES

[1] M. H. Fleming, Issues in measuring the efficacy of a suspicious activity reports (SARs) regime, Amicus Curiae 70 (2007) 9.

[2] D. Hughes, P. Rayson, J. Walkerdine, K. Lee, P. Greenwood, A. Rashid, C. May-Chahal, M. Brennan, Supporting law enforcement in digital communities through natural language analysis, in: S. N. Srihari, K. Franke (Eds.), Computational Forensics, Springer, Berlin, Heidelberg, 2008, pp. 122–134.

[3] M. Schraagen, F. Bex, Extraction of semantic relations in noisy user-generated law enforcement data, in: 2019 IEEE 13th International Conference on Semantic Computing (ICSC), 2019, pp. 79–86. doi:10.1109/ICOSC.2019.8665497.

[4] A. Dixon, D. Birks, Improving policing with natural language process- ing, in: A. Field, S. Prabhumoye, M. Sap, Z. Jin, J. Zhao, C. Brockett (Eds.), Proceedings of the 1st Workshop on NLP for Positive Impact, Association for Computational Linguistics, Online, 2021, pp. 115–124. doi:10.18653/v1/2021.nlp4posimpact-1.13.

[5] S. Raza, S. Haider, Suspicious activity reporting using dynamic bayesian networks, Procedia Computer Science 3 (2011) 987–991, world Conference on Information Technology. doi:10.1016/j.procs.2010.12.162.

[6] R. Desrousseaux, G. Bernard, J.-J. Mariage, Predicting financial suspicious activity reports with online learning methods, in: 2021 IEEE International Conference on Big Data (Big Data), 2021, pp. 1595–1603. doi:10.1109/BigData52589.2021.9671716.

[7] E. Hayble-Gomes, The use of predictive modeling to identify relevant features for suspicious activity reporting, Journal of Money Laundering Control 26 (2023). doi:doi.org/10.1108/JMLC-02-2022-0034.

[8] M. Shanahan, Talking about large language models, Communications of the ACM 67 (2) (2024) 68–79. doi:10.1145/3624724.

[9] A. Vaswani, N. Shazeer, N. Parmar, J. Uszkoreit, L. Jones, A. N. Gomez, L. Kaiser, I. Polosukhin, Attention is all you need, in: Proceedings of the 31st International Conference on Neural Information Processing Systems, NIPS'17, Curran Associates Inc., Red Hook, NY, USA, 2017, pp. 6000–6010.

[10] A. Pen˜a, A. Morales, J. Fierrez, I. Serna, J. Ortega-Garcia,´I. Puente, J. Co ´rdova, G. Co´rdova, Leveraging large language models for topic classification in the domain of public affairs, in: M. Coustaty, A. Forn´es (Eds.), Document Analysis and Recognition – ICDAR 2023 Workshops, Springer Nature Switzerland, Cham, 2023, pp. 20–33.

[11] L. Waidelich, M. Lambert, Z. Al-Washash, S. Kroschwald, T. Schuster, N. Do¨ring, Using large language models for the enforcement of consumer rights in germany, in: J. Ma´slankowski, B. Marcinkowski, P. Rupino da Cunha (Eds.), Digital Transformation, Springer Nature Switzerland, Cham, 2023, pp. 1–15.

[12] E. M. Bender, T. Gebru, A. McMillan-Major, S. Shmitchell, On the dangers of stochastic parrots: Can language models be too big? in: Proceedings of the 2021 ACM Conference on Fairness, Accountability, and Transparency, FAccT '21, Association for Computing Machinery, New York, NY, USA, 2021, pp. 610–623. doi:10.1145/3442188.3445922.

[13] H. Brown, K. Lee, F. Mireshghallah, R. Shokri, F. Tram`er, What does it mean for a language model to preserve privacy?, in: Proceedings of the 2022 ACM Conference on Fairness, Accountability, and Transparency, FAccT '22, Association for Computing Machinery, New York, NY, USA, 2022, p. 2280–2292. doi:10.1145/3531146.3534642.

[14] P. Lewis, E. Perez, A. Piktus, F. Petroni, V. Karpukhin, N. Goyal, H. Ku ¨ttler, M. Lewis, W.-t. Yih, T. Rockta¨schel, et al., Retrieval augmented generation for knowledge-intensive nlp tasks, Advances in Neural Information Processing Systems 33 (2020) 9459–9474.

Chapter 3

A Comprehensive Survey of Technological Approaches in the Detection of CSAM

Devangana Sujay, Vineet Kapoor, and Shishir Kumar Shandilya

3.1 INTRODUCTION

Child Sexual Abuse Material is at the utmost depth of the dark side of what digital society has led to. "It is important to remember that CSAM consists of much more than just images and video files. While CSAM is seen and transmitted on computers and through other technology, these images and videos depict actual crimes being committed against children." - Quotes National Centre for Missing and Exploited Children (NCMEC) [1] - one of the leading organizations working in the fight against online evil. Upon a classified survey, the response from victims suggested that the propagation of the image caused as much psychologically detrimental effect as the physically committed crime itself.

Being aware of the issue certainly does not solve it. This clearly is not a geographically or community-bound or any kind of classification-based issue; it is spread out globally. Reports, statistics, and research point out the exact same bitter truth that the influx of CSAM content increases by the minute and, thus, the more who are violated. Global strategies aim to combat the forces of this "epidemic," as it was seen in the graph hiking plotted against viewers and generators over the period of time.

Fighting fire with fire is a common usage, ironically having quite an insightful effect here. Technology to beat technology, it is. Now, it is evident that the media of generation, propagation, duplication and any other operation associated with the traversal of a single CSAM from one individual to another or storage of the same with oneself is performed with the help of the Internet. As commonly understood, the Internet is not a confined little space from where one can pick up the rotten apples and keep the good ones. The detection, investigation, and further removal of such undesirable content, thus, becomes more than just a tedious task. Even if our capabilities skyrocket to such heights, the prevention of even more content spreading through the Internet being stopped is almost a hypothetical notion for now. So, in fact, how do we stop this? Child safety and

 DOI: 10.1201/9781003471103-3

protection-oriented organizations especially have been enduring years of efforts for the aforementioned.

3.2 GLOBAL EFFORTS

NCMEC, or National Center for Missing & Exploited Children [2], was one of the earliest organizations that took the problem into account and pro-actively functioned for its prevention. The organization serves as a repository of information and a resource for communities, schools, parents, children, law enforcement agencies, and organizations in order to promote public awareness regarding preventive measures against child sexual abuse and abduction and to aid in the recovery of missing children. Child Exploitation and Online Protection Command (CEOP) Safety Centre is another leading organization working for the same cause under the UK's National Crime Agency (NCA). The IWF, or Internet Watch Foundation, was the first to bring about a hotline for the reporting of potentially illegal recordings and images depicting child sexual abuse. The International Centre for Missing & Exploited Children (ICMEC) took a step forward by collaborating with 196 member countries in successful Anti-CSAM regulation with regular progress reports keeping a consistent track record. [3] Thorn is an NGO founded in the year 2009 with the title "Digital Defenders of Children" that showcased progressive yields in this domain. [4] The contributions they make are comprehensively discussed in further sections of the chapter. A useful intelligence and investigative tool that enables specialized investigators to exchange information on child sexual abuse cases is the International Child Sexual Exploitation (ICSE) image and video database. This was the innovation developed by INTERPOL. [5].

3.3 STATISTICS

Current President and Chief Operating Officer of NCMEC, Michelle DeLaune, stated that it is more than just alarming; the count of around 100 per week in the year 2001 has skyrocketed to 70,000 reports per day two decades later. [6] Ayat A Najjar et al. state in their mini-review that, as per the FBI, the most used propagation media are chat rooms and instant messaging platforms. [7] The significant spike, specifically 64%, was noticed transitioning from the year 2020 to 2021 in URLs that promote or incorporate CSAM, and experts speculated the reason being the location shift of servers that aided CSAM propagation that now improved the amount of traffic influx it could handle (specific to western countries). [8] Table 3.1 depicts the number of pieces of CSAM content reported on online services in 2022. [9]

Table 3.1 Number of Pieces of CSAM Content Reported on Online Services

Platform	*Number of Reports*
Facebook	21,165,201
Instagram	5,007,902
Google	2,174,548
WhatsApp	1,017,555
Omegle	608,601
Snapchat	551,086
TikTok	288,125
Discord	169,800
X/Twitter	98,050

3.4 METHODOLOGY

Global efforts seem to be taking the bad guys down. But how exactly is it being executed? The solution was or is never a singular approach in this context. These efforts required technological backing - some kind of math that works against whatever powers CSAM. The following diagrams (Figure 3.1) represent a step-by-step approach that may be seen via this lens:

Detection itself cannot be a single step. Assuming that Stage 1 (see Figure 3.1 (A) Stage 1) is achieved, there are two ways to proceed to the next stage; a human analyst could visually demarcate between CSAM and non-CSAM, and secondly, automate this process. Both point to two different scenarios and their respective constraints:

Upon the discovery of the impact and influx caused by CSAM content all over the Internet, multiple authorities tried to stretch their capabilities into combating its expansion, running a global cleanse and bringing culprits to courts, starting off with this initial phase. One of the earliest methods to go about this was to use human vision and intellect to solve the dilemma, and someone out there did. Employees were tasked with sieving the worst from the bad by analyzing images and reporting them if confirmed to be CSAM. This just resulted in inhuman psychological trauma, eventually calling off the mission.

The theory of lowering harm, caused to a human, led to another human being mentally harmed. Lesser human interaction for better CSAM detection, investigation and associated tasks was encouraged. Though the motive stood high on its intent, it was not without its flaws. The answer to this intent was automation, and the inadequacy lay in false positives. Scenarios drive towards improper algorithms resulting in even the green flagging of true positive CSAM as well. Now, how would we make sure that these automated solutions are indeed "perfect" at their task? Zero Trust Principle was proposed to be a remedy.

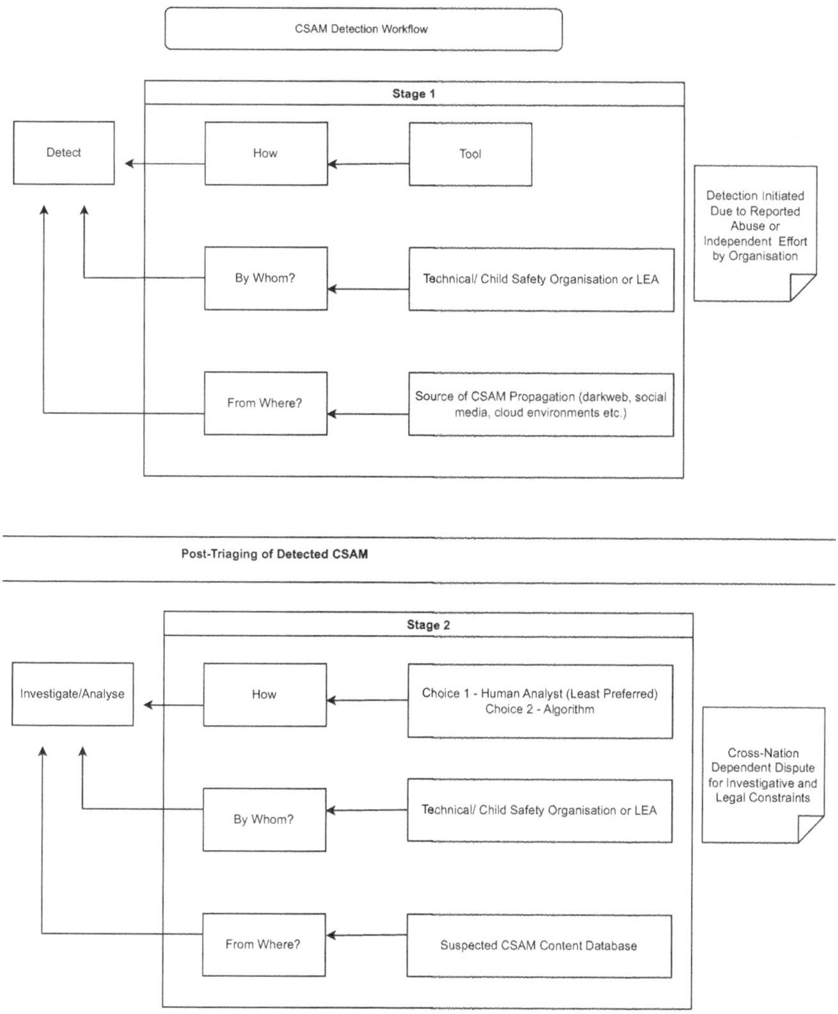

Figure 3.1(A) All stages of CSAM detection workflow.

Stage 2 (See Figure 3.1 (A) Stage 2) was sought to go by least human exposure, for sure. In the following section, the solutions are comprehensively discussed. The next part of the process deals with informing the authorities notifying the presence or existence of CSAM on their platform. From the point of view of such a platform providing service organization, there was more than one way to go about this. Direct reporting was the most straightforward in its earliest periods, but recently most organizations

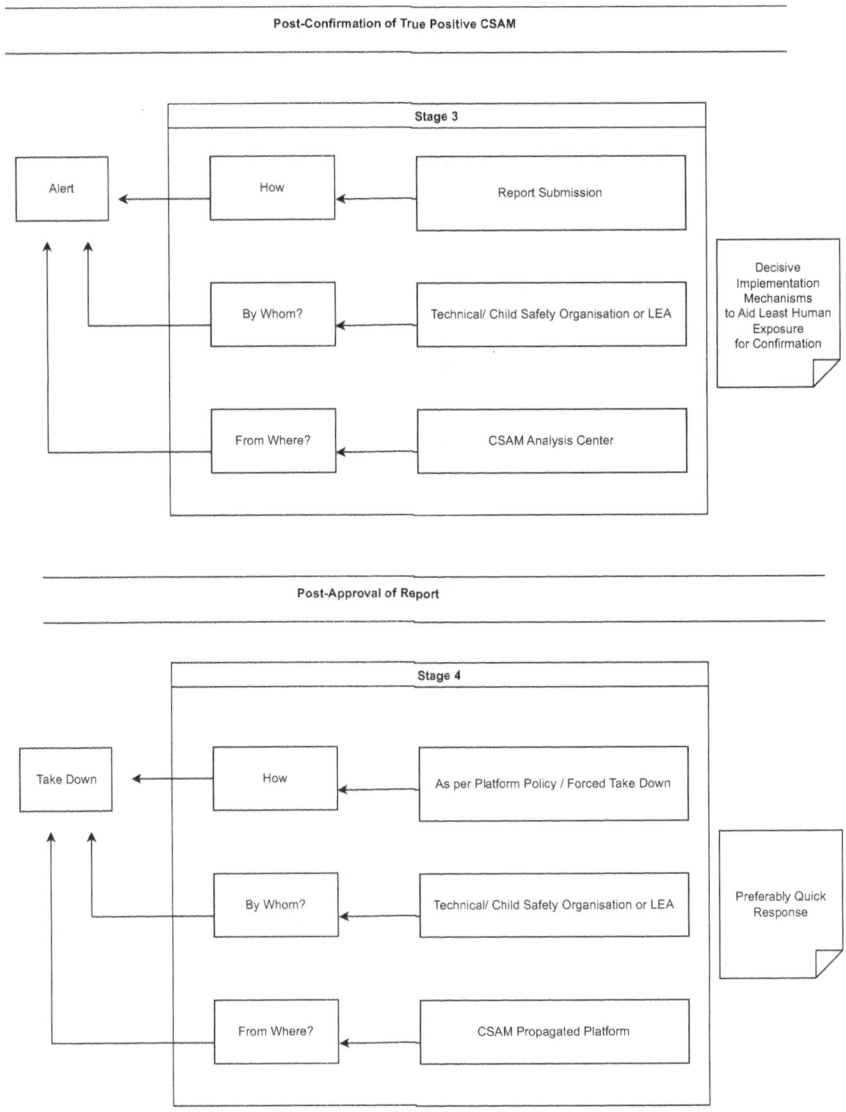

Figure 3.1(B)

adopted the strategy of a special team or a reporting portal that handles the CSAM reports and related affairs; this clearly suggests the world is taking the problem more seriously.

Taking the content down is now under the discretion of the platform, national and/or international regulatory bodies, government and so on. The

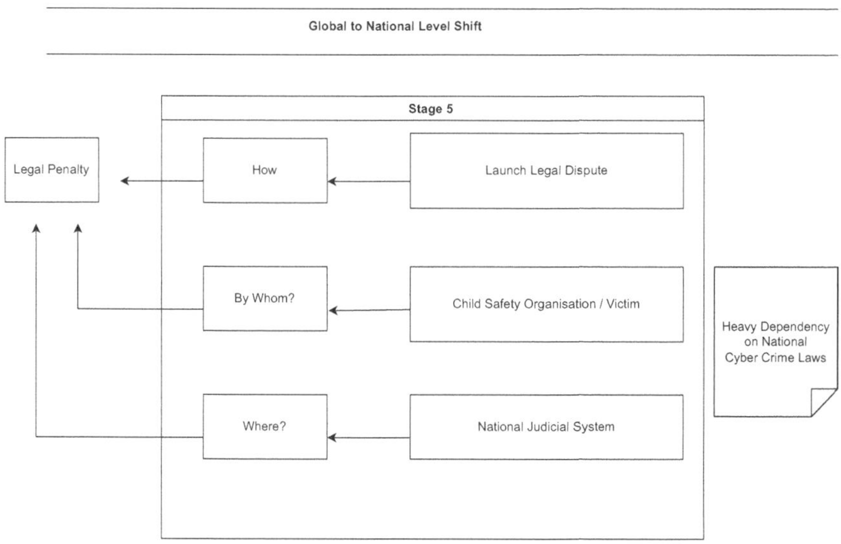

Figure 3.1 (C) i

culprits facing legal repercussions have a massive dependency on numerous factors such as the severity of cyber laws existing within the nation, which entity is fighting against the cybercriminal, how the investigation is carried on, etc.

3.5 PHOTODNA

The first-of-its-kind solution was born by the combined efforts of Microsoft and Dartmouth College. Ever since its inception, it has been the frontrunner of all existing tools in this category of detection. The tool gained massive popularity at a spark. LEAs, other tech giants and many more vouched for the same as well. It was put on a pedestal with titles such as "the robust hashing technology" surpassing the traditional image hashing technologies. An important point to be noted is that, in the end, the detection was reported (after cross-evaluation by Microsoft's expert(s) for report validation purposes) directly to NCMEC. A multitude of variants, upgrades and so on were performed on PhotoDNA, but it continues to be a firm base for CSAM detection across the globe.

3.5.1 Functioning of PhotoDNA

The task performed by PhotoDNA is to generate specific hashes or unique digital signatures. These signatures are evaluated against hashes of other images available online, and if they coincide, respective authorities are reported to, and the image shall be taken down. The technology was donated to NCMEC. A NCMEC study states that PhotoDNA has a false negative rate of less than 2% and a false positive rate of less than 1 in 1 trillion.

A deeper dive into the math behind PhotoDNA could be explained in this way - PhotoDNA is a perceptual fuzzy hash technology. Before proceeding, the full-resolution color image is reduced in resolution and converted to grayscale in order to increase consistency and speed. The process proceeds by applying a high-pass filter to accentuate significant image attributes, partitioning the high-pass image into squares, and generating a PhotoDNA hash by assigning a value to each square in the grid according to its visual characteristics. In order to verify that the hash value matches previous hashes in the law enforcement database, the similarity between the two is evaluated against a predetermined threshold. Internet service providers (ISPs) may be provided with these hashes; by comparing them to the hashes of images hosted on their platforms, ISPs may identify duplicates and remove them. Additionally, law enforcement may acquire new victims in order to aid in the pursuit of the criminals through the identification of previously undetectable duplicates of similar images. For videos, the fundamental method remains unchanged. PhotoDNA is utilized to generate a distinct hash for crucial video frames containing CSAM. The aforementioned CSAM hashes are subsequently comparable to other keyframe hashes.

3.5.2 Challenges Faced by PhotoDNA

The hashing algorithm is not accompanied by decryption capabilities. This suggests that if CSAM is present in an encrypted format, there lies no option other than skipping detection there. Secondly, if modification or manipulation is made to the content, there lies a high chance of not being flagged to be CSAM. Thus, two loopholes or escape routes are already open to perpetrators. [10]

3.6 BEYOND PHOTODNA

- Fuzzy hashing, or approximate hash-based matching, is another technique used to find intricate, unorganized information that shares some byte-level resemblance. Approximate Matching techniques consist of three sub-classifications, namely,
  - (a) Perceptual
  - (b) Content
  - (c) Hash-Based

    Out of them, the foremost is the most relevant in this context owing to its capabilities with respect to visual data content. [11]

- Multiple approaches have been tried over the years, and one that gave semi-successful results was "Colour Histograms." It provides a representation of the overall color distribution within an image and is highly sensitive to even minute changes. The biggest flaw found in this method is the high rate of false positives it generates with the reason being the absence of inclusion of spatial information. [12]
- With legal authorization being the first step that could be time-consuming, many researchers resorted to methodologies that involved no direct or actual use of the sensitive content itself but its peripheral yet significant information, here, namely, metadata. Metadata-based CSAM detection was raised as an idea. [13]
- However, the technology and the math behind its working is explained, there lies a specific point that has not been addressed yet, that is, a location-specific identification of CSAM. With this focus at hand, an idea is explored, which is powered by a custom-crafted web crawler and snowball sampling specifically for Child Sexual Abuse Image or CSAI, a sub-classification within CSAM. [14]

3.7 PROJECT ARACHNID

Project Arachnid is a highly respectable initiative launched in the year 2017 at a global scale. It relies on the automation of CSAM detection. "Shield" is the most remarkable undertaking within this project owing to the fact that it is one of the only no-cost tools for industry out there. In essence, it is an API that organizations can avail for proactive detection. Arachnid Orb is the second avenue under this project, which essentially formulated a device that could aid in the collaborative functioning of child protection organizations and hotlines. Significant backing was provided by the Government of Canada for this particular project as well. [15]

3.8 GOOGLE'S TECH

The two major innovative moves advanced by Google are the Industry Hash Sharing Platform and Hash Matching API. [16]

The following are the keywords in Google's digital strive against CSAM:

1. Industry Hash-Sharing Platform
2. Hash Matching API
3. Content Safety API
4. CSAI Matching

Google's Transparency Report handed over to NCMEC is focused on diligence dealing with YouTube as a platform combating CSAM. One of the key challenges that earlier detection methods lacked was the ability to foresee what the next-generation CSAM may look like. In other words, a totally new genre of CSAM taking over may be found cumbersome to classify. This is exactly where Content Safety API comes into play. CSAI Matching technology primarily deals with previously known content.

3.9 APPLE'S INITIATIVE

The following is a summary of Apple's work for CSAM detection [17]:

In Apple's technical summary of 2021, these were the following keywords Apple vouched for:

1. Neural Hash
2. Private Set Intersection
3. Cryptographic Safety Voucher
4. Threshold Secret Sharing
5. Hyperplane Locality Sensitive Hashing
6. Synthetic Matching Vouchers
7. Safety Voucher Mechanics

Neural Hash has the ability to match even images that are possible variants of the original hash itself. A certain amount of size and quality variations shall not cause hindrance to the matching probability, as per the technical summary. This apparently is made possible by another underlying cryptographic technology termed Private Set Intersection. A match result is accompanied by a digital entity named Cryptographic Safety Voucher.

To sum up, Apple has a pre-made database of CSAM image hashes. Now, this gets coupled with each and every user device via their cloud platform, iCloud Photos, where they use the Safety Voucher Generation module. Now, to answer the question of whether Apple takes magnifying glasses onto every visual content accumulated in the user's device, the answer is - No. For this exact purpose, it is said that they brought into effect the Threshold Secret Sharing Technology. What underlies the supervision part of this detection methodology is the Safety Voucher Generation module which is not accessed by Apple until this threshold is passed. Neural Hash technology by Apple is now built into iOS devices, crosschecking for CSAM content.

How does Neural Hash differ from the traditionally used images with hash-matching approaches? What they lacked is the Hyperplane Locality Sensitive Hashing (LSH) process. This predominantly falls under the Perceptual Hashing concept itself. They have significant reliance on image descriptors. The basic idea is pretty straightforward. What human eyes observe to be similar, the technology must be able to match the similarities and likewise for the ones that are not.

Math Behind Neural Hash

Step 1: CNN
: The output of the floating point descriptor along with the N-dimensional, floating point descriptor is obtained after the image passes through the CNN.

Step 2: Hash
: Conversion of N floating point numbers to M bits with the use of a hashing scheme.

Private Set Intersection or PSI:
This is the Zero Knowledge Proof solution in the form of a cryptographic protocol.

Steps Involved:

Step 1 - Matching Database Setup
Step 2 - On-device PSI Protocol
Step 3 - Server-side PSI Protocol

As a conclusion about Apple's CSAM detection approach, it can be said that the introduction of new terminologies and newer ideas backing it in a combined format seemed striking. But the true determinant of innovative technology definitely does not rely on eye-catching terminologies and complicated multilayered procedures to make it work but rather the efficiency that the methodology practically yields. The search for better and better technologies at the end of the day is to make sure that a day will come when fewer, least and no minors are burdened by being robbed of their rights to privacy. And to make that happen it is entities holding power over the so-called Internet who need to respond the way they should.

3.10 ORGANIZATION V/S EFFORT(S)

Table 3.2 Organization vs Efforts

Organization	*Effort*
NCMEC	Repository
ICMEC	International Regulation
IWF	Hotline
Thorn	Classifier Algorithm
INTERPOL	ICSE Database
Microsoft	PhotoDNA
Google	Industry Hash Sharing Platform, Hash Matching API
Apple	Neural Hash
Project Arachnid	Sheild, Arachnid Orb

3.11 AI-GENERATED CSAM OR AIG-CSAM

The advent of AI gave birth to many more non-human-generated entities. The tug of war, whether AI is going to be the savior of all or the devil itself, is a debate on its own. The multitudes of things that we humans are able to do with the click of a fingertip the high-tech innovations are truly awe-inspiring but as a world-known fact - all is a two-faced coin. The good finds its bad on the other side. Here is a peek at the scary competency of AI.

A buzzword that was outspoken as a pitfall of AI, "Deepfake" is truly notorious for its all-power. The reason is that the duplication of an already available specimen (such as a single disturbing image) is possible by AI- generation specifically for images, video or any other multimedia form. This is what produces the so-called deepfakes. The output of this maleficent breakthrough is of such a degree of similarity with respect to its source or predecessor, i.e., for example, a human-generated photograph, that even the human eye could be deceived in classifying one from the other. Thus, the name "Deep-Fake."

This is an area requiring intense research as the threat it poses is higher than the rest of its counterparts. Our current capabilities may find its function cloudy by the nature of AIG-CSAM. ML/AI models are an umbrella solution, especially when it comes to the identification of synthetic content. [18]

3.12 THORN'S ALGORITHM

With AI in the picture, more pinpointed and efficient algorithms are a necessity to give rise to powerful tools of detection. One of them was brought into effect by Thorn, introducing Thorn's CSAM Classifier Algorithm. The highlight here is that once a true positive CSAM (both in the case of image and video), it continually learns from it, thus, keeping a loop of learning to get smarter. The highest merit claimed by this technology is the efficacy against the time it is prophesied to revert. [19]

3.13 CONCLUSION

AI taking over this era of technology with certain aspects of its capabilities unknown is quite cannibalistic unless thoroughly comprehended and controlled. This would specifically aid in reducing newer versions of non-human generated or synthetic CSAM from being produced and propagated. A medical pandemic has left the world enough in pieces; an electronic one taking us over shall cause more harm than what can be foreseen.

> I fear the day that technology will surpass our human interaction. The world will have a generation of idiots.

Sir Albert Einstein spoke the remarkable words, though in an era much earlier than the worse-to-worst state of affairs of technology was reached - quite arguable. One cannot simply put up points on how chaotic an ever-evolving society, humans are building - this is always how it has been and always will be. The good part is we are blessed with an intellect that judges the difference between good and bad and it is our hands and heads to make the conscious choice of which and which not to choose.

Sadly, a high number of online users make the undesirable choice, leading the greater number of ones in the desirable paths to enter the ring to put up a battle. It is evident that the Internet though can be used for good with millions of ways to do so, perpetrators are never on the sinking count. The net effect, the fight is definitely not at equilibrium and as optimist technologists, we mostly like to see that we are on the winning side. Surely, an appreciable chunk of human brains function the tireless number of hours to fight the e-evil without no doubt yield handsome results. The outcomes churned out by exceptional initiatives starting from PhotoDNA [20], a semi-technological idea of opening a window of help via hotlines providing immediate attention to victims from IWF [21], national operations such as CEOP [22] are remarkable progress of technological giants, child safety-focused organizations, national missions and so on have risen up to. A collective strive from people involved in this form of act of service, irrespective of their role, without themselves knowing, are making a safer home within the virtual cobwebs.

Ending loops of mistreatment is the aim, but surely "The End" is not near, Every new ounce of effort made is scaling us closer and closer to a better world, though it might not be visible as abundantly as daylight. The fight is not stopping, and neither is our grit to fight back. A new tool, a new idea, a new armor rises up.

REFERENCES

1. National Center for Missing & Exploited Children. (n.d.). Retrieved May 10, 2024, from www.missingkids.org/home
2. Missing Kids. (n.d.). Child Sexual Abuse Material. Retrieved May 10, 2024, from www.missingkids.org/theissues/csam
3. Ward, K. (n.d.). Child Sexual Abuse Material: Model Legislation & Global Review. International Centre for Missing & Exploited Children. Retrieved May 10, 2024, from www.icmec.org/child-pornography-model-legislation-report/
4. Thorn. (n.d.). Home. Retrieved May 10, 2024, from www.thorn.org/
5. Interpol. (n.d.). International Child Sexual Exploitation Database. Retrieved May 10, 2024, from www.interpol.int/en/Crimes/Crimes-against-children/International-Child-Sexual-Exploitation-database
6. Google Safety Centre. (n.d.). How Hash Matching Technology Helps NCMEC. Retrieved May 10, 2024, from https://safety.google/intl/en_uk/stories/hash-matching-to-help-ncmec/

7. ResearchGate. (n.d.). A Mini-Review of Combat Online Child Abuse Using PhotoDNA Technology. Retrieved May 10, 2024, from www.researchgate.net/profile/Ayat-Najjar/publication/358497140_A_mini-review_of_combat_online_child_abuse_using_PhotoDNA_technology/links/6204f4aa4d47431e1f532511/A-mini-review-of-combat-online-child-abuse-using-PhotoDNA-technology.pdf
8. RAINN. (n.d.). What is Child Sexual Abuse Material (CSAM). Retrieved May 15, 2024, from www.rainn.org/news/what-child-sexual-abuse-material-csam
9. Statista. (n.d.). CSAM Content Reported Online 2022. Retrieved May 10, 2024, from www.statista.com/statistics/1448957/pieces-csam-content-reported-online-platforms/
10. Article from ACM Digital Library. (n.d.). An Analysis of PhotoDNA. Retrieved May 10, 2024, from https://dl.acm.org/doi/pdf/10.1145/3600160.3605048
11. Bjelland, P. C., Franke, K., & Årnes, A. (2014). Practical Use of Approximate Hash Based Matching in Digital Investigations. *Digital Investigation*, 11, S18–S26. https://doi.org/10.1016/j.diin.2014.03.003Apple
12. Jing Huang, S. Kumar, R., Mitra, M., Zhu, W.-J.& Zabih, R. Image Indexing Using Color Correlograms. In *Proceedings of the IEEE Computer Society Con-ference on Computer Vision and Pattern Recognition (CVPR '97)*, 762–768, 1997.
13. IEEE. (n.d.). Metadata Based Child Sexual Abuse Material. Retrieved May 10, 2024, from https://ieeexplore.ieee.org/stamp/stamp.jsp?tp=&arnumber=10283988
14. Guerra, Enrique & Westlake, Bryce G. (2021). Detecting Child Sexual Abuse Images: Traits of Child Sexual Exploitation Hosting and Displaying Websites. *Child Abuse & Neglect*, 122, 105336.
15. Project Arachnid. (n.d.). Home. Retrieved May 10, 2024, from www.projectarachnid.ca/en/
16. Google Safety Centre. (n.d.). How Hash Matching Technology Helps NCMEC. Retrieved May 10, 2024, from https://safety.google/intl/en_uk/stories/hash-matching-to-help-ncmec/
17. Apple. (n.d.). CSAM Detection Technical Summary. Retrieved May 10, 2024, from www.apple.com/child-safety/pdf/CSAM_Detection_Technical_Summary.pdf
18. Thorn. (2023). How Thorn's CSAM Classifier Uses Artificial Intelligence to Build a Safer Internet. Retrieved May 10, 2024, from www.thorn.org/blog/how-thorns-csam-classifier-uses-artificial-intelligence-to-build-a-safer-internet/
19. Thorn. (n.d.). Generative AI: Now is the Time for Safety By Design. Retrieved May 10, 2024, from www.thorn.org/blog/now-is-the-time-for-safety-by-design/
20. Microsoft. (n.d.). PhotoDNA. Retrieved May 10, 2024, from www.microsoft.com/en-us/photodna

21. Internet Watch Foundation. (n.d.). Our History. Retrieved May 10, 2024, from www.iwf.org.uk/about-us/why-we-exist/our-history/#:~:text=The%20Internet%20Watch%20Foundation%20
22. Wikipedia. (n.d.). Child Exploitation and Online Protection Command. Retrieved May 10, 2024, from https://en.wikipedia.org/wiki/Child_Exploitation_and_Online_Protection_Command

Chapter 4

Advanced Mobile Forensics

Beyond Tool Automation

Luca Cadonici

4.1 INTRODUCTION

4.1.1 The Mobile Communication Revolution

The evolution of mobile communication has marked two fundamental revolutions over the years. Starting from the 1980s with the introduction of the Motorola DynaTAC 8000x in 1983, the first mobile phone, mobile telephony revolutionized communication by expanding user possibilities. Over time, mobile technology has continued to grow both numerically and technologically. The first revolution occurred in the early 2000s with the unstoppable proliferation of mobile communication devices. The year 2007 was a milestone with Apple's announcement of the iPhone, defining the standard for smartphones with its innovative combination of phone, media player, and internet access. Shortly after, Android was introduced, leading to the launch of the HTC Dream in 2008, the first Android smartphone. These events mark a second turning point in the history of mobile devices, ushering in an era of interconnectedness and advanced functionalities that has not ceased since. Globally, there were around 15 billion active mobile devices in 2021, as opposed to slightly more than 14 billion the year before. By 2025, there will be 18.22 billion mobile devices worldwide, an increase of 4.2 billion above 2020 levels, according to predictions (see Figure 4.1). [1]

4.1.2 Mobile Devices: A Definition

We can use the National Institute of Standards and Technology's (NIST) rules to describe mobile devices. The NIST is a unit of the U.S. Department of Commerce tasked with promoting the American economy through collaboration with industry to develop standards, technologies, and methodologies that enhance production and trade. The following definition is taken from NIST's "Guidelines for Managing the Security of Mobile Devices in the Enterprise." [2]

 DOI: 10.1201/9781003471103-4

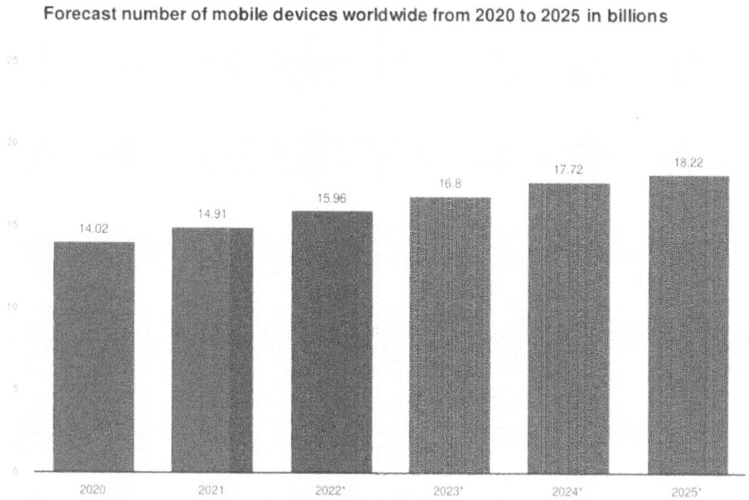

Figure 4.1 Forecast Number of Mobile Devices Worldwide From 2020 to 2025 in Billions.

> *A portable computing device that has a small form factor such that it can easily be carried by a single individual; is designed to operate without a physical connection (e.g., wirelessly transmit or receive information); possesses local, non-removable data storage; and is powered on for extended periods of time with a self-contained power source. Additionally, mobile devices may have built-in microphones for voice communication and sensors that let them record, take pictures, record videos, and locate information, and\or built-in features for synchronizing local data with remote locations.*

From a forensic perspective, the widespread use of smartphones and tablets has increased their significance, making them essential tools in various investigative scenarios. Recognizing the crucial role of these devices, gaining an advanced understanding of their operations and forensic acquisition methods becomes fundamental for modern investigators.

4.1.3 From Mobile Devices to Mobile Forensics

Mobile devices have become privileged channels for accessing individuals' personal information. However, this growing reliance on mobile devices is balanced by robust dedicated security measures. This equilibrium between extensive use as personal archives and the presence of advanced security measures underscores the crucial nature of privacy and security in the digital era. Technology has played a fundamental role in transforming smartphones and tablets into not only sophisticated communication tools but also reliable guardians of users' personal information. While this reassures us as users that our data is protected, it also presents significant technical challenges for analysts.

4.1.4 Role of Forensic Suites: Acquisition, Automation, and AI Application

Recognizing the capabilities of forensic suites available in the market in terms of acquisition, analysis support, and automation is essential for extracting, acquiring, and validating data within a forensic context. Gone are the days when a complete copy of the file system was easily obtainable through rooting and jailbreaking procedures. Similarly, especially in the Android world, native backup solutions do not allow the acquisition of the often most interesting part of a mobile device – namely, the contents of messaging apps. Forensic acquisition suites play a crucial role, primarily in the critical phase of forensic acquisition, where they use vulnerabilities in chipsets, devices, and operating systems to gain maximum privileges on the system and make a complete copy of the stored data or, alternatively, a logical copy of only the applications supported by the acquisition agents.

Then, the automation provided by the graphical interfaces of tools also allows analysts to speed up and optimize device analysis, proving highly user-friendly in diverse investigations. It correlates contacts, messages, and multimedia files to simplify and make the analyst's work more intuitive. Particularly useful in this regard is the use of artificial intelligence, now firmly integrated into analysis tools concerning the analysis and categorization of images and videos. Tools have long allowed the categorization of multimedia files based on predetermined categories through automated analysis of photos and videos, enabling the analyst to set a minimum threshold to reduce the risk of false positives. Multimedia classification allows the reporting of images and videos based on the presence of objects or individuals of interest, considering depicted locations, graphics, context, or meaning. Also highly valuable are the functions for recognizing colors in photos and videos to identify the percentage of skin present, which is of paramount importance in handling cases related to Child Sexual Abuse Material (CSAM) or any other sexual crime. Finally, particularly useful when available, is the facial recognition function that allows for the automated identification and categorization of subjects portrayed in the photos on devices. It categorizes them based on age, gender, and physical characteristics, enabling the verification of the presence of images related to a specific individual. It is easy to imagine how this can be beneficial, for example, in cases of *kidnapping*, *stalking*, *sextortion*, or *revenge porn*.

4.2 A LOOK INSIDE MOBILE DEVICES

4.2.1 iOS vs Android

The technological advancement in the mobile device sector has given rise to the simultaneous development of the two predominant operating systems: Apple's iOS and Google's Android (see Figure 4.2). Both aim to provide an optimal user experience on smartphones and tablets but follow distinct approaches in their design and development philosophy. The proprietary operating systems of Blackberry, Nokia, and Windows, on the other hand, failed to withstand the competition and were discontinued after several years of attempts.

4.2.1.1 iOS

The debut of iOS in 2007, with the launch of the iPhone, marks an epochal moment in the history of mobile devices. Apple conceived iOS as an intuitive and integrated operating system, tailor-made for its hardware devices, such as the iPhone, iPod Touch, and iPad. Over the years, iOS has undergone several major versions, each introduced with new features and improvements, seamlessly integrated with the native Apple iCloud environment, forming

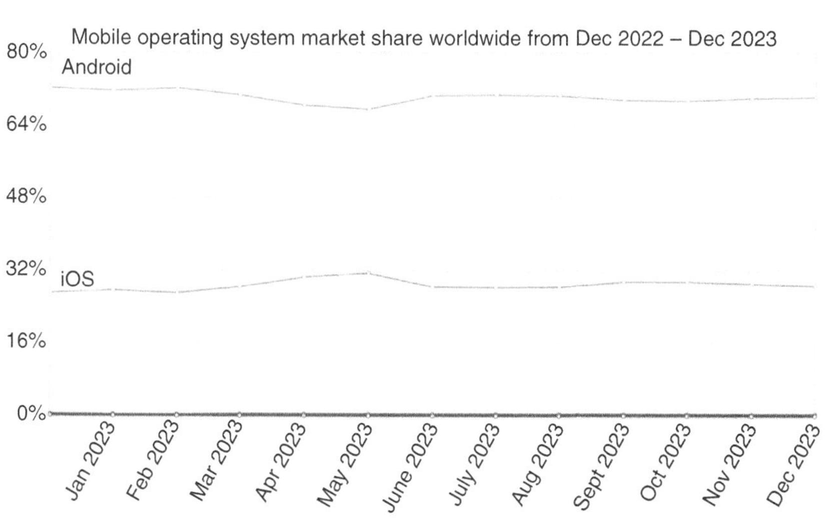

Figure 4.2 Mobile Operating System Market Share Worldwide from December 2022 to December 2023 [3].

a true digital ecosystem with the highest level of integration and efficiency. Additionally, iOS has laid the foundation for the development of three specialized operating systems: iPadOS for iPad, tvOS for Apple TV, and watchOS for Apple Watch. Each of them has been adapted to meet the specific needs of their respective devices, further expanding the Apple ecosystem.

4.2.1.2 Android

Primarily developed by Google within the Open Handset Alliance, Android follows a more open approach compared to iOS. Its launch in 2008 quickly propelled Android to become the dominant operating system in the mobile device market. The open-source nature of Android has facilitated the adoption and customization of the operating system by many manufacturers, leading to a notable variety of Android devices available in the market. This flexibility has made Android the preferred choice for many manufacturers, contributing to its extraordinary success. As of December 2023, Android smartphones held a 70% share of the global mobile operating system market, while iOS accounted for 28.8%. The continuous evolution of both operating systems has driven significant innovations in the world of mobile devices, offering users a wide range of options and ongoing technological progress.

4.2.2 The Artifacts of Mobile Forensics

> Every contact leaves a trace. – Dr. Edmond Locard

This fundamental principle of forensic science, formulated by the pioneer of forensic sciences, Dr. Edmond Locard, emphasizes that every interaction leaves a trace. In other words, during contact between two objects or individuals, there is an exchange of materials that can constitute valuable evidence for forensic investigations. In Mobile Forensics, the term *artifact* refers to any element of forensic value produced by the device, the operating system, or third-party applications during the operation of the mobile device and/or interaction with the user. Typically, every investigator faces the need to answer a comprehensive set of questions, including *Who*, *What*, *When*, *Where*, *Why*, and *How*. Data on modern mobile devices play a crucial role in resolving such inquiries. By leveraging specific artifacts for Android and iOS devices, it becomes possible to determine with whom a user of the device has communicated and the places visited by the device. Through the analysis of device usage, it is also possible to establish whether a person was using the device during a fatal road accident, as well as to pinpoint the timeline of a death in cases of suicide, homicide, or overdose by identifying the user's last interactions (e.g., device lock or unlock, reboot, charging, response to a message or call, etc.).

According to Magnet Forensics [4], mobile forensics artifacts are classified into the following five categories:

1. Geolocation Artifacts
2. Communication Artifacts
3. Multimedia Files
4. Web Browsing Activity Artifacts
   To these five macro-categories, at least two more can be added:
5. Log Files
   Produced by applications and the operating system, log files prove particularly useful both for reconstructing users' usage history and for detecting potential compromises and malware infections.
6. Configuration Files
   In this category, we include files – typically in ABX, XML, .list or .txt format for Android and .plist for iOS – that the operating system uses to store device identification information or details related to its configuration and selected settings. Examples of such information encompass Android ID, Serial Number, Model, IMEI, Wi-Fi MAC address, Bluetooth device name, hotspot device name, factory reset date, and the date of the device's initial complete configuration after formatting.

4.3 SQLITE DATABASE ARTIFACTS

4.3.1 SQLite Databases in Mobile Forensics

The management of data organized alphabetically, typologically, or chronologically on mobile devices occurs through the organization of information collected in databases managed by third-party applications or directly by the operating system. Both Android and iOS resort to the creation and querying of SQLite databases to handle information related to communications, web searches, and the management of contacts and multimedia files, just to name a few common scenarios. SQLite artifacts, therefore, constitute a source of paramount importance regarding the forensic analysis of mobile devices. Consequently, the manual parsing of SQLite databases is one of the key skills required of Mobile Forensics analysts to verify the information collected by analysis suites, as well as to extract or correlate new information. This enables the integration of findings from automatic analysis with those detected through manual analysis.

SQLite is a lightweight, serverless SQL database engine widely used for its simplicity and ease of use. Due to its limited resource consumption, it can be embedded directly into applications, making it particularly suitable for mobile devices. However, desktop applications, such as web browsers (Chrome, Firefox, Brave, etc.), also use SQLite for managing bookmarks, favorites, and browsing history.

4.3.2 SQLite Queries

Queries are utilized to handle data stored in SQLite files. These queries are authored in the Structured Query Language (SQL), which is specifically designed for interacting with the SQLite database. A query might consist of one or several clauses that define the desired actions, such as selecting, inserting, updating, or deleting data.

The retrieval of data analyzed by forensic tools is often the result of specific selection queries inserted by developers. Typically, these queries are not specified in the final output, where tables and analyzed columns are usually reported. Therefore, the ability to recreate the necessary queries to acquire the data of interest is one of the primary skills that an advanced-level analyst must possess. This skill is essential for verifying the results of reports and, if necessary, enhancing the collected information with new data obtained from queries created to meet specific analysis needs.

Although SQLite has various main categories of parameters (insertion, updating, deletion, table creation), in forensic contexts, queries and selection parameters are practically exclusively used. The main statements employed in almost any analysis query are SELECT, FROM, and WHERE:

- SELECT: A parameter used to retrieve data from one or more tables in the database. It allows for queries to obtain specific information from the data stored in the tables.
- FROM: A clause typically used within a SELECT query to specify the table or tables from which to retrieve data.
- WHERE: A clause used within a SELECT query to filter data based on specific conditions.

A basic example of using the three parameters could be the following query applied to the **sms.db** database used by iOS to store SMS messages[1]. We query the database to retrieve all outgoing messages (column **is_from_me** = 1) (see Figure 4.3). Note that the use of a semicolon at the end of queries is optional but recommended for formatting and comprehension purposes.

Other statements of interest for forensic analysis include the following:

- DISTINCT: A parameter used within a SELECT query to return unique results, eliminating any duplicates from the data retrieved

SELECT ROWID, text, is_from_me FROM message WHERE is_from_me = 1;	*ROWID*	*text*	*Is_from_me*
	34	Test iMessage. I hope this is a blue bubble!	1
	36		1
	38	Here is Heather's paper from DFIR Review.	1
	41	It is. But there was some weird stuff at the end.	1

Figure 4.3 Output of the SQLite Query: Outgoing SMS in the sms.db Database.

from the table. In other words, DISTINCT allows obtaining a list of distinct values for one or more columns specified in the SELECT clause.

- JOIN: Statement used to combine rows from two or more tables based on a related column between them. The JOIN operation allows you to retrieve information from multiple tables in a single query, creating a result set that includes columns from both tables.
- INNER JOIN: Type of join operation that combines rows from two or more tables based on a specified condition and only returns the rows where the specified condition is true.
- ORDER BY: Statement used to specify the order in which the result set should be sorted. The ORDER BY clause can be applied to one or more columns, and it can sort the result set in ascending (default) or descending order.

A first simple example could be a query to ask **knowledgeC.db** for timeframes related to iOS Camera usage (column **ZVALUESTRING = 'com.apple.camera'**) (see Figure 4.4).

```
SELECT DISTINCT
ZVALUESTRING as "App",
datetime('2001-01-01', "ZSTARTDATE" || ' seconds') as "Start date",
datetime('2001-01-01', "ZENDDATE" || ' seconds') as "End date"
FROM ZOBJECT
WHERE "App" = "com.apple.camera";
```

A little more complex option is to create a query on the **Photos.sqlite** database used by iOS to organize multimedia files present in the device's gallery. Let's query the database to retrieve the name and trashed date of multimedia files moved to the trash (column **ZTRASHEDSTATE = 1**):

App	*Start, date*	*End, date*
com.apple.camera	2020-03-22 11:45:21	2020-03-22 11:45:21
com.apple.camera	2020-03-23 15:50:24	2020-03-23 15:50:24
com.apple.camera	2020-03-24 01:01:17	2020-03-24 01:01:20
com.apple.camera	2020-03-25 02:01:54	2020-03-25 02:01:56
com.apple.camera	2020-03-25 18:35:27	2020-03-25 18:35:29
com.apple.camera	2020-03-27 21:53:59	2020-03-27 21:53:59

Figure 4.4 Output of the SQLite Query:Time-Frames Related to iOS Camera Usage From knowledgeC.db Database.

```
SELECT
Z_PK,
ZFILENAME AS "File",
ZTRASHEDSTATE,
datetime('2001-01-01', "ZTRASHEDDATE" || ' seconds') AS "Trashed Date",
datetime('2001-01-01', "ZDATECREATED" || ' seconds') AS "Creation Date",
datetime('2001-01-01', "ZADDEDDATE" || ' seconds') AS "Added Date"
FROM ZASSET
WHERE ZTRASHEDSTATE = 1
ORDER BY Z_PK;
```

The earlier examples are straightforward illustrations. However, as we delve deeper, we can enhance the results and expand correlation possibilities through more sophisticated queries.

4.4 ADVANCED TECHNIQUES

4.4.1 Validating Data: An Example of Manual Analysis

The myriad possible variations in requests posed to the mobile forensic analyst necessitate the proficiency to manually parsing SQLite artifacts. This ensures the recovery of information not routinely encompassed in the analysis results of forensic suites, or, as an alternative, validates such findings. For instance, the analyst may be required to verify not only if a WhatsApp message has been delivered but also if it has been viewed. To validate this assertion, and possibly testify in court, it is imperative that the analyst understands the underlying mechanics of the application, particularly the logics governing the SQLite database where such information is stored.

Z_PK	File	ZTRASHEDSTATE	Trashed Date	Creation Date	Added Date
16033	!MG_4681.HEIC	1	2023-07-24 11:34:38	2023-07-24 11:34:22	2023-07-24 11:34:23
16034	!MG_4682.HEIC	1	2023-07-24 11:34:40	2023-07-24 11:34:22	2023-07-24 11:34:23
16102	!MG_4750.HEIC	1	2023-07-29 18:38:38	2023-07-29 18:28:07	2023-07-29 18:28:08
16149	!MG_4797.HEIC	1	2023-08-05 20:49:29	2023-08-04 00:11:04	2023-08-04 00:11:05
16150	!MG_4798.HEIC	1	2023-08-05 20:49:29	2023-08-04 00:11:04	2023-08-04 00:11:05

Figure 4.5 Output of the SQLite Query: Name and Trashed Date of Multimedia Files Moved to the Trash From iOS Photos.sqlite Database.

ZMESSAGESTATUS	*ZTEXT*
6	io lavoro
6	ce no ho per un po'
6	scusa
6	usciamo dopo cena
6	passeaaiata io e te
8	senza cani
8	così non rompono
8	i miei
8	non i cani..

Figure 4.6 ChatStorage.sqlite – ZWAMESSAGE Table, ZMESSAGGESTATUS = 8 (message read).

To address the question, for an iOS device, we can analyze the ZWAMESSAGE table in the **ChatStorage.sqlite** using an SQLite browser, *DB browser for SQLITE* [6] in this case. For each sent message (column ZISFROMME =1), in column ZMESSAGESTATUS for each sent text message we may have, and a value of '8' corresponds to 'read' (see Figures 4.5 and 4.6).

Note that if the user has not enabled read receipts, commonly known as 'blue ticks,' the messages will only have a value of 6, as the sender is never notified of their reception (see Figure 4.7). The same behavior has been noticed for messages edited by the sender itself, as is it is possible to do since May 2023.

ZMESSAGESTATUS	*ZTEXT*
8	allora ok
8	cerco i voli
8	e il viaggio lo facciamo a Malta
8	ti può andare?
8	Ok.. quanti giorni siamo fuori?
6	Ora sento Alìs.

Figure 4.7 ChatStorage.sqlite – ZWAMESSAGE Table, ZMESSAGGESTATUS = 6 (message unread or edited).

4.4.2 Advanced SQLite Queries

We can enhance the query to retrieve the screen time for various time intervals of the WhatsApp application on iOS by querying the RMAdminStore-Local.sqlite database (see Figure 4.8).

Its structured organization, particularly within tables like ZUSAGETIMEDITEM, ZUSAGECOUNTEDITEM and ZUSAGEBLOCK, provides forensic analysts with a granular view of app usage patterns, device pickups, notification counts, and more.

Located at the path **/private/var/mobile/Library/Application Support/com.apple.remotemanagementd** this database serves as a repository of interesting insights into application screen time and user interactions on iOS devices.

The query we are about to propose retrieves detailed information for each time block, focusing on local time. It includes data such as screen time, number of notifications, number of pickups, block duration, and timestamps for the start, end, first pickup, last event, longest session start, and longest session ends in Universal Time Coordinated (UTC) time zone.

In the query, some additional analysis elements are included:

- **LEFT JOIN**: A type of join operation that combines rows from two tables based on a specified condition and includes unmatched rows from the left (or first) table. This means that even if there are no matching rows in the right (or second) table, the rows from the left table will still be included in the result set, with NULL values in the columns from the right table.
- **Datetime**: A function, which returns the date and time as text in this formats: YYYY-MM-DD HH:MM:SS.
- **strftime**: A function, which returns the date formatted according to the format string specified as the first argument.

```
SELECT
  datetime('2001-01-01', "ZSTARTDATE" || ' seconds') AS "Start date
(UTC)",
  ZUSAGETIMEDITEM.ZBUNDLEIDENTIFIER AS "App",
  ZUSAGETIMEDITEM.ZTOTALTIMEINSECONDS AS "Screen time in
seconds (single app)",
  ZUSAGECOUNTEDITEM.ZNUMBEROFNOTIFICATIONS AS "Number
of notifications",
  ZUSAGECOUNTEDITEM.ZNUMBEROFPICKUPS AS "Number of
Pickups",
  ZUSAGEBLOCK.ZDURATIONINMINUTES AS "Block duration in
minutes",
  ZUSAGEBLOCK.ZNUMBEROFPICKUPSWITHOUTAPPLICATIONUS
AGE AS "Number of pickups without application",
  strftime('%M:%S', ZUSAGEBLOCK.ZSCREENTIMEINSECONDS,
'unixepoch') AS "Total block screen time (mm:ss)",
  datetime('2001-01-01', "ZUSAGEBLOCK.ZFIRSTPICKUPDATE" || '
seconds') AS "First pickup date (UTC)",
  datetime('2001-01-01', ZUSAGEBLOCK.ZLASTEVENTDATE || '
seconds') AS "Last event date (UTC)",
  datetime('2001-01-01', ZUSAGEBLOCK.ZLONGESTSESSIONENDDATE
|| ' seconds') AS "Longest session end date (UTC)",
  datetime('2001-01-01', ZUSAGEBLOCK.ZLONGESTSESSION
STARTDATE || ' seconds') AS "Longest session start date (UTC)"
FROM
  ZUSAGETIMEDITEM
JOIN
  ZUSAGECATEGORY ON ZUSAGETIMEDITEM.
ZCATEGORY = ZUSAGECATEGORY.Z_PK
JOIN
  ZUSAGEBLOCK ON ZUSAGECATEGORY.
ZBLOCK = ZUSAGEBLOCK.Z_PK
LEFT JOIN
  ZUSAGECOUNTEDITEM ON ZUSAGETIMEDITEM.
ZBUNDLEIDENTIFIER = ZUSAGECOUNTEDITEM.
ZBUNDLEIDENTIFIER AND ZUSAGECATEGORY.
ZBLOCK = ZUSAGECOUNTEDITEM.ZBLOCK
WHERE ZUSAGETIMEDITEM.ZBUNDLEIDENTIFIER = "net.whatsapp.
WhatsApp"
ORDER BY
  ZUSAGECATEGORY.ZBLOCK ASC;
```

This type of query can be used for various purposes. One example is checking the iOS camera usage within a specific period. In a forensic investigation, I was tasked with illustrating the creation of a video, subsequently removed, related to a serious criminal case – specifically, one

Start date(UTC)	*App*	*Screen time in seconds (single app)*	*Number of notifications*	*Number of Pickups*	*Block durabon in minutes*	*Number of pickups without application*	*Total block*
2023-06-18 15:00:00	net.whatsapp.WhalsApp	20	0	1	60	3	30:44
2023-06-18 17:00:00	net.whatsapp.WhalsApp	34	0	1	60	3	06:56
2023-06-18 18:00:00	net.whatsapp.WhalsApp	55	5	3	60	10	13:20
2023-06-18 19:00:00	net.whatsapp.WhalsApp	833	10	3	60	2	26:40
2023-06-18 21:00:00	net.whatsapp.WhalsApp	33	5	1	60	4	36:32
2023-06-19 08:00:00	net.whatsapp.WhalsApp	341	2	3	60	5	25:36
2023-06-19 09:00:00	net.whatsapp.WhalsApp	1147	25	2	60	1	58:24
2023-06-19 10:00:00	net.whatsapp.WhalsApp	1248	12	4	60	2	54:32
2023-06-19 12:00:00	net.whatsapp.WhalsApp	1218	22	1	60	1	39:16
2023-06-19 11:00:00	net.whatsapp.WhalsApp	205	11	5	60	0	18:04
2023-06-19 13:00:00	net.whatsapp.WhalsApp	116	11	0	60	4	05:32
2023-06-19 14:00:00	net.whatsapp.WhalsApp	190	8	3	60	7	39:24

Figure 4.8 RMAdminStore-Local.sqlite – Time Block Information.

involving the nighttime use of an iPhone camera to capture footage of a violent incident.

Employing manual SQLite analysis, I thoroughly examined the **RMAdminStore-Local.sqlite** database, revealing a 40 second window of camera activity between 04:00 and 05:00 A.M. This led to an in-depth exploration of the iOS **knowledgeC.db** database. Specifically, I chose to query the ZOBJECT table containing detailed information on app usage start and end times, facilitating the calculation of comprehensive usage patterns. Aligning data from both **knowledgeC.db** and **RMAdminStore-Local.sqlite** databases, I methodically reconstructed camera usage patterns, establishing a precise timeline for the alleged incident. This involved determining both the start and end times of camera usage, narrowing down the timeframe to the minute, and discerning the sequence of events leading to the commencement and conclusion of the recorded footage. To accomplish this, I utilized the following query on **knowledgeC.db**:

```
SELECT DISTINCT
ZVALUESTRING as "App",
datetime('2001-01-01', "ZSTARTDATE" || ' seconds') as "Start date",
datetime('2001-01-01', "ZENDDATE" || ' seconds') as "End date"
FROM ZOBJECT
WHERE "App" = "com.apple.camera"
```

You can see the query applied in the attached snapshots, capturing information about the iOS camera usage from the **knowledgeC.db** database extracted from Josh Hickman's iOS 13 image on Digital Corpora (see Figures 4.9 and 4.10).

4.4.3 Python Scripting

4.4.3.1 An Introduction to Python

Python, created by Guido van Rossum in 1991, is a programming language that is interpreted, object-oriented, and high-level. It is recognized for its dynamic semantics. The presence of integrated data structures, dynamic typing, and binding capabilities make it well-suited for Rapid Application Development and as a scripting language for linking components. The straightforward syntax of Python emphasizes legibility, hence decreasing the expenses associated with program upkeep. The software provides support for modules and packages, allowing for the organization of code into separate components for increased modularity and the ability to reuse code. The Python interpreter and standard library are readily accessible for all major platforms.

	App	*Start date*	*End date*
1	com.apple.camera	2020-04-11 13:55:59	2020-04-11 13:57:22
2	com.apple.camera	2020-04-12 10:22:51	2020-04-12 10:23:48
3	com.apple.camera	2020-04-12 10:22:53	2020-04-12 10:23:48
4	com.apple.camera	2020-04-12 10:24:51	2020-04-12 10:25:16
5	com.apple.camera	2020-04-12 10:24:53	2020-04-12 10:25:16

Figure 4.9 knowledgeC.db – Detected Camera Usage Periods (DB Browser for SQLite).

The versatility of Python is crucial for professionals seeking to quickly gain programming expertise, not only in the fields of digital forensics and cybersecurity, but also in various scientific and professional domains, including Economics, Physics, Big Data analysis, data science, data analysis, machine learning, data engineering, web development, software development, and more.

4.4.3.2 Python Modules for Mobile Forensics

Files containing code on a specific topic are known as Python modules. These modules consist of built-in functions, classes, and variables, each serving a specific purpose and can be imported into scripts using the "import" command to fulfill specific functions.

Modules are a fundamental organizational tool in Python, providing a structured way to group related code and enhance code reusability. Conceptually, a module can be thought of as a code library or a file containing a set of functions meant for inclusion in applications. Below are some of the most common Python modules:

- **datetime:** Manipulating date and time data.
- **html:** Parsing HTML pages.
- **random:** Generating pseudo-random number generators for various distributions.
- **re:** Detecting and parsing regular expressions.

While "module" refers to a single Python file containing reusable code, "library" is often used to describe a broader collection of related modules that provide cohesive functionality.

Python plays a fundamental role in crafting tailored scripts for queries posed to mobile forensics analysts. Below is a list, certainly not exhaustive, of some particularly useful modules and libraries for mobile forensic analysis activities:

Figure 4.10 knowledgeC.db - Pictures Taken During Detected Camera Usage Periods (Oxygen Forensic Detective Preview).

- **androguard**: A Python library used for analyzing and inspecting Android applications. It provides features for extracting information from bytecode, analyzing Android Application Package (APK) files, and conducting reverse engineering tasks.
- os: This module provides operating system-related functionality in Python. It includes operations to manipulate files and directories, interact with the system environment, obtain information about the platform, and more.

- **pathlib**: Module in that provides the *Path* class for manipulating file and directory paths in a more objective and object-oriented manner compared to traditional string-based methods. It was introduced in Python version 3.4 and offers a clearer and more powerful interface for handling path-related operations.
- **pyMobileDevice**: A Python library that provides an interface for interacting with iOS devices through the *usbmuxd*[2] service. It is used to perform operations like extracting data from Apple devices.
- **sqlite3**: An interface to interact with the SQLite database.
- **tarfile:** A module that provides support for manipulating tar archives. It is often used to compress or extract files and directories in tar format.
- **ZipFile**: This module offers support for manipulating zip archives. It is used to create, read, or extract compressed files and directories in zip format.

4.4.3.3 Python Scripting for Mobile Forensics

Python's seamless integration and interaction with SQLite databases make it a versatile and highly efficient tool for analyzing and correlating artifacts in Mobile Forensics. By developing custom tools, analysts can finely select and verify data extraction, offering a more granular approach compared to the standardized reporting provided by acquisition and analysis suites. This allows for tailoring results to meet specific investigative needs.

Below are three Python scripts developed by the author to address various analysis needs for the Android WhatsApp application:

- **Android WhatsApp vCard Filtering**
- **Android WhatsApp Message Exchange Reporter**
- **Android WhatsApp Self-Destruction Messages Reporter**

There might be a scenario where an analyst needs to extract all electronic business cards (vCard) exchanged in the WhatsApp chats. One possible approach would be to manually extract the data using the graphical user interface of a forensic suite. However, this method would be highly time-consuming and, more significantly, could result in inaccuracies.

A quicker and less error-prone approach would be to create a dedicated Python script that automatically extracts all vCards and produces a result like the one shown in Figure 4.11.

In other situations, it could be beneficial to swiftly identify all contacts engaging in interactions via WhatsApp or to pinpoint contacts with the message auto-destruction timer enabled. Filtering the databases of WhatsApp for Android, specifically **msgstore.db** (which pertains to exchanged messages) and **wa.db** (which contains contact information), allows for a

```
= RESTART: C:\Users\UTENTE\AppData\Local\
Number of distinct vCards: 4
------------------------------
FN: Emeka Swe
Phone Number: +39242
Label: Mobile
------------------------------
FN: Pango
Phone Number: +39325
Label: Mobile
------------------------------
FN: Uche
Phone Number: +393232
Label: Mobile
------------------------------
FN: Young
Phone Number: +3915324
Label: Mobile
------------------------------
```

Figure 4.11 Android WhatsApp vCard Filtering.

```
Script to generate a report of all phone numbers involved in WhatsApp message exchanges.

Results are sorted by Message Count (descending) and then by Display Name.

Please ensure that 'msgstore.db' and 'wa.db' databases are in the same directory as this script. Press Enter to continue...
Display Name:  ANAYO Madam
Phone Number:  2349
Message Count:  394
Raw String:  2349@s.whatsapp.net
------------------------------
Display Name:  None
Phone Number:  status
Message Count:  81
Raw String:  status@broadcast
------------------------------
Display Name:  Oty
Phone Number:  3935
Message Count:  49
Raw String:  3935@s.whatsapp.net
------------------------------
Display Name:  Young
Phone Number:  39153
Message Count:  35
Raw String:  39153@s.whatsapp.net
------------------------------
```

Figure 4.12 Android WhatsApp Message Exchange Reporter.

rapid retrieval of the requested details, as illustrated in the provided outputs shown in Figures 4.12 and 4.13.

The three scripts are available at the following GitHub paths:

https://github.com/cadonici/android_python-scripts/blob/main/whatsapp/vcards/android_wa-vcard_filtering.py

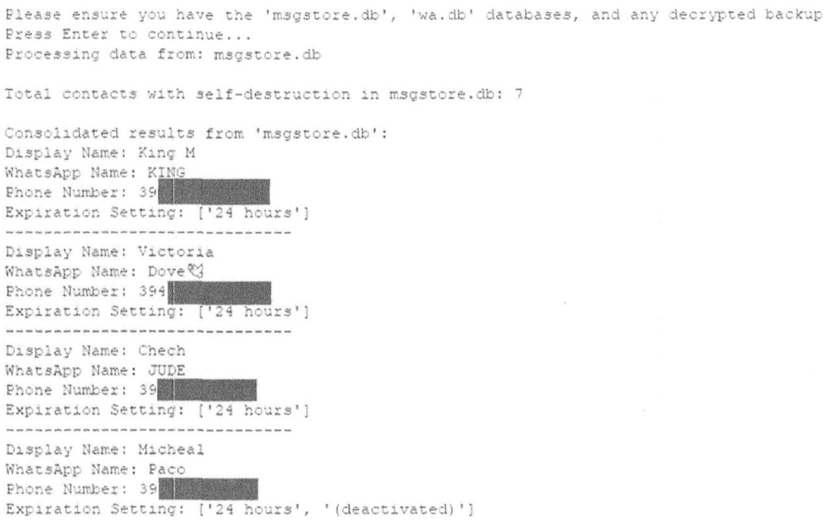

Figure 4.13 Android WhatsApp Self-Destruction Messages Reporter.

https://github.com/cadonici/android_python-scripts/blob/main/whatsapp/messages/android_wa-self-destruction_messages_reporter.py
https://github.com/cadonici/android_python-scripts/blob/main/whatsapp/messages/android_wa-self-destruction_messages_reporter.py

These scripts are primarily based on SQLite queries applied to the **msgstore.db** database: straightforward in the first case (*vCard Filtering*), more complex in the second and third (*Message Exchange reporter* e *Self-Destruction Messages Reporter*).

```
SELECT
DISTINCT vcard
FROM message_vcard
```

Android WhatsApp vCard Filtering

```
SELECT jid.user AS "Phone Number",
    COUNT(*) AS "Message Count",
    jid.raw_string AS "Raw String"
FROM jid
INNER JOIN chat ON chat.jid_row_id = jid._id
INNER JOIN message ON chat._id = message.chat_row_id
GROUP BY jid.user, jid.raw_string
ORDER BY "Message Count" DESC, jid.user;
```

Android WhatsApp Message Exchange Reporter

```
SELECT
        jid.raw_string,
        jid.user AS "Phone Number",
        CASE
          WHEN message_ephemeral_setting.setting_duration = 0 THEN
    '(deactivated)'
          WHEN message_ephemeral_setting.setting_duration > 86400 THEN
            CAST(message_ephemeral_setting.setting_duration / 86400 AS
    VARCHAR) || ' days'
          WHEN message_ephemeral_setting.setting_duration >= 3600 THEN
            CAST(message_ephemeral_setting.setting_duration / 3600 AS
    VARCHAR) || ' hours'
          WHEN message_ephemeral_setting.setting_duration >= 60 THEN
            CAST(message_ephemeral_setting.setting_duration / 60 AS
    VARCHAR) || ' minutes'
          ELSE
            CAST(message_ephemeral_setting.setting_duration AS
    VARCHAR) || ' seconds'
        END AS "Expiration Setting"
      FROM
        message
      INNER JOIN
        chat ON message.chat_row_id = chat._id
      INNER JOIN
        message_ephemeral_setting ON message._id = message_ephemeral_
    setting.message_row_id
      INNER JOIN
        jid ON chat.jid_row_id = jid._id
```

Android WhatsApp Self-Destruction Messages Reporter

The examples provided are just a taste of Python's capabilities, specifically applied to querying and correlating information extracted from SQLite artifacts. The applications are numerous, and as we will see in the next section, they lend themselves to creating more sophisticated tools.

4.4.3.4 Python Advanced Tools

In the realm of mobile device forensics, the significant contributions from analyst-developers, particularly in the use of Python, are noteworthy. The following tools are highlighted, without the presumption of offering an exhaustive list, but rather encouraging readers to supplement it:

- ALEAPP (Android Logs Events And Protobuf Parser)
  A full-fledged Android analysis suite with numerous plugins, developed by FBI Special Agent Alexis Brignoni.

- **APOLLO (Apple Pattern of Life Lazy Output'er)**
  A potent tool for examining a user's pattern of life on macOS and jailbroken iOS devices. It streamlines the analysis of information pertaining to device states, connections, and application usage developed by SANS author and senior instructor Sarah Edwards.
- **ccl_abx**
  A Python module developed by Alex Caithness principal Digital Analyst at CCL Group for reading Android Binary XML (ABX) files and converting them back to XML for processing.
- **iLEAPP (iOS Logs, Events And Plist parser)**
  The equivalent of ALEAPP for iOS, also developed by FBI Special Agent Alexis Brignoni.
- **iOS_sysdiagnose_forensic_scripts**
  Scripts to parse various iOS *sysdiagnose* logs. Based upon the forensic research of Mattia Epifani, Heather Mahalik and Cheeky4n6monkey.
- https://github.com/python-for-mobile-forensics
  A GitHub repository with private members, which dedicated to the development of Mobile Forensics scripts in Python.

4.4.4 Hexadecimal Search

Hexadecimal, often abbreviated as Hex, is a base-16 numerical system utilized to streamline the representation of binary data. It employs 16 characters, including 0-9 and A-F (equivalent to values from 00 to FF). By conducting a Hex search, examiners can uncover numerous artifacts that have yet to be explored.

Hexadecimal representations of prevalent artifacts on mobile devices are valuable in this context. Tables 4.1 and 4.2 show some of the most common ones.

Table 4.1 bplist, gif, jpeg

bplist
62 70 6C 69 73 74
gif
47 49 46 38 37 61
47 49 46 38 39 61
JPEG
FF D8 FF DB
FF D8 FF E0 00 10 4A 46
49 46 00 01
FF D8 FF E0
FF D8 FF EE

Table 4.2 pdf, SQLite, XML

PDF
25 50 44 46 2D

SQLite
53 51 4C 69 74 65 20 66
6F 72 6D 61 74 20 33 00

XML
3C 3F 78 6D 6C 20
3C 00 3F 00 6D 006C 00 20
00 3C 00 3F 00 78 00 6D00 6C 00 20
3C 00 00 00 3F 00 00 00
78 00 00 00 6D 00 00 00
6C 00 00 00 20 00 00 00
00 00 00 78 00 00 00 6D
00 00 00 6C 00 00 00 20

Figure 4.14 Renamed PDF File – Oxygen Forensic Detective (File View).

Hex searching enables examiners to analyze paired groupings associated with files that constitute their unique file signatures. This file signature is directly linked to the specific file type, including its file extension. In situations where files are corrupted or deleted, their signatures can be significantly compromised. The resulting broken or incomplete file may not fully parse with the tool we are utilizing. This is where hex searching for specific file signatures becomes crucial. One commonly employed technique involves identifying damaged files that may have evaded automated searches within the analysis suite.

Another application of this technique proves beneficial when addressing anti-forensics. In such instances, we can search for signatures of renamed files. In the provided example, you can see a file with the apparent extension *.dll.mui* actually turning out to be a PDF, identified by the file signature 25 50 44 46 2D (see Figures 4.14 and 4.15).

Ultimately, hexadecimal analysis is of paramount importance for verifying the accuracy of extracted results, such as the temporal values or other values of interest detected in the metadata of acquired images (see Figure 4.16).

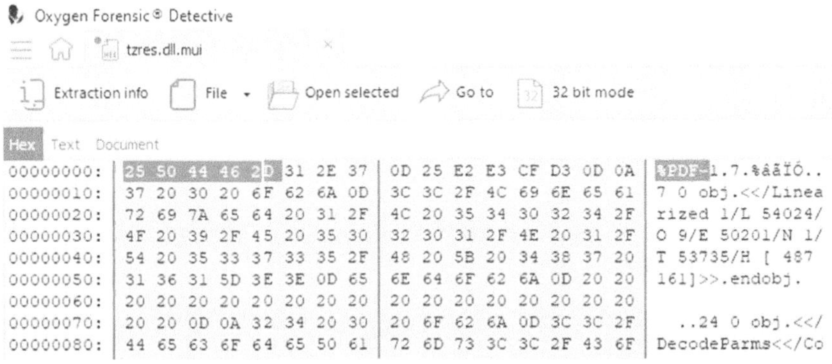

Figure 4.15 Renamed PDF File Header – Oxygen Forensic Detective (Hexadecimal View).

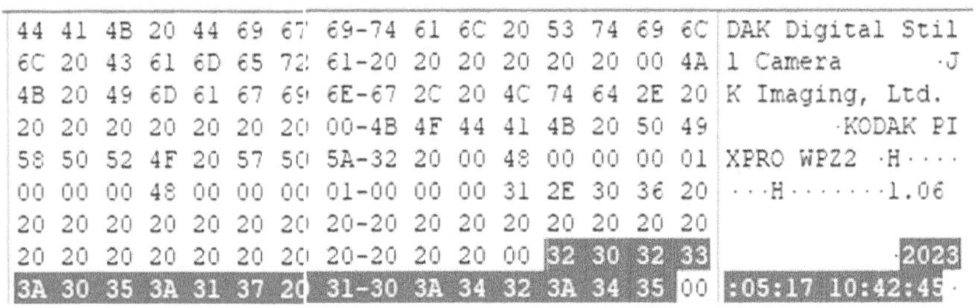

Figure 4.16 Renamed PDF File Metadata – Oxygen Forensic Detective (Hexadecimal View).

4.5 CONCLUSION

Mobile Forensics is one of the most rapidly evolving areas of study among the various disciplines that make up forensic sciences. Its significance has been exponentially increasing, fueled by the constant and rapid expansion of the mobile market. This field requires continuous knowledge updates from analysts, along with a certain mental flexibility and the ability to gather valid information in a short period. Moreover, it requires a creative component that not only refines the process but ultimately makes the work more captivating, which can manifest in manual analysis and the creation of one's own work tools. Mobile Forensics, therefore, thrives on the combination of perpetual research and improvement, dedication, and a touch of creativity, making it not just a necessity in the digital realm but also a compelling and challenging pursuit.

Notes

1 From the set of iOS 13 images and files provided by Joshua Hickman at [5].
2 *usbmuxd* stands for "USB multiplexing daemon". This daemon oversees multiplexing connections over USB to an iOS device.

REFERENCES

[1] Statista (2024) Multiple Mobile Device Ownership Worldwide. www.statista.com/statistics/245501/multiple-mobile-device-ownership-worldwide/
[2] National Institute of Standards and Technology (2024) Guidelines for Managing the Security of Mobile Devices in the Enterprise. https://nvlpubs.nist.gov/nistpubs/SpecialPublications/NIST.SP.800-124r2.pdf
[3] StatCounter (2024) Mobile OS Market Share Worldwide. https:\\gs.statcounter.com\os-market-share\mobile\worldwide\
[4] Magnet Forensics (2024) Mobile Device Artifacts: Exploring Geolocation, Communication, Application, and Media Evidence. www.magnetforensics.com/blog/mobile-device-artifacts-exploring-geolocation-communication-application-and-media-evidence/
[5] Digital Corpora (2024) iOS 13 Cell Phone Corpora. https://digitalcorpora.org/corpora/cell-phones/ios-13/
[6] SQLite Browser (2024) DB Browser for SQLite. https://sqlitebrowser.org/

Chapter 5

Digital Forensics

Extracting Information From Devices

Abhishek Pradhan and Bhag Dei

5.1 INTRODUCTION

In this era of rapid technological advancement, the significance of both knowledge and data has escalated. Unfortunately, a considerable number of individuals remain unaware of how to safeguard their personal information, making them susceptible to cyber crimes. According to the NCRB 2022 report, there were 65,893 reported cyber crimes in the year 2022, reflecting a 24.4% increase compared to the 52,974 cases in 2021 and 50,035 cases in 2020. It is important to note that these figures likely underestimate the actual prevalence, as many cases go unreported. The growth of network technology and widespread internet access has heightened the risk, particularly with the hiking use of Internet of Things (IoT) devices and drones. These steps of progress in technology have led to advancements that have expanded the vulnerable surface area, posing challenges for investigators. As the market size continues to grow at a tremendous rate, the urgency to address and mitigate these cyber threats becomes increasingly apparent [1]. The accessibility of technology has integrated it into various aspects of criminal activities. Consequently, the function of a digital forensic examiner is essential in researching and analyzing digital evidence to extract relevant information efficiently and in a manner that meets forensic standards [2]. Given the diverse nature of cyber crimes, digital artifacts vary, necessitating specific extraction and search procedures tailored to each case. The success of the investigation relies heavily on the skills and experience applied by the analyst.

5.1.1 Digital Forensics and Fundamentals

The simplest explanation of what digital forensics is, would be that it is taking a deep glance into what has happened and/or what is happening in a digital device, which is executed through forensically sound techniques and tools. It is more of a reactive approach. As per SWGDE and NIST IR 8006, "Digital forensics as a science is the process used to acquire,

DOI: 10.1201/9781003471103-5

preserve, analyze, and report on electronically stored information using scientific methods that are demonstrably reliable, verifiable, and repeatable, such that they may be used in judicial and other formal proceedings." The investigation of digital forensics is also based on the very basic principle of forensics, the Locard's principal of exchange, even the slightest use of a digital device leaves a trace. Digital forensics works of its four pillars namely skillset, procedure, integrity and ethics [3]. The expertise of a digital forensic examiner plays a critical role in guiding investigations in the right direction. Opting for the appropriate procedure to extract evidence yields more effective results. In digital forensics, upholding integrity is paramount and is verified through the chain of custody [4]. Preserving digital evidence from tampering is achieved by using write blockers and generating hash values. Ethics is crucial in forensic examinations, acknowledging that there exist chances of involving breach of privacy. While these examinations are executed to solve crimes, they must be within ethical and moral bounds. Respecting fundamental rights, human rights, and basic morals is essential for the pursuit of justice. The core process of digital forensics comprises five essential stages: identification of digital evidence, gathering of digital evidence, extraction of digital data, analysis of digital data, and the creation of a legally admissible report [5].

Digital forensics can be classified into five distinct categories: Computer forensics, Mobile forensics, Network forensics, Drone forensics, and IoT Forensics as shown in Figure 5.1.

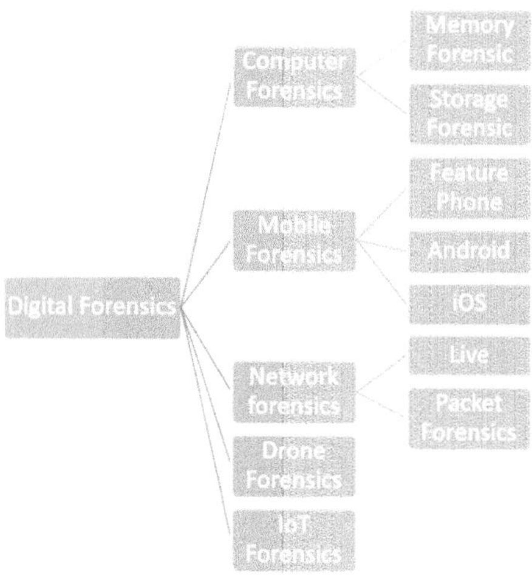

Figure 5.1 Types of Digital Forensics.

5.1.2 Importance of Digital Forensics

An example of a crime scene is considered to understand the importance of digital forensics: in a crime scene, there is a victim, a suspect, and a witness or evidence which sets a link between a victim and accused. This can be either visible or invisible [6]. Likewise, in a digital crime scene, the witness is the channel through which the crime has happened, such as messaging apps, network ports, cameras, registries, log files etc. In the present world digital forensics is as important as delivering justice to the victim.

Digital forensics holds paramount importance in the realm of cyber security and criminal investigations, playing a pivotal role in various aspects [7]. One essential feature is the collecting and preservation of evidence, guaranteeing the integrity of electronic evidence for legal procedures [4].

For instance, in cases involving hacking, digital forensics revolves around preserving server logs, network traffic, and malware samples to trace the origins of cyber-attacks. It also is instrumental in incident response procedures to swiftly identify the scope and nature of security breaches, aiding in the prevention of future incidents. Criminal investigations benefit significantly from digital forensics, as it assists law enforcement in solving crimes involving digital evidence (example: cases of cyberstalking or online fraud). Intellectual property theft is another area where digital forensics finds its utility, enabling the identification and proof of such theft and safeguarding businesses from financial losses. It ensures legal compliance by adhering to standards and regulations related to electronic evidence handling. Malware analysis is a critical domain where digital forensics aids in dissecting and understanding malicious software, contributing to the development of effective countermeasures.

The scope of digital forensics is very vast and isn't restricted to forensic laboratories; it is used in financial fraud investigations; private companies (Enterprise Forensics) have separate forensic branches for the investigation of breaches and cyberattacks. They work in coordination with cyber forensic professionals to keep the organization safe.

5.2 DIGITAL EVIDENCE AND CRIME RELATED TO THEM

5.2.1 General Definition: Evidence

Evidence refers to the information, materials, or facts presented in a legal context to establish the truth or falsity of a claim, assertion, or argument. It acts as the cornerstone for making informed decisions within the judicial system, aiding in the determination of guilt or innocence, the resolution of disputes, or the validation of legal rights. Evidence includes testimony, documents, physical objects, or electronic records etc.

As per the Indian Evidence Act of 1872, evidence refers to any statements made by witnesses in court regarding matters of fact being investigated. These statements are known as oral evidence. Additionally, evidence also includes any documents presented to the court for examination, which are referred to as documentary evidence.

5.2.2 Digital Evidence

The legal concept of digital evidence lacks a precise definition in Indian law. The admissibility of electronic evidence was established by the inclusion of Sections 65A and 65B into the Indian Evidence Act, 1872, in the year 2000. Section 65A specifically addresses electronic records, treating them as admissible evidence. Meanwhile, Section 65B outlines a special procedure, employing a deeming fiction, for determining the admissibility of electronic records in the court. The provisions pertaining to electronic or digital records, their specific treatment in evidence, and their admissibility are now outlined in Clause 61 (Electronic or digital record), Clause 62 (Special provisions regarding evidence related to electronic records), and Clause 63 (Admissibility of electronic records) of The Bhartiya Sakshya Adhiniyam, 2023. These clauses collectively establish the legal framework for handling electronic evidence in accordance with the updated legislation.

Digital evidence can be derived from various sources, encompassing any device containing digital data. The digital evidence can be categorized into two groups: one is volatile data and another one is non-volatile data. The data, which is perishable is volatile and is stored in a RAM, Cache, Registers or a primary memory, and the data which is stored in secondary storage and retains even after power off is non-volatile data [8]. Among the notable and well-known sources are computers and computer-related devices, both fixed and portable data storage devices, CDs, printers, scanners, faxes, photocopiers, smartphones, cameras, modems, firewalls, switching devices (such as switches), and emails.

5.2.3 Comparison Between Digital Evidence and Other Physical Evidence

Digital evidence is distinguished by its intangible, invisible, and virtual nature, setting it apart from other forms of evidence. Its meaning is realized only through relevant hardware. Unlike concrete physical evidence, digital evidence exists in the abstract, represented by 0s and 1s. It cannot be seen or touched directly; instead, visibility and touch-ability pertain to the hardware storing the digital evidence. In contrast, physical evidence like written documents, blood, saliva, and hair is visible and tangible.

Recovering deleted data from digital evidence is feasible with specific tools, whereas obtaining physical evidence after excluding it from a crime scene is challenging unless traces are left behind. Manipulating digital evidence may be more intricate to comprehend compared to manipulating other physical evidence. Digital evidence cannot serve as a basis for conclusive and 100% certain proof, unlike physical evidence such as DNA, which can yield definitive results.

5.2.4 Difference Between Digital Evidence and Electronic Evidence

The distinction between digital evidence and electronic evidence is frequently blurred, with the terms being interchangeably used both in practical application and theoretical frameworks. The term "electronic device" covers a wide range, including devices storing information in two formats: digital form (characterized by 0s and 1s, as seen in computers and mobile phones) and analog form (encompassing devices like radios, televisions, and video recorders). When an electronic device, containing information in digital format, is presented as evidence in court, it is referred to as digital evidence.

5.2.5 Crime Related to Digital Evidence

The rise of cyber crime, thanks to digital technologies, has created a whole new world of criminal activities. Digital evidence plays a pivotal role in investigating and prosecuting these offenses. Different types of cyber crimes involve digital evidence, like cyberattacks, financial fraud, identity theft, and online harassment. Cybercriminals often use tactics such as malware, phishing, and ransomware to gain unauthorized access to sensitive information. In financial crimes, digital trails left by online transactions or electronic banking activities become important evidence. Identity theft, where personal data stored digitally is compromised, is also on the rise. Online harassment and cyberbullying cases leave behind digital communication as crucial evidence.

Digital evidence comes from various sources like computers, mobile devices, online platforms, and communication channels. Law enforcement and cybersecurity experts use advanced forensic techniques to collect, preserve, and analyze this evidence [9]. It's important to ensure that digital evidence is admissible, and its integrity maintained in legal proceedings. This emphasizes the need for specialized skills in both forensic analysis and legal interpretation. As technology keeps advancing, the landscape of digital crime changes too, making it crucial for legal systems to adapt and effectively use digital evidence to achieve justice.

5.3 DIGITAL CRIME SCENE INVESTIGATION

5.3.1 Introduction

In today's era, it is highly challenging for individuals to avoid leaving a digital footprint. In a technological age where humans are constantly surrounded by electronic devices, it becomes nearly impossible for a crime scene to remain completely untouched. Digital devices have seamlessly integrated into various aspects of criminal activities. Even in offline crimes, mobile devices contain extensive data and evidence, including call details, location history, messages, social media chats, emails, web history, photos, videos, and more. Managing a digital crime scene requires additional caution due to the vulnerability of digital data to destruction or loss [8]. Experts must prioritize digital evidence over physical evidence, isolating it from the network to prevent any potential tampering.

The fundamental principles of managing a crime scene with digital devices align with those of other crime scenes. These include isolating the crime scene, documenting findings, capturing photographs and videos, marking evidence, reconstructing the crime scene, and maintaining the chain of custody [2]. In a digital crime scene, additional crucial tasks distinguish it from others. These tasks involve isolating evidence from the network, safeguarding it against static charge, minimizing potential losses, ensuring the integrity of the evidence, and facing the significant challenges of accurately identifying digital evidence. The sheer volume of evidence and data presents both facilitative and challenging aspects to this task [8].

The process of investigating a digital crime scene and its evidence involves identification, collection, preservation, extraction, analysis, and reporting or documentation [2]. There is a slight variation in this process when dealing with live forensics. In cases like so, the extraction process is conducted before collecting the evidence, and these facets will be explained in detail further in this chapter.

5.3.2 Steps of Crime Scene Investigation

5.3.2.1 Access the Digital Crime Scene

The initial step in forensic investigation is crucial. Upon arriving at a digital crime scene, the First Responder Officer must possess proper authorization and follow guidelines to initiate the investigation process. Prior to commencing the investigation, the Investigating Officer (IO) should secure consent from the victim or suspect who possesses the suspected electronic device, obtaining their signature. The IO must procure a warrant for search and seizure issued by a magistrate. The search warrant specifies the individuals or items and the location to be searched. A seizure memo is then prepared,

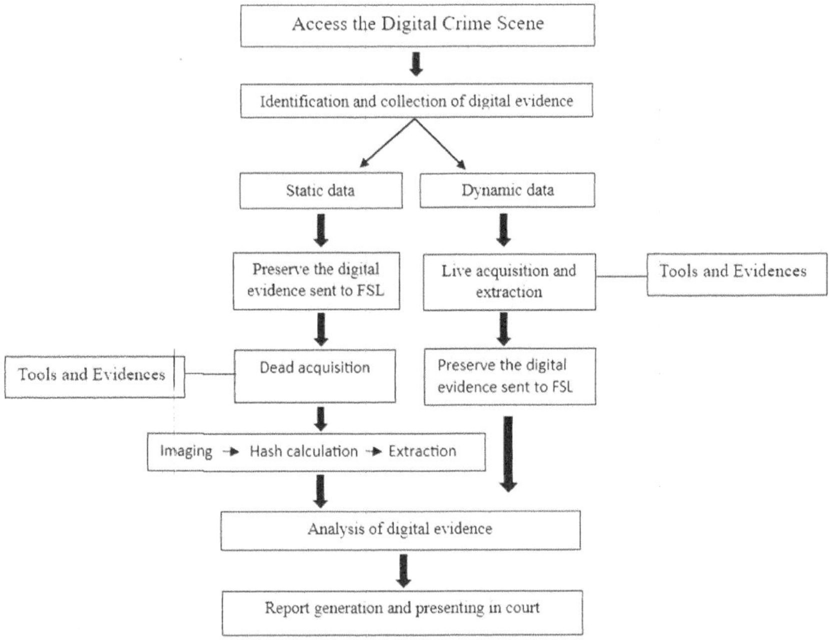

Figure 5.2 Stages of Forensic Investigation.

providing a detailed description of the seized article and the location where it was found. In the event of a password-protected device, the IO requests the password from the owner (victim or suspect) and documents it in the seizure memo [8].

A thorough evaluation of the scene is conducted, ensuring that the surrounding area connected to the incident is also secured, in addition to the computing systems and other electronic devices. The crime scene is meticulously documented through note-taking, photography, and videography (see Figure 5.2). It is imperative to accurately record the location and condition of computers, digital storage media, and other electronic devices, including their power status [8]. Details such as capturing a photograph of the computer monitor's screen and noting the displayed content are also documented. In some countries, for real-time scene capturing, Audio-Video Recording is performed using Spy Specs High-definition Camera.

5.3.2.2 Identification and Collection of Digital Evidence

The most important step is correctly identifying the device. Check for every possible evidence like IoT devices, mobile phones, smart watches, storage devices (HDD, SSD, NAS, raid servers), laptops and desktops, drones etc. [10]. Accurate identification of digital evidence during the collection process enhances its effectiveness. For instance, when collecting an IoT device like a smartwatch as evidence, it is crucial to also gather the associated mobile phone. In case of a turned-off smartphone or portable computer system, it is advisable to collect its charger as well [8].

At a crime scene, two categories of digital data may be encountered: static or non-volatile, and dynamic or volatile. Non-volatile data encompasses items like Hard Disk, Floppy drives, CD/DVD, external storage devices, etc. [10]. Meanwhile, volatile data consists of memory, open files, running processes, and all network connections. Therefore, acquisition process varies accordingly.

Live acquisition

Live acquisition is employed for volatile data, with RAM holding all such information [11]. Hence, if a suspected device is powered on, RAM capture is conducted, with that some of the important files and data such as cache data, temp files, prefetch files, event log file, registry hives are taken. In this a device called Digital Collector is also used specifically for Mac and Windows operating systems. Prior to this, a photograph of the screen is taken, documenting running programs and open files of evidentiary value. If a screen saver is displayed, the mouse is gently moved without any button presses before capturing the screen. Once the volatile data has been gathered, the machine is shut down and unplugged from all networks. For a feature phone, the screen, date and time, and all files of evidentiary value are documented using a camera [12].

Dead acquisition

It is essential to isolate digital evidence from the external environment. In crime scenes where computers or smartphones are discovered, the primary step involves disconnecting the device by activating airplane mode and subsequently turning it off [11]. Any removable media is removed, collected, and preserved separately. All items are then packaged in antistatic or Faraday bags. The collected pieces of evidence are kept away from magnets, high temperatures, radio signals, etc., to prevent any compromise to its integrity [12].

5.3.2.3 Preservation and Laboratory Procedure

After collection of digital evidence, they are preserved in static-free bags and sent to forensic science labs (FSLs) for further analysis. Upon receiving a case at the FSL, various checks are conducted, including the examination of seals, exhibits, the originating police station's name, figure lists, postmortem report, FIR, etc. If any crucial report is absent, seals are insufficient, or if a seal is broken or unrecognizable, the case is returned to the respective police station. Otherwise, it is received, the case number is assigned to it and forwarded to the Cyber Division or Digital Forensics Division.

In the division, the case is opened, and each step is documented using a camera. The chain of custody is diligently maintained throughout the process. The officer responsible for opening the case signs the chain of custody form. Following case opening, the extraction and examination or analysis of digital evidence are performed using the appropriate tools.

5.3.2.4 Extraction

Data acquisition involves employing well-established methods to extract electronically stored information (ESI) from a suspected computer or storage media, providing insights into a crime or incident. In forensic data acquisition, information is imaged or collected from various media in adherence to specific standards to assess its forensic significance [8]. Subsequently, investigators meticulously process and scrutinize the gathered data to extract information relevant to a particular case or incident while ensuring the integrity of the data is maintained. This stage is pivotal in digital forensics, as any improper acquisition could potentially modify data in evidence media, rendering it inadmissible in the court of law.

Forensic investigators must possess the ability to confirm the accuracy of obtained data, and the entire process should be deemed acceptable and reproducible in a court of law. Prior to acquiring the data, the investigator is required to guarantee the forensic cleanliness of their storage device and subsequently activate write protection using physical or software (Soft Block by Cellebrite) write blockers to safeguard and preserve the original evidence.

5.3.2.5 Analysis

Data analysis involves reviewing the data to identify evidential information and its relevance to the crime. It encompasses the examination, identification, separation, conversion, and modeling of data to isolate valuable information [8]. In forensic investigation, data analysis aids in the collection and examination of data to determine its relevance to the incident, facilitating the submission of findings to authorities for conclusions and decision-making.

The stage of analysis involves the following tasks:

- Examining file content to understand data usage
- Reviewing the time and date of file creation and modification
- Identifying users linked to file creation, access, and modification
- Establishing the physical storage location of the file
- Generating a timeline
- Discovering the root cause of the incident

5.3.2.6 *Report/Documentation*

Following the completion of the analysis, a technical review is conducted by another examiner. The evidence is carefully packed, sealed with the FSL seal, and labeled accordingly. Two copies of each forwarding letter and intimation letter are generated. One copy is dispatched to the respective police station, while the other serves as an office copy.

A final report is compiled, including the extracted data report, and both reports are organized in a case file. This case file, along with the packed exhibits, is stored in the outgoing case almirah. Ultimately, it is received by the messenger from the respective police station.

5.4 EXTRACTION AND ANALYSIS OF DIGITAL EVIDENCE

Following the identification and collection of evidence, the subsequent step involves analyzing the data for artifacts. Forensic examiners may either analyze the collected evidence on-site at the crime scene or submit it to forensic laboratories for extraction and analysis. The term "digital" encompasses anything capable of storing and transferring information in the form of bits, making digital forensics inherently more challenging. Every item present at the crime scene associated with digital devices holds the potential to be evidence. Each piece of digital evidence must undergo examination tailored to its specific characteristics and the state in which it was discovered, such as live and dead forensics in computer forensics [8].

The extraction and imaging process is efficiently carried out using digital forensic software such as Cellebrite UFED, MSAB XRY, Magnet Axiom, MobileEdit Forensics, Access Data Forensic Tool Kit, and Belkasoft. Hardware tools, including Tableau TX1, Tableau Forensic Write Block Bridge, and others, are also employed in this procedure. In addition, this section will subsequently examine open-source programs such as FTK Imager, Encase Imager, Magnet RAM Capture, Avila Forensics, iTunes, iLeep, Magnet Acquire, and others. Preserving the integrity of the evidence is paramount throughout the extraction process, emphasizing the utmost importance of write blockers and hash values to prevent any tampering with the evidence [8]. For ease of comprehension, we have categorized this information based on commonly encountered digital evidence and the proprietary and open-source software utilized for extraction.

5.4.1 Computer Forensics

Computer forensics is a specialized field within digital forensics that involves the extraction and analysis of all evidence related to computers, including Random-Access Memory (RAM), Hard Disk Drives (HDD), Solid State Drives (SSD), Registry, event logs, and system files such as Page file and

Hibernation file [7]. A comprehensive understanding of operating systems like Windows, Macintosh, and Linux, as well as their respective file systems, is essential for practitioners in computer forensics. This also includes knowledge of primary and secondary storage drives such as RAM, HDD, SSD, SD Card, Compact Disk, etc. [8].

In computer forensics, evidence is handled in two broad ways, depending on the state of encounter. This involves Live Forensics when the system is in a switched-on state and Dead Forensics when the system is in a switched-off state.

5.4.1.1 Case 1: Device Is Switched-On

At the crime scene, when the investigators encounter the digital evidence in switched on state, specifically the computer system, then the first thing that should be done is the live capture of that system instead of switching it off or pulling all the connections out [13]. The live system contains important data in the volatile memory, such as the running processes, network connections etc. Through this an investigator can know a lot of information concerning the case. While the system is running the non-volatile data can also be taken. The tools used are for capturing and analyzing RAM. For RAM capturing there are various software such as Dump it, Magnet Forensics RAM capture, FTK Imager (also captures the page file) [14]. LiMe is used for capturing RAM in Linux computers, while DD is used for capturing RAM in Mac systems. For open-source software analysis, some available options include volatility3, Redeye's Redline [15], and bulk extractor. For the proprietary one there are Magnet Axiom, Belkasoft and Digital collector.

The analysis of RAM becomes important in a way that it provides a lot of data and can be used for malware forensics also, the reconstruction of the evidence gives the whole real time scenario of the victim's or the attackers' system, sometimes the encryption key can also be found [1, 6]. Let's see the capturing process and analysis using open- source software.

Extraction and Analysis Using Open-source Software

For capturing the RAM run the Magnet ram capture.exe (Figure 5.3) file at the target system and run it by providing the location. And for Redline (Figure 5.4), it has its own customizable collector having memory, disk, system, network and other collectors.

5.4.2 Analysis of Captured RAM

Volatility3 has been used, which is a CLI-based tool written in python and developed by the volatility foundation, and can easily be installed through git hub [16]. This has various python plugins for mac, linux and windows operating systems, such as netscan, pslist, psscan, registry, malfind, hashdump

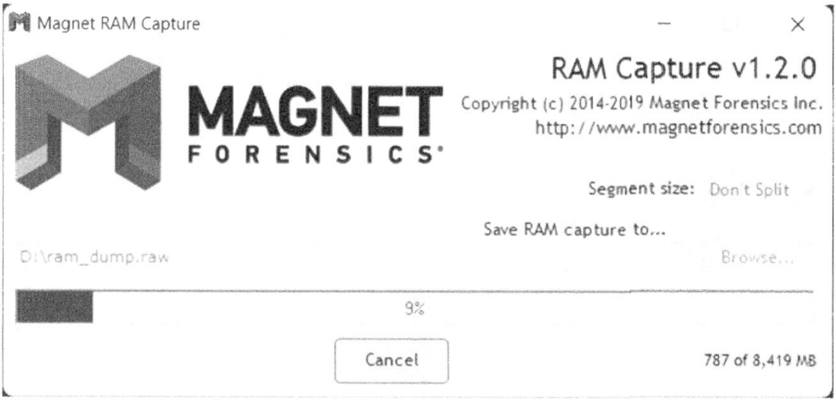

Figure 5.3 Magnet RAM Capture.

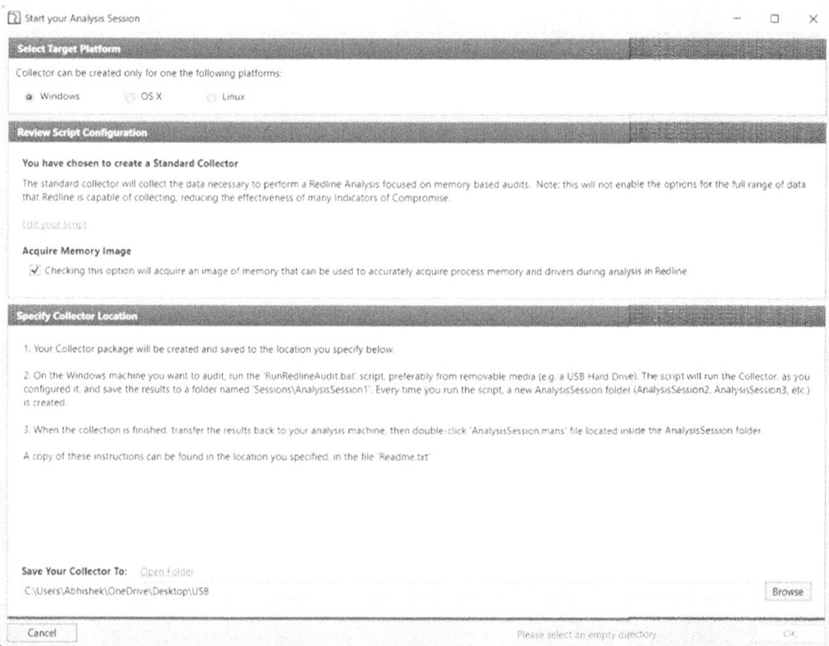

Figure 5.4 Redline RAM Capture.

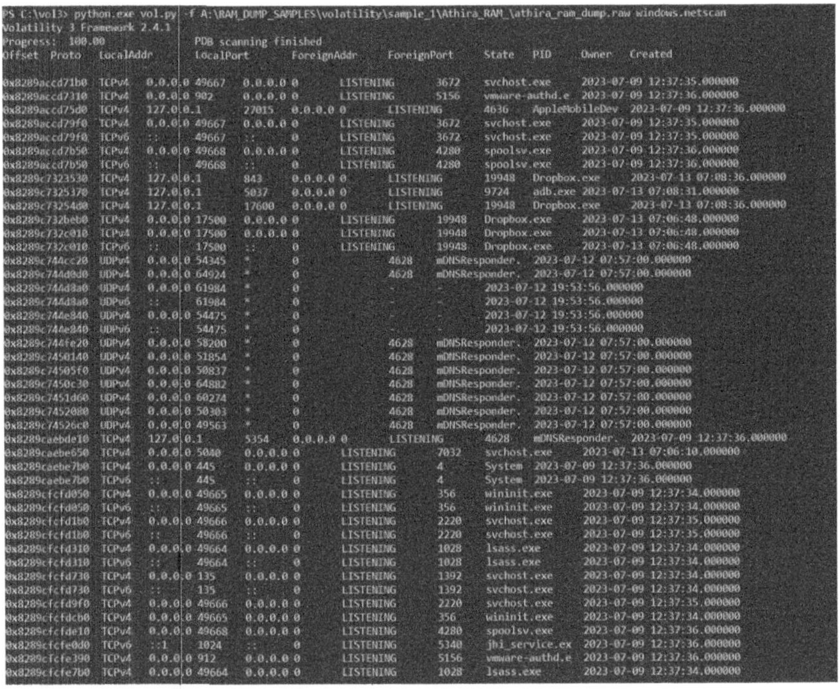

Figure 5.5 Network Scan Result in Volatility3.

etc. Volatility gives a free hand to the examiner while analyzing the RAM (see Figures 5.5–5.7).

In proprietary software, there are Magnet and Belkasoft, Magnet Outrider, Magnet Axiom, triage tools such as OS forensics, Cyber triage and Digital collector also analyses the RAM. They help in carving out the artifacts present in the RAM with time line creation also.

5.4.2.1 Case 2: Device Is Switched-Off

In dead forensics, or when the system is switched off, the source from which data can be extracted is the internal secondary drive, which may either be an HDD or an SSD, it is crucial to be mindful of the type of interfaces the drive employs, such as ATA/PATA, SCSI, SATA, PCIe. Forensic imaging of these drives is accomplished through a bit-by-bit copy, utilizing various software and hardware tools [5].

When performing forensic imaging, several considerations must be kept in mind. The system should not be powered on, and the drive must be write-blocked. Other important factors include the image format, ensuring that

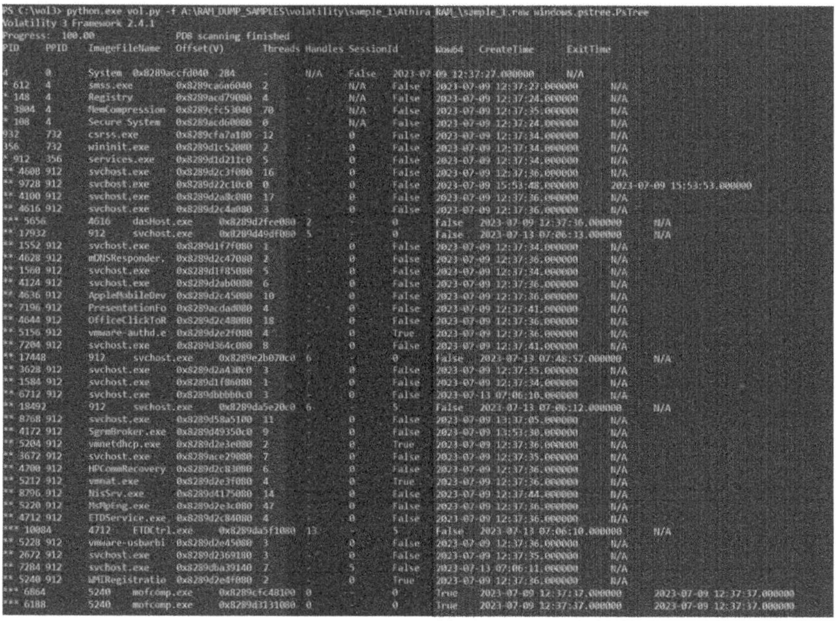

Figure 5.6 Process Tree Result in Volatility3.

Figure 5.7 Hash Dump Result in Volatility3.

the destination drive is larger than the source drive, formatting the destination drive beforehand, placing the setup on an anti-static mat, specifying whether the imaging is done on a physical, logical, or components of a folder level, and ensuring that the resulting image is hashed.

There exists a list of proprietary and open-source software used for imaging and analyzing computer forensics evidence:

- Proprietary software: Magnet Axiom Process, Belkasoft, AccessData FTK, Tableau TX1, Falcon
- Open-source software: FTK Imager, EnCase Imager, Magnet Acquire, Autopsy

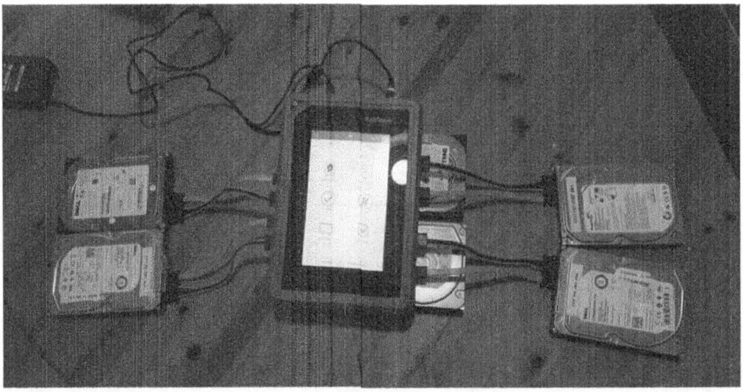

Figure 5.8 Forensic Imaging Using TX.1.

The image files are subsequently analyzed using specific software like Access Data FTK and Magnet Forensics' Axiom Process. Analysis configurations are chosen stemming from the required artifacts and the type of the cases. Imaging encompasses data from slack space, deleted data, bad clusters, and carved files, streamlining the investigative process. The range of artifacts found on a drive is extensive, including media files, registry data, page files, hibernation files, carved files, timeline analysis, web files, hash sets, and more [5].

FTK is the most frequently employed software for disk forensics analysis and provides a plethora of customizable checks, as illustrated in Figures 5.8 and 5.9 [13]. The evidence processing of a disk image file is demonstrated in Figures 5.10 and 5.11.

After making the forensic image of the evidence drive in the properly wiped or formatted destination drive using FTK Imager, Encase Imager or Tableau TX1 in the acceptable image format such as e01, the destination drive is plugged into the workstation through a write blocker. The image is then uploaded to the software such as FTK. Magnet Axiom Process. These software have diverse technical specifications that help in carving out the data irrespective of the operating systems [5].

Artifacts that can be obtained from the storage drives are listed below (see Figures 5.12 and 5.13):

- Image files
- Document files
- Archives
- Databases
- Mobile phone attachments

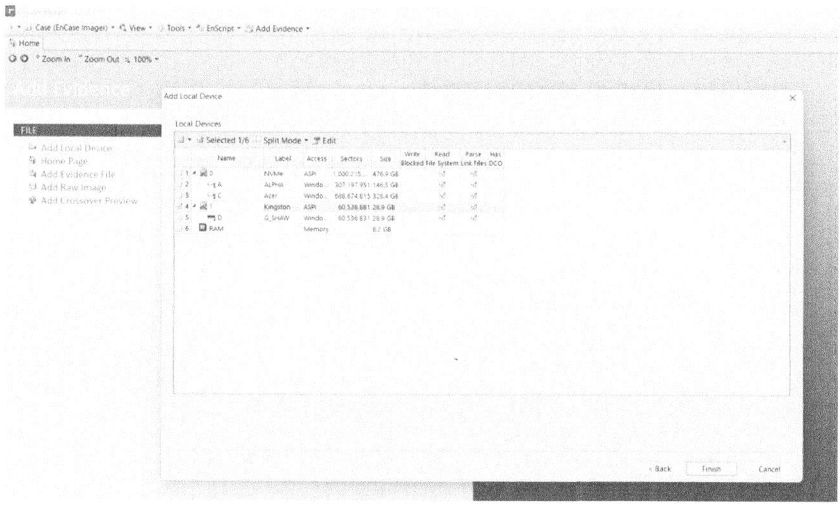

Figure 5.9 Forensic Imaging Using EnCase Imager.

- Web browser details
- E-mail/browser files
- Cookies
- Deleted files / carved files
- Files from slack space
- Bad extension files

For the drives that are either Full Disk (FDE) or File Based (FBE) Encrypted, for analyzing them a decryption key is needed to read the data stored inside it. In Magnet Axiom it shows a lock icon ahead of encrypted drive it also asks for the Recovery key, or it can decrypt in case of clear key decryption (Figure 5.14) [17]. In FTK we can check by mounting the image files.

5.5 MOBILE FORENSICS

In this technological world, mobile phones are the most accessible devices, and it is extremely rare for a crime scene not to involve a mobile phone. Therefore, it becomes a crucial piece of evidence to study. Digital evidence on mobile devices can be easily altered, deleted, or destroyed, so an examiner is advised to handle it with caution. A significant amount of data is parsed from mobile phones, depending on the level of extraction performed (Figure 5.15) [18]. The extent of data extraction is influenced by the AFU (After First Unlock) and BFU (Before First Unlock) states. The BFU state becomes challenging due to encryption compared to the AFU mode. Some

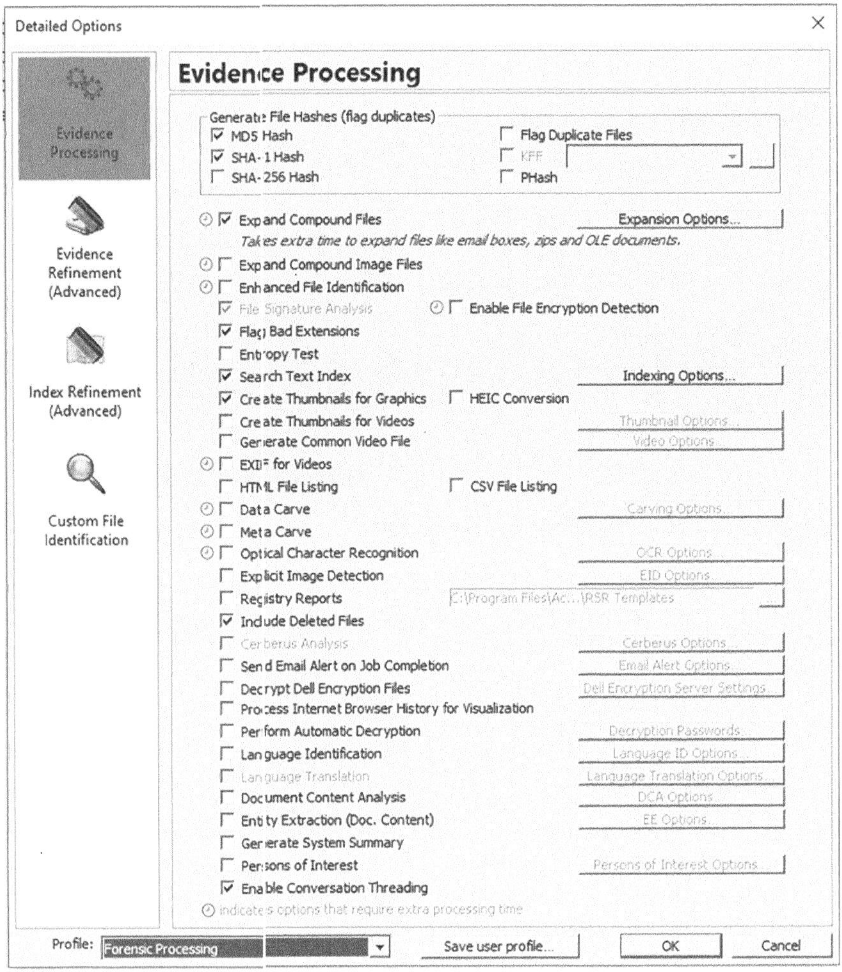

Figure 5.10 Evidence Processing in FTK.

software also provides data extraction from locked mobile phones or BFU mode such as Cellebrite Premium [8].

Different types of information can be gathered from a mobile phone, including stored and deleted media files, cloud authentication tokens, and cloud data. Additionally, chat messages, backup files of system and third-party applications, contacts, messages, connected devices, Wi-Fi passwords, etc., are collected separately from three different sources: SIM, mobile phone, and Micro SD card [18]. The types of extraction that are performed on a mobile phone are:

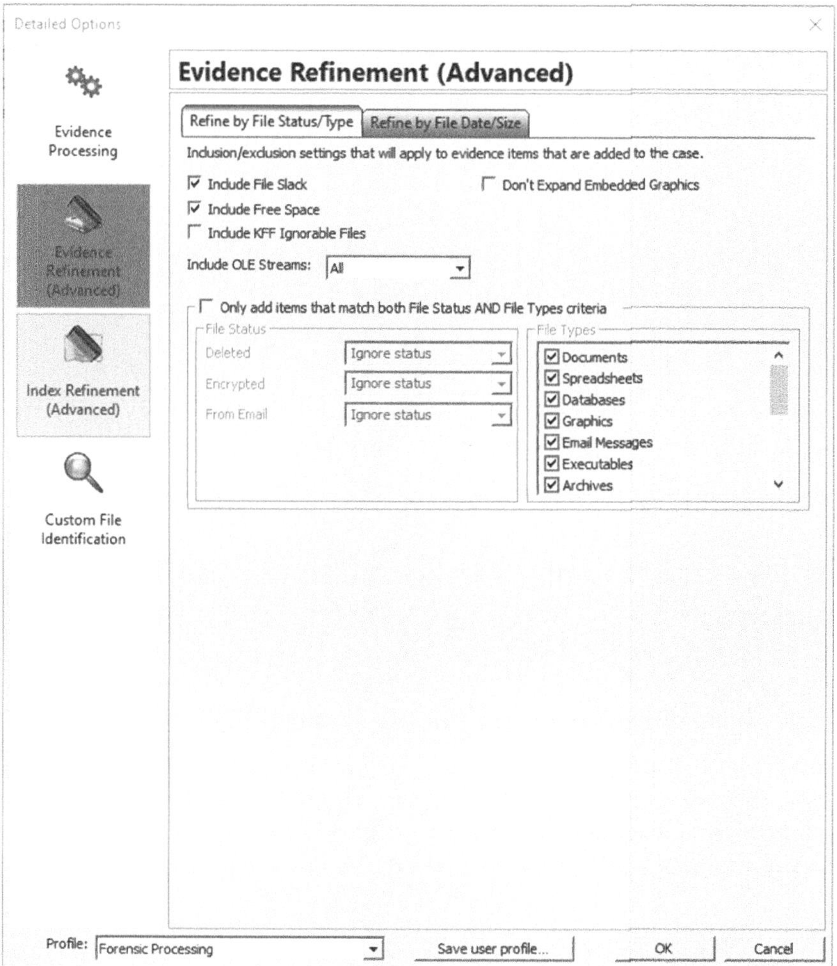

Figure 5.11 Evidence Processing in FTK.

5.5.1 Logical Extraction

In mobile forensics, logical acquisition refers to the creation of a bit-by-bit copy of the logical storage on a mobile device. The logical storage contains objects such as directories and files that are accessible to the user. Logical acquisition generally recovers data that is not deleted. System files and deleted data cannot be captured under logical acquisition [8].

Live data that can be acquired using logical acquisition includes call logs, text messages, passwords to active social media accounts, IMEI and

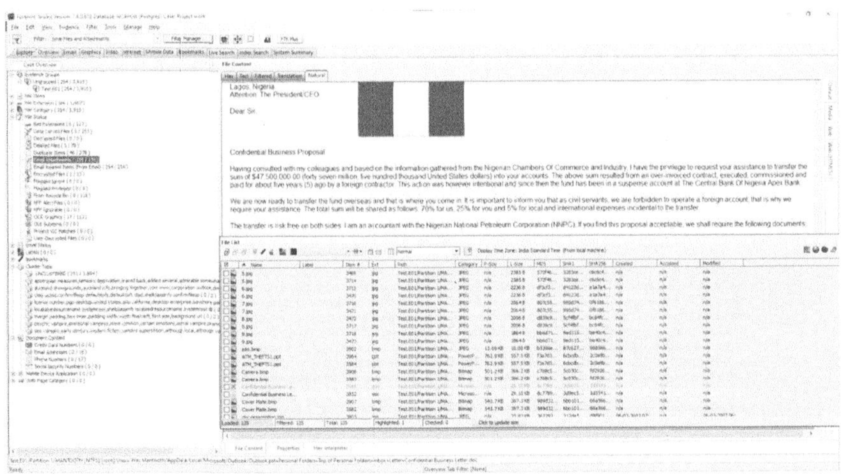

Figure 5.12 Analysis Dashboard of FTK.

ESN (Electronic Serial Number) data, contact lists, data from installed applications, and saved photos and videos. A full device back-up can also be considered as a logical acquisition [5].

5.5.1.1 File System Extraction/ Full File System (FFS)

Mobile devices use file systems to organize and store data. Extracting data at the file system level allows forensic investigators to retrieve a wide range of information, including user files, application data, system files, and metadata, along with hidden files and deleted files in some models [13].

5.5.1.2 Physical Extraction

Physical acquisition entails generating a bit-by-bit copy of the data stored in the physical storage media of mobile phones, encompassing hidden files, system files, and deleted data. If performed successfully, physical acquisition can help forensic investigators obtain information such as deleted text messages, contacts, call logs, deleted passwords, location tags, GPS information, deleted files, photos, and videos. It eliminates the risk of compromising the data integrity [13].

5.5.1.3 JTAG (Joint Test Action Group)

JTAG forensics represents an alternative approach to physically extracting data from mobile devices [13]. This method is employed in situations where

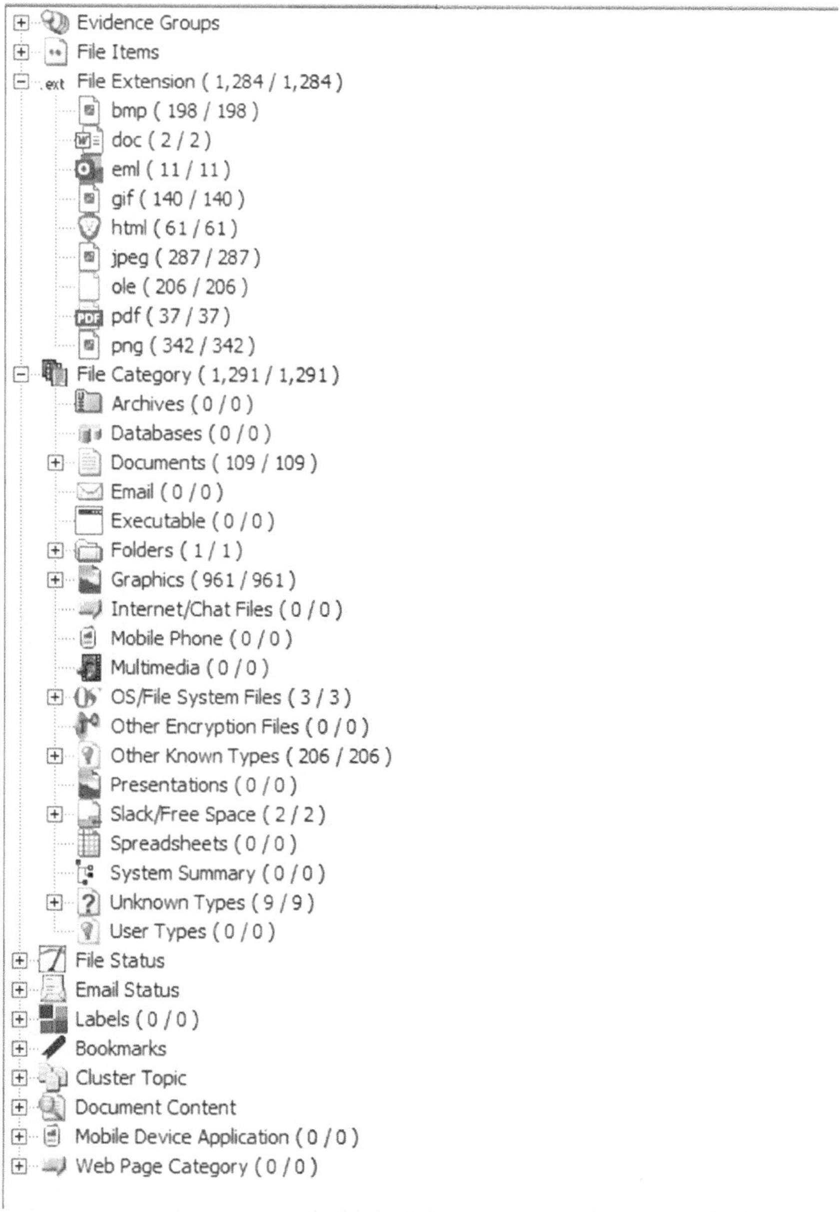

Figure 5.13 Classification of Data Extracted From a Storage Drive.

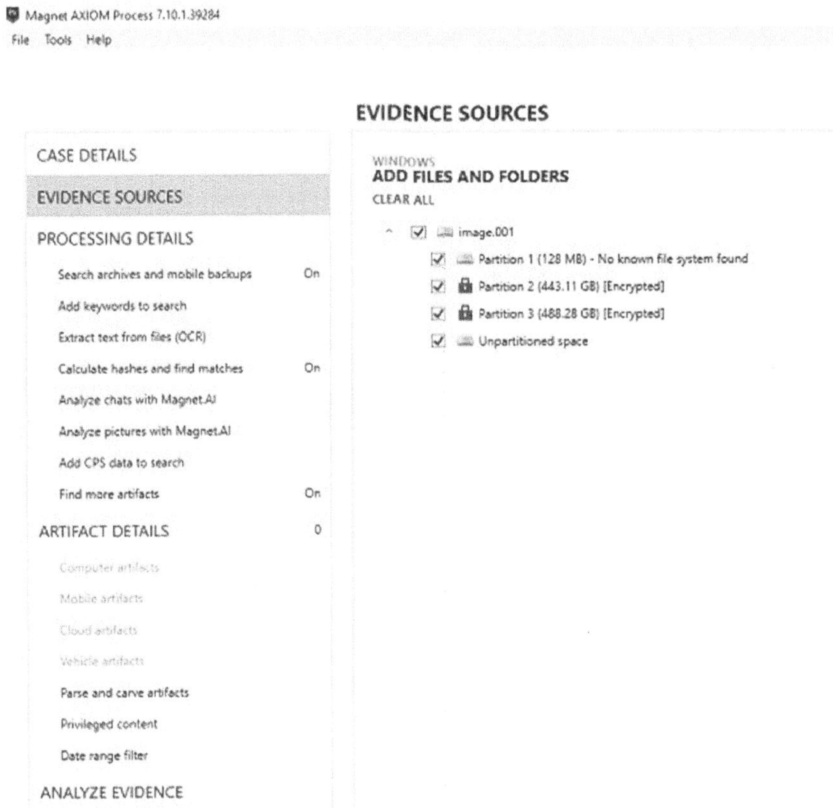

Figure 5.14 Encrypted Drive Identification in Magnet Axiom Process.

there are no compatible or suitable tools supported by a specific device. JTAG involves disassembling a phone and directly soldering wires to the Test Access Port (TAP) on the phone's circuit board. Examiners intending to employ this technique must possess proficient electronics skills and undergo specialized training.

5.5.1.4 Chip-Off

The chip-off procedure involves physically removing the flash memory from mobile devices to acquire data. Investigators can create a binary image of the detached chip and conduct chip-off forensics. This method is important for extracting data from devices with pattern/PIN locks or those that are damaged or dismantled (see Figure 5.16).

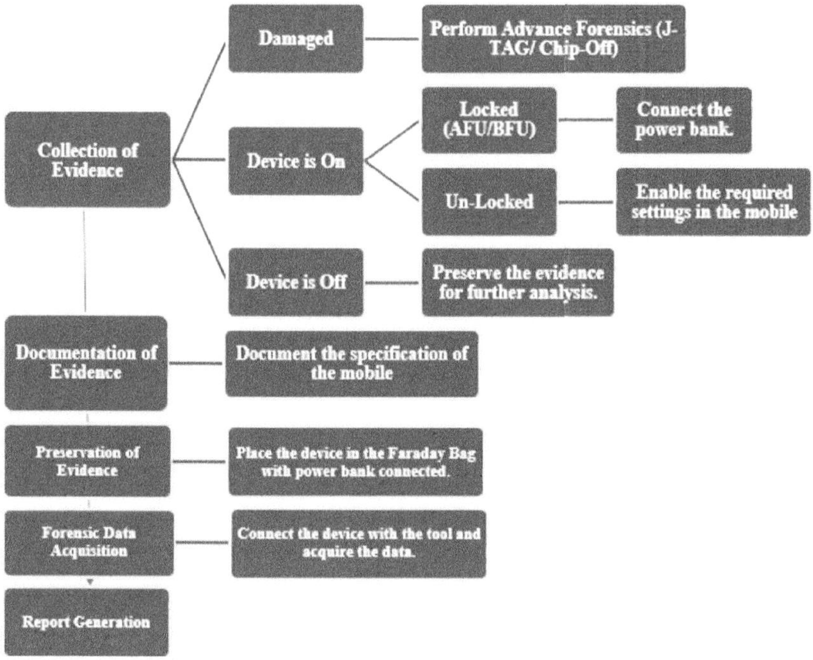

Figure 5.15 Mobile Data Extraction Flow.

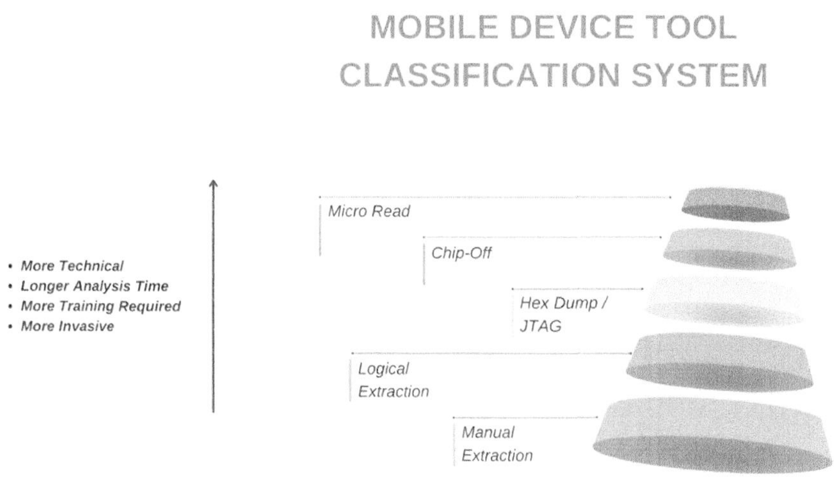

Figure 5.16 Extraction Processes - Android Debug Bridge.

The Android Debug Bridge (ADB) is a command-line tool that establishes a USB connection between a mobile device and a computer. ADB commands facilitate a range of actions on the device, such as transferring files, installing and uninstalling applications, and running shell commands [5].

These commands enable investigators to obtain the root shell of the device, allowing them to execute various commands. ADB functions as a client-server program comprising three components:

Client: This component operates on the forensic workstation, issuing ADB commands to install or uninstall applications and extract data from the device.

Daemon: It is a background process responsible for executing commands on the device.

Server: This component runs in the background on a forensic workstation, overseeing communication between the client and daemon.

Steps that should be followed in an Android mobile phone before extraction: (see Figure 5.17)

1. Removing of all sim cards from the device before switching it on
2. Putting the device in airplane mode
3. Switch off location, bluetooth, wi-fi & hotspot services
4. Follow the following steps to enable developer options

   SETTINGS -> ABOUT PHONE/SOFTWARE INFORMATION -> TAP 07 TIMES BULD NUMBER/VERSION/KERNEL VERSION (After the above mentioned Steps the developer option should be enabled inside System Setting/Additional Setting)

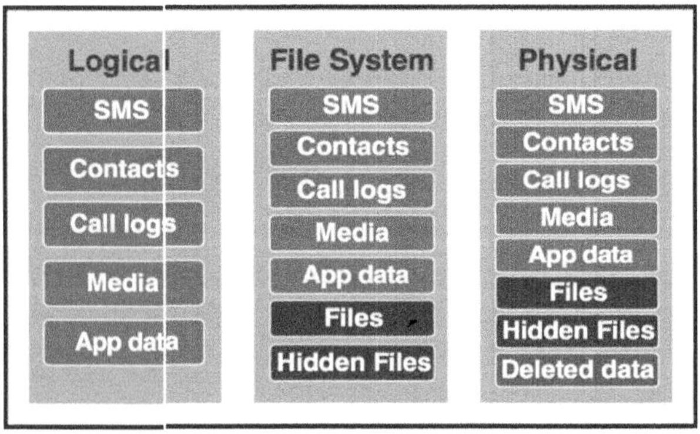

Figure 5.17 Extraction Types.

- For Developer Option, the following settings should be enabled

STAY AWAKE-	ON
OEM UNLOCKING-	ON (If not asking to reset the device)
USB DEBUGGING-	ON
VERIFY APPS/APPLICATION OVER USB	OFF
VERIFY BYTECODE DEBUGGER	OFF
DEFAULT USB CONFIGURATION-	FILE TRANSFER
AUTO LOCK	MAXIMUM

There are two types of software commonly used for extracting and analyzing mobile evidence:

a. Proprietary
   UFED 4PC, MSAB XRY, MAGNET AXIOM
b. Open-source
   Avilla Forensics for Android and itunes, iBackup viewer, iLeapp for iPhone

5.6 EXTRACTION AND ANALYSIS OF AN ANDROID DEVICE

5.6.1 Using Proprietary Software (UFED)

Three types of extraction are performed on an Android device using proprietary software (UFED), i.e., File system, logical or advanced logical and physical extraction [19]; there are generic profiles also based on the chipset Qualcomm or Mediatek. Another few options: Camera, Screenshot, and Chat capture are also present and are used when the device can be accessed using the mentioned three extraction methods (see Figures 5.18 and 5.19) [2, 8].

5.6.2 Analysis of Extraction Report

The extraction report displays all the artifacts (Figures 5.20–5.23) retrieved from the device depending upon the type of extraction, encompassing both current and deleted phone data. The obtained artifacts after extraction include:

- Calendar
- Call Logs
- Cell Towers
- Chatting applications

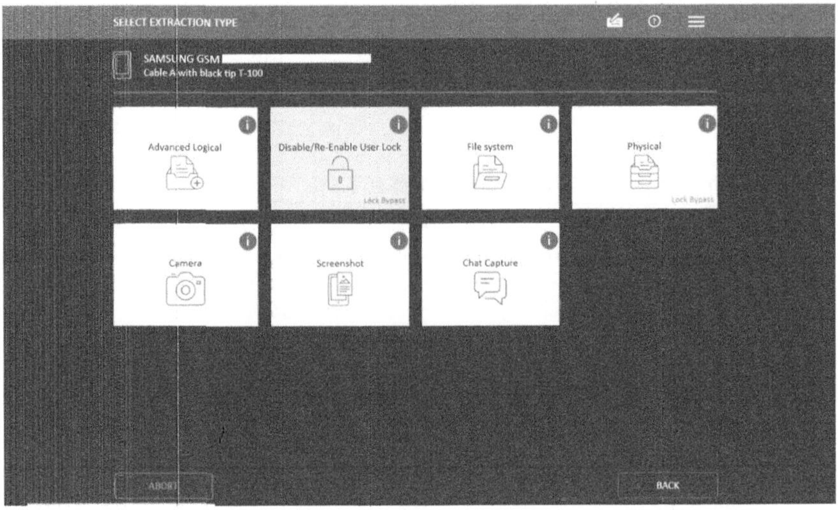

Figure 5.18 UFED Android Extraction Interface.

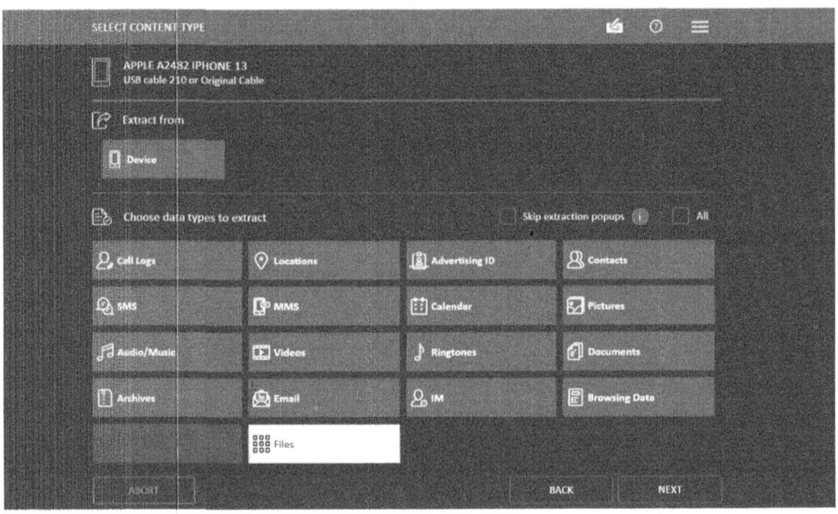

Figure 5.19 Logical Extraction Interface.

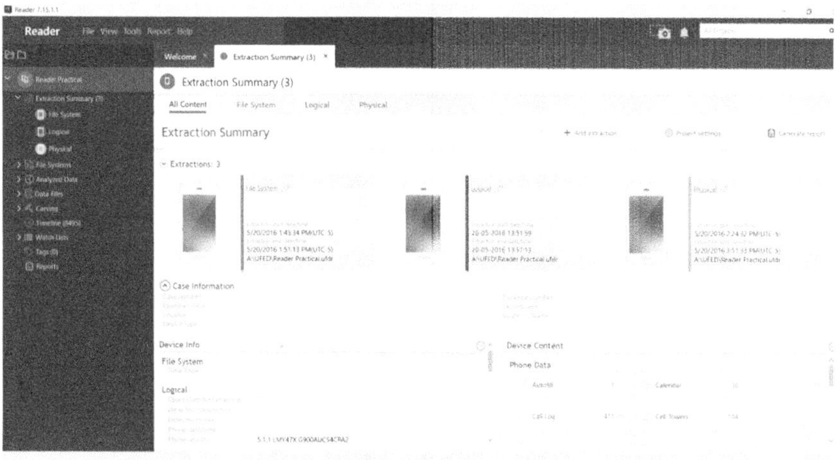

Figure 5.20 Extraction Summary of Android Device.

- Email
- Installed Applications
- Cookies
- Instant Messages
- Device Users
- Locations
- MMS Messages
- Passwords
- Powering Events
- SMS Messages
- User Accounts
- Web History
- Wireless Network
- Data Files
- Timeline
- Applications
- Audio

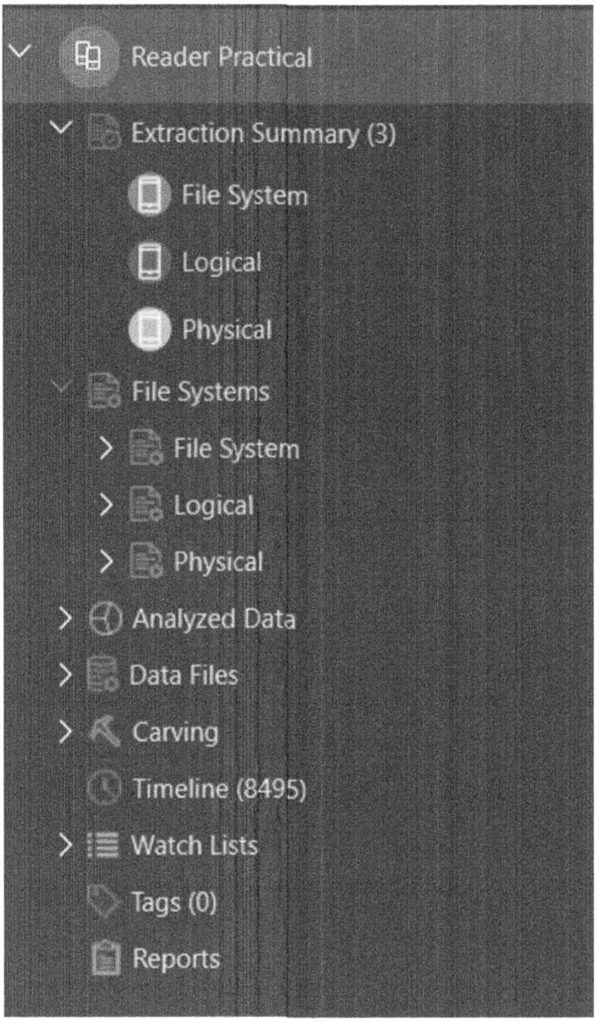

Figure 5.21 UFED Evidence Tree.

5.7 USING OPEN-SOURCE SOFTWARE (AVILLA FORENSICS 3.5)

5.7.1 Process of Extraction From Avilla

1. Verify the connection by examining the Avilla interface for the visibility of information such as model number, release version, vendor build version, and build version.

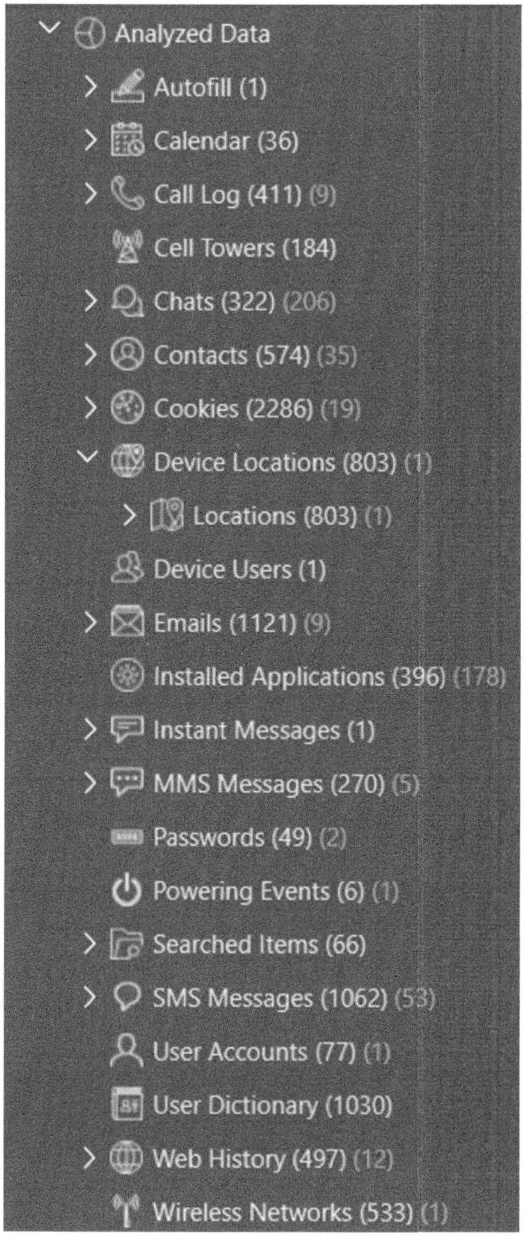

Figure 5.22 UFED Evidence Tree.

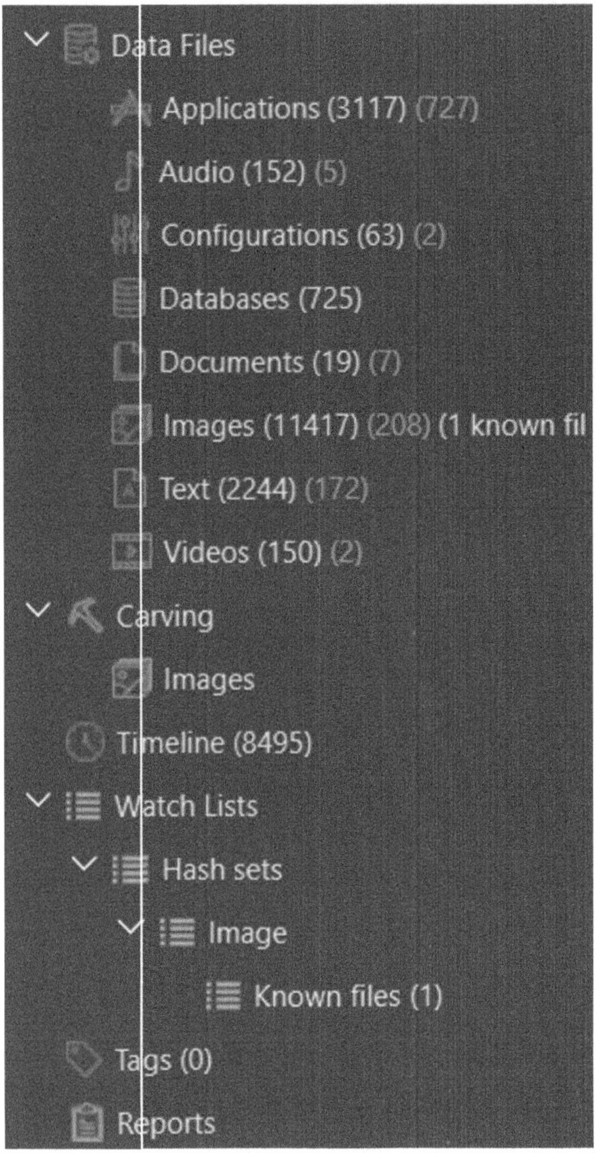

Figure 5.23 UFED Evidence Tree.

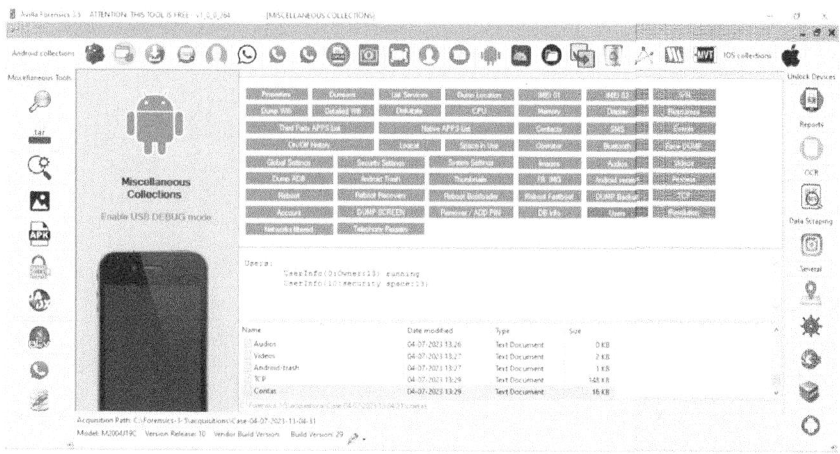

Figure 5.24 USB Debugging Mode Checked in Avilla.

2. Create a new case and select "Miscellaneous Collections" (see Figure 5.24) on the Avilla interface to initiate the extraction of artifacts from an Android device.
3. After the extraction process is finished, review the extracted data. The extracted data may include:

- Properties data, dumpsys, list service, dumplocation
- IMEI 01 & IMEI 02
- Serial no., dumpwifi, detail wifi, diskstat, CPU, Memory, display
- Third party app, Native app, SMS, Events, logcat, space in use, operator, Bluetooth, images, vedios
- Contacts, Audio, Facedump
- Globalsetting, system setting, security setting, Android trash, process, reboot, TCP, account, users, telephony registry

5.7.2 Extraction and Analysis of iPhone Device

5.7.2.1 Data Extraction Using iTunes

5.7.2.1.1 Logical Backup of iPhone Using iTunes

The iPhone should be connected to the laptop via an iPhone USB data cable. Once connected iTunes detect and identify the connected iPhone by displaying the iPhone icon displayed under the Devices on the left sidebar of the iTunes homepage (see Figure 5.25). By clicking on iPhone icon on the

Figure 5.25 Homepage of iTunes.

iTunes homepage, it displays the summary of the iPhone, such as its Name, Capacity, software version, Phone number and Serial number.

The iTunes application creates a backup of the iPhone data during the sync process. When the iPhone mobile is synced with the laptop, the device's configuration, address book, calendar, images, SMS database, email accounts, web history, and other sorts of personal details are saved on the laptop in backup files in a single directory. When iTunes syncs the iPhone with the laptop, it copies data from the iPhone to the PC and vice versa to ensure that the content is the same on both [20].

Extracting artifacts through iTunes

- Photo and video files
- Contact information
- Application used by user

5.7.2.2 Backup of iPhones

The backup process starts by selecting the "Back Up" option by right-clicking the iPhone icon. After the backup process is completed, the iPhone is disconnected from the laptop. The backup data created from iTunes is saved in*Windows-SSD-(C)\Users\Username\AppData\Roaming\AppleComputer\MobileSync\Backup*

1. Logical Image Extraction and Analysis with iBackup Viewer iBackup Viewer of version 4.27.20 gets downloaded and installed.

5.7.2.3 *iBackup Viewer Summary Information of Backup*

The iTunes backup of iPhone displays a thumbnail in iBackup Viewer, iBackup Viewer lists the backups for the iPhone, providing summary information such as name and iOS version (see Figure 5.26). Each iOS backup exhibits a thumbnail, and the details encapsulated in the thumbnail are as follows:

- Name of the iPhone device in which the backup was created
- iOS version of the iPhone at the time of backup
- Creation Date of backup
- Folder icon will show the location of the backup folder

Clicking on the thumbnail leads to the content of the backup.

5.7.2.4 *Contents of Backup*

- Contacts: Extraction of each contact is done by selecting "Selected to vCard file" from the Export option on the top right of the iBackup viewer toolbar. The exported contacts are then saved by selecting the destination folder
- Call history
- Messages
- Calendar
- Voicemails
- Notes
- Voice recording
- WhatsApp Messages
- Safari & bookmarks
- Photos and videos

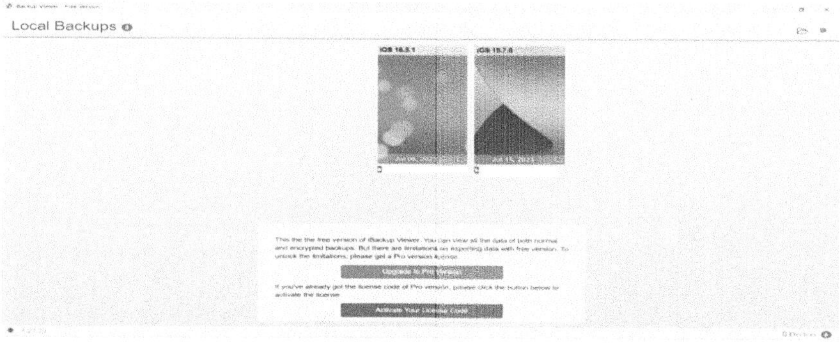

Figure 5.26 iBackup Viewer.

By clicking each of the items it has displayed the contents inside the item from the backup. On the top side of the toolbar of iBackup Viewer it displayed the name, model, iOS version, IMEI number, unique ID, serial number, iTunes version, backup created date, and phone number. iBackup Viewer exports the selected data and can examine the data.

5.7.2.5 Analysis Using iLEAPP

The HTML report is produced by the iLEAPP. The homepage of the html report produced by iLEAPP is shown in Figure 5.27.

The following information can be analyzed using ileapp:

1. Device details: The device details tab provides the information about the device, such as built version, device name, ICCID, IMEI, last backup date, MEID, phone number, Product name, Product type, Product version and Serial number
2. Calendar Identity Report
3. Apps per screen report
4. Paired Bluetooth
5. Paired low-energy Bluetooth, which is also known as Bluetooth Low Energy (BLE)
6. Other LE: All Bluetooth LE has either a public address or random address. Random address enables a device to hide its identity
7. Google Duo - Call history
8. Google Duo – Contacts
9. Account data
10. TCC- Permission: TCC refers to Transparency, Consent, and Control. The database contained the permissions allowed and denied for apps and services, defined by the PPPC (Privacy Preferences Policy Control) settings

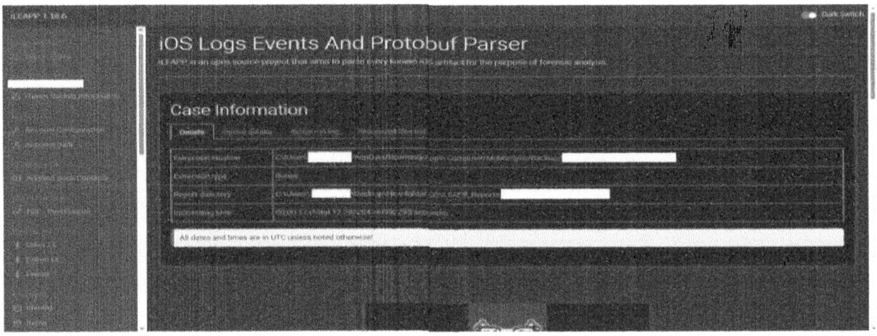

Figure 5.27 Homepage of iLEAPP Html Report.

11. Address book contacts
12. Messages
13. Bookmarks
14. Voice recordings

5.8 DRONE FORENSICS

Drones, also known as Unmanned Aerial Vehicles (UAVs), have gained popularity among the general public due to their accessibility and affordability. This increased popularity has also raised concerns for internal security, as non-state actors utilize drones for illicit activities like cross-border smuggling. This sheds light on the significance of extracting and analyzing information from these devices.

Extraction of drone data can be accomplished through a variety of methods, including direct physical extraction through the USB port of the drone, extraction via network connection (WIFI), retrieval from the SD card, chip-off extraction, and obtaining drone application data through ADB backup. The initial effort involves pulling the data from user applications and performing physical extraction via USB, followed by subsequent data analysis. Artifacts are obtained from the flight logs, media files stored in the SD card, and user applications to retrieve credentials for cloud data extraction. Key artifacts include parameter values tied to the timeline, encompassing speed, altitude, longitude, latitude, yaw, roll, and pitch; historical flight path data; GPS information; media data; and timeline creation details.

Several software tools, including MD Drone by GMD Soft, UFED 4PC, and Belkasoft, aid in the extraction of drone data. The extracted data is formatted as a .bat file, which can be further analyzed using open-source tools like Autopsy, CSV View, and Dat Con. Given the diverse landscape of do-it-yourself (DIY) drone configurations, not all software can accommodate every model. In such cases, extraction is carried out using a generic profile.

For demonstration purposes, the drone dump files were outsourced from the project and then analyzed using Autopsy, CSV View, and Dat Con.

5.8.1 Analysis of Drone Data Using Autopsy

In Autopsy, after initiating a new case, the logical files must be chosen under data source types [21]. Subsequently, all DAT files are selected, followed by the appropriate selection of ingest modules like GPx parser, DJI_Phantom_Drone, DJI Drone, exif parser, etc., and the ingest process is executed. Once the ingest modules is completed, the parsed data could be observed on the left side in a tree structure. Additionally, utilizing the Geo-location module allowed for a graphical representation of the flight history, incorporating

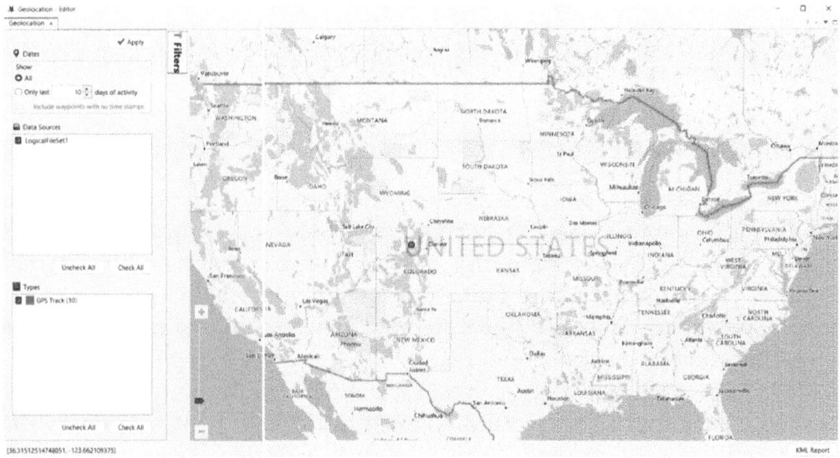

Figure 5.28 Geolocation Tab.

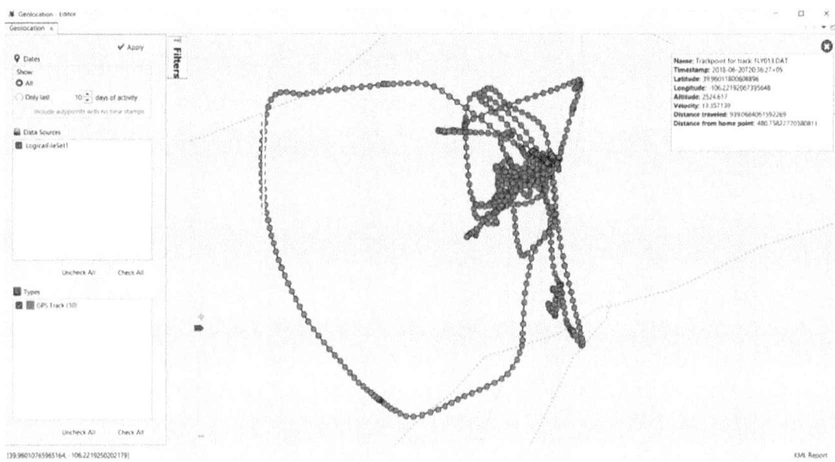

Figure 5.29 Geolocation Tab Showing Trails.

supplementary data such as speed, time, latitude, and longitude (see Figures 5.28 and 5.29).

For the media file the micro-SD card and the application data base has to be extracted and parsed.

5.8.2 Analysis of Drone Data Using Csv View and Dat Con

CsvView and DatCon are freely available offline applications that offer the capability to analyze log files generated by various drones, including

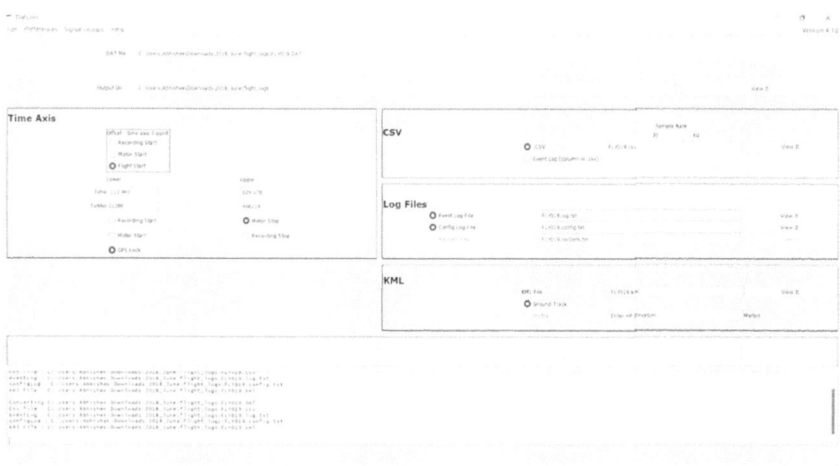

Figure 5.30 Dat Con Interface.

Phantom 3, Phantom 4, Phantom 4 Pro, Inspire 1, Spark, and Mavic Pro. To utilize either or both of these applications, simply download and install them on your PC, Mac, or Linux machine. DatCon was developed and released starting in January 2016, while CsvView is an ongoing project, with distribution commencing in June 2016. Many DatCon users may discover that CsvView provides the features they need and is also more user-friendly. CsvView employs a SigPlayer to display flight variables, and this SigPlayer can also present flight status information. Users can download KML files using Dat Con and visualize them using Google Earth (see Figures 5.30 and 5.31).

5.9 IOT FORENSIC

The extraction of data from the Internet of Things needs a deep knowledge of various fields, such as hardware forensics, mobile forensics, network forensics, and cloud forensics [22]. All these are the layers of an IoT architecture; an examiner must know from which layer data can be extracted and how [9]. In the Internet of Things – "all the devices which can be connected over the network" – act as data receivers from the physical world are called nodes, which can be amazon alexa, smart watches, vehicular IoT, DIY IoT's etc [23].

If we look at smart watches, Mobile Edit software is there, which provides the extraction of smartwatches such as Samsung, Garmin and Apple with their kit. Data such as GPS locations, recent contacts and messages, tracking, and recent activities can be pulled out of the watches

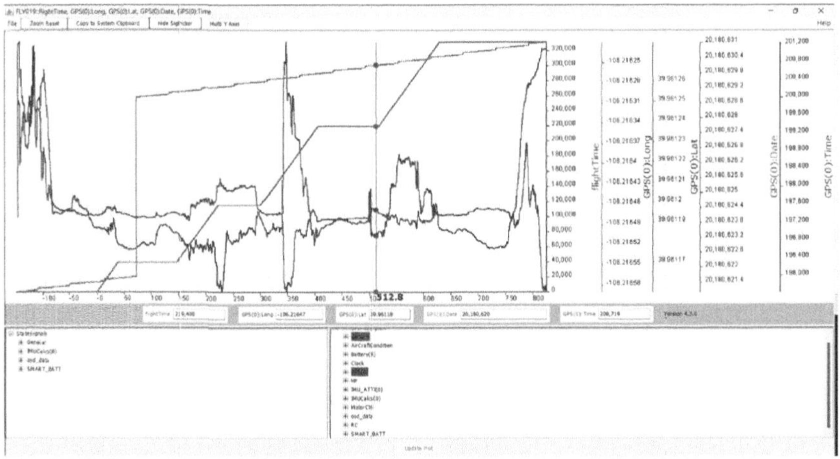

Figure 5.31 CsV View Module Showing Flight Data.

[17]. It also depends on the type of watch; some have internal storage, and some possess SIM [24].

And with the Amazon's Alexa systems the examiner has to look into the applications database for the last activities, search list, and cloud authorization tokens amazon related data. And from alexa itself he/she can gather the evidence via physical extraction, chip-off.

For the DIY IoT's examiners have to do hit and trial for the extraction of data by diving through different layers of an IoT.

5.10 LIST OF OPEN-SOURCE TOOLS FOR HANDS-ON

Table 5.1 List of Open-Source Tools for Hands-On

No.	*Company/ OEM*	*Package*	*Brief Info*	*Download Link*
1.	Sleuthkit	Autopsy	Autopsy is an easy to use, GUI-based program that allows you to efficiently analyze hard drives and smart phones.	Download
0.	-	Autopsy-Plugins	Python Plugins for Autopsy.	Download
0.	NirSoft	NirSoft Package (Password: nirsoft9876$)	NirSoft Package having more than 200 portable freeware utilities for Windows.	Download

Table 5.1 (Cont.)

No.	*Company/ OEM*	*Package*	*Brief Info*	*Download Link*
0.	Parmavex Services	WinAudit	WinAudit is an inventory utility for Windows computers. It creates a comprehensive report on a machine's configuration, hardware and software.	Download
0.	Passware	Encryption Analyser	It is a GUI Based that can quickly and non-intrusively check for encrypted volumes on a computer system during incident response.	Download
0.	Magnet Forensic	Magnet RAM Capture	Magnet RAM Capture is an imaging tool designed to capture the physical memory.	Download
0.	Magnet Forensic	Encrypted Disk Detector	Encrypted Disk Detector is a command-line tool that can quickly and non-intrusively check for encrypted volumes on a computer system during incident response.	Download
0.	Magnet Forensic	Magnet Acquire	Magnet ACQUIRE lets digital forensic examiners quickly and easily acquire forensic images of any iOS or Android device, hard drive, and removable media.	Download
0.	CDAC	F-Ran	F-Ran is a Forensic Registry Analysis tool.	Download
0.	CDAC	F-DAC	F-DaC is a Forensic data carving tool, to carve different files with optimized search engine for identifying files based on headers and footers.	Download
0.	CAINE	CAINE	CAINE (Computer Aided INvestigative Environment) is an Italian GNU/Linux live OS having a collection of Forensic Tool used Investigation.	Download
0.	Passmark Software	Volatility Workbench-GUI	Volatility Workbench is a graphical user interface (GUI) for the Volatility tool. Volatility is a command line memory analysis and forensics tool for extracting artifacts from memory dumps.	Download
0.	Passmark Software	OSFClone	**OSFClone** is a free, self-booting solution which enables you to create or clone exact raw disk images quickly and independent of the installed operating system.	Download

(*continued*)

Table 5.1 (Cont.)

No.	*Company/ OEM*	*Package*	*Brief Info*	*Download Link*
0.	Passmark Software	OSFMount	OSFMount allows you to mount local disk image files (bit-for-bit copies of an entire disk or disk partition) in Windows as a physical disk or a logical drive letter.	Download
0.	iMAC Tool	iBackup Viewer	iBackup Viewer works with full features, includes extracting contacts, exporting and printing SMS & iMessage messages to PDF files, exporting phone call history, add safari visit history and bookmarks to desktop safari, viewing and recovering photos and videos.	Download
0.	-	iLeapp	Backup tool for Apple phones.	Download
0.	Andriller	Andriller	Andriller - is software utility with a collection of forensic tools for smartphones. It performs read-only, forensically sound, non-destructive acquisition from Android devices. It has features, such as powerful Lockscreen cracking for Pattern, PIN code, or Password; custom decoders for Apps data from Android (some Apple iOS & Windows) databases for decoding communications. Extraction and decoders produce reports in HTML and Excel formats.	Download
0.	Google TakeOut	--	-	Download
0. 22	Access Data	FTK Imager	-	Download
23	HASH CALC		-	Download
24	Avilla Forensics	Avilla Forensics (Mobile forensics utility)	https://github.com/AvillaDaniel/AvillaForensics.	Download
25	Encase Imager	Open text	-	Download
27	Forensically	-	Forensically is a set of free tools for digital image forensics. It includes clone detection, error level analysis, meta data extraction and more. It is made by Jonas Wagner.	https://29a.ch/photo-forensics/
28	Csv View and Dat Con	-	Open tools to analyze the .dat files of Drones.	Download

REFERENCES

1. K. Kaushik, R. Tanwar, S. Dahiya, K. K. Bhatia, and Y. Wu. *Unleashing the Art of Digital Forensics*. CRC Press, 2022.
2. N. Pansari and D. Kushwaha. Forensic analysis and investigation using digital forensics-an overview. *International Journal of Advance Research, Ideas and Innovations in Technology*, 5(1): 471–472, 2019.
3. A. Singh et al. Extraction and analysis of forensic deleted data from digital evidence using the sleuthkit. *International Journal of Multidisciplinary Educational Research*, 9(10): 107–120, 2020.
4. Z. Baig et al. Future challenges for smart cities: Cyber security and digital forensics. *Digital Investigation*, 22: 3–13, 2017.
5. M. Bader et al. iPhone 3gs forensics: Logical analysis using apple iTunes. *Small Scale Digital Device Forensics Journal*, 4(1): 4–6, 2010.
6. M. S. Bahir and M. N. A. Khan. Triage in live digital forensic analysis. *The International Journal of Forensic Computer Science*, 1: 35–44, 2013.
7. C. Tankard. The security issues of the internet of things. *Computer Fraud & Security*, 9: 11–14, 2015.
8. J. Annies Mary Jeyaseeli and C. Shanthi. Forensic data extraction using sleuthkit tools. *Nevo-Nat. Volatiles & Essent. Oils*, 8(5): 1913–1922, 2021.
9. M. I. Alghamdi. Digital forensics in cyber security - Recent trends, threats, and opportunities. *Periodicals of Engineering and Natural Sciences*, 8(3): 1321–1330, 2020.
10. F. Freiling et al. Advances in forensic data acquisition. *IEEE Design & Test*, 35(5): 63–74, 2018.
11. H. Srivastava and S. Tapaswi. Logical acquisition and analysis of data from android mobile devices. *Information and Computer Security*, 23(5): 450–475, 2015.
12. A. Agarwal et al. Systematic digital forensic investigation model. *International Journal of Computer Science and Security (IJCSS)*, 5(1): 124–127, 2011.
13. T. B. Tajuddin et al. Forensic investigation and analysis on digital evidence discovery through physical acquisition on smartphone. In *2015 World Congress on Internet Security (WorldCIS)*. IEEE, 2015
14. A. Case et al. Memory forensics: The path forward. *Digital Investigation*, 20: 23–33, 2017.
15. S. Li et al. IoT forensics: Amazon echo as a use case. *IEEE Internet of Things Journal*, 6(4): 6487–6497, 2019.
16. P. Jain and A. Mishra. Extraction of data using cellebrite UFED 4PC. *International Journal of Multidisciplinary Educational Research*, 9(10(7)): 225–230, 2024.
17. R. Tamma, O. Skulkin, H. Mahalik, and S. Bommisetty. *Practical Mobile Forensics: Forensically investigate and analyze iOS, Android, and Windows 10 devices*. Packt Publishing Ltd., 2020.
18. D. Ali, O. Bernard, and B. Chukwuemeka. Performance of android forensics data recovery tools. In *Contemporary digital forensic investigations of cloud and mobile applications*, 91–110. Elsevier, 2016.
19. Q. Do et al. Exfiltrating data from android devices. *Computers & Security*, 48: 74–91, 2015.

20. Y. Yusoff et al. Common phases of computer forensics investigation models. *AIRCC's International Journal of Computer Science and Information Technology*, 3(3): 1–11, 2011.
21. M. Parekh and S. Jani. Memory forensic: Acquisition and analysis of memory and its tools comparison. *International Journal of Engineering Technologies and Management Research*, 5(2): 90–95, 2018.
22. A. Dhaqm, R. A. Ikuesan, V. R. Kebande, et al. Digital forensics subdomains: The state of the art and future directions. *IEEE Access*, 9: 152476–152502, 2021.
23. A. S. Abdul-Qawy, P. J. Pramod, E. Magesh, and T. Srinivasulu. The internet of things (iot): An overview. *International Journal of Engineering Research and Applications*, 5(12): 71–82, 2015.
24. B. K. Sharma et al. Emerging trends in digital forensic and cyber security-an overview. In *2019 Sixth HCT Information Technology Trends (ITT)*, 309–313. IEEE, 2021.

Chapter 6

Data-Driven Forensics

Unveiling the Hidden Depths of Financial Crime

Mukund Purohit and Haresh Barot

6.1 DEFINING FRAUD

The term "Fraud" gives waves of images in which one witnesses people who have lost money because they have been victims of various scams like phishing, vishing, or social engineering. Most prominent is shoulder surfing, in which, while making any transaction via UPI or withdrawing money from an ATM, fraudsters take a peek from the shoulder/arms of the victims and indulge them in conversation while easily replacing the cards. The end result is the loss of hard-earned money. The same applies to the organizations.

The ACFE (Association of Certified Fraud Examiners) has defined *fraud* as "any activity that relies on deception in order to achieve a gain." Fraud becomes a crime when it is a "knowing misrepresentation of the truth or concealment of a material fact to induce another to act to his or her detriment." In other words, if you lie in order to deprive a person or organization of their money or property, you are committing fraud. (*What Is Fraud*, n.d.)

There are numerous explanations as to why people commit fraud. A famous criminologist, Dr. Donald Cressey, gave three explanations. These are pressure, opportunity and finally, rationalization (Figure 6.1). Interestingly, they were given in 1970 but are still valid, and with time, some other modifications have also evolved. (Prasmaulida, 2016)

The components of the fraud triangle are the reasons that tell us about the mentality of the fraudster and why he/she has committed the fraud. The opportunity explains the conditions in terms of absence/less strict internal control or no strict punishment for financial fraud. Such favorable conditions give rise to frauds as the perpetrator commits the crime as he/she has been able to bypass the system or found a loophole to extract monetary gain. The pressure experienced by fraudsters provides insights into their mental health, namely whether they were facing financial strain due to debts from loans or gambling, or if they had dependencies on alcohol or drugs that required financial support. A striking point is that it is not just loans,

DOI: 10.1201/9781003471103-6

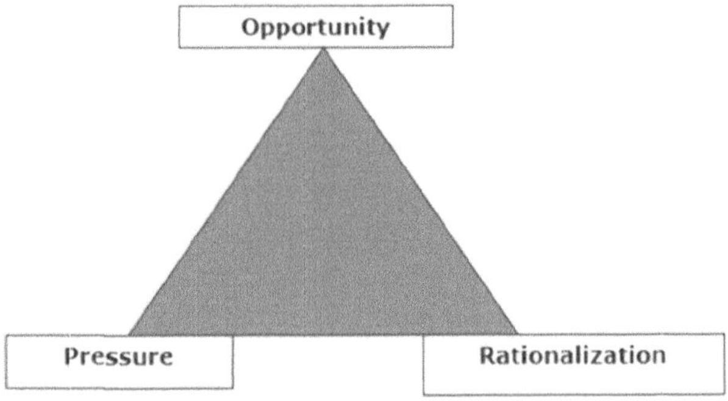

Figure 6.1 Dr Donald Cressey's Explanation for People Committing Fraud.

sometimes peer pressure also forces a person to indulge in such activities as living a high-end lifestyle.

The third and last reason is rationalization, as criminals justify their reason for committing fraud. They also try to showcase it as the right act. They sometimes call it their due raise, which they were supposed to get in the form of an increment, or they believe that they are borrowing it for a short duration and will give it back soon. All such frauds are done very carefully and shown as genuine expenditures in the name of paying the due bills or paying a vendor for its products or services. (*Schuchter and Levi - 2016 - The Fraud Triangle Revisited.Pdf*, n.d.) If we reflect back on the reason, specifically "Opportunity," we learn that fraudulent acts are executed when there is the absence of internal control or less strictness in terms of punishment; but what precisely are internal controls, and how do they prevent fraud from happening? Internal controls can be defined as safety measures that are kept in order to prevent fraud from happening. Let's take an example.

6.1.1 Example

David is an employee in a big firm and has a routine traveling job; his work requires him to visit different client sites and spend some days or even weeks if required. After every trip, he produces his traveling expenditures, which include fares of flights, hotel, and restaurant. After producing such bills, company personnel verify with clients and hotels regarding his visit and pay him after proper due diligence. If David is paid without verifying the bills, then there is a high chance that he may exaggerate the amount on bills and cash an extra amount that will go to his pocket. That is the reason why proper checks and balances are required to verify the claims.

This example has shown us the point that if opportunity is present, then employees may commit fraud, and it will incur not only monetary losses to the company but also to the brand image or reputation, along with motivating other employees to commit fraud.

An important question that arises is how employees can become aware of opportunities regarding loopholes or weak internal controls.

6.2 WHITE COLLAR CRIMES

The answer is directed towards another term, "white collar crime." White-collar crime refers to the crime committed by employees who possess decision-making power or can influence the decisions in the company. It could be monetary or any other medium that results in any transaction. Such employees are with the company for a longer period of time, which enables them to understand the day-to-day operations, and thus, they can easily find loopholes in the system and exploit it for their personal benefit. Whereas a new employee will hesitate to commit such acts as he is not aware of the internal controls that have been kept in the system. (Gottschalk & Gunnesdal, 2018).] There have been many cases where the employees from top management were involved in making fraudulent invoices or paying money to shell companies, which were created in their relatives or friend's names and sometimes even disappeared after receiving the payments. One such hypothetical exemplary case is Mars Financials.

6.2.1 Example

The embezzlement scheme at Mars Financials took place in the prestigious hallways of the investment firm, which, during the course of its thirty years of existence, was known for its cautious investing tactics and steadfast client care. At the center of this tale was Mark Stevens, a seasoned 15-year Chief Financial Officer (CFO) who was trusted and respected by the company's leaders. Sarah Thompson, a senior accountant with five years of tightly entwined service, and Michael Greene, a junior accountant with two years of direct reporting to Sarah.

Money was siphoned from the customers' accounts into a whole network of fake accounts in a tightly orchestrated plan that Stevens had devised and executed in 2018-2023. Early during 2023, routine checks in Thompson's work uncovered inconsistencies that set up an "epic battle of wits," as she later put it, with Stevens who minimized the apparent errors as a temporary blip that she was diligently looking into. Thompson kept finding more such errors that confirmed her suspicion that something was going awry. In turn, she shared her woes with Greene, whose worries kept mounting, and led to Thompson passing an anonymous communication with the authorities later in the same year. The subsequent investigation stripped away layers of Stevens' complicated scam, peeling back veil after veil through the sober lenses of forensic accountants. Records suggested a life of extravagant purchases funded by embezzled money, used to fuel an array of dedicated options in Stevens' quest for a luxuriant lifestyle over a number of years: from opulent cars to expensive trips abroad. A succession of court appearances ensued, and Stevens was arrested and handed down a number of convictions for fraud, money laundering and embezzlement. While Thompson demonstrated her dedication to justice by cooperating with authorities and was kept under a witness protection program, Greene was protected by law as a whistleblower. Stevens's 20-year federal jail sentence brought an end to his deceptive behavior, but Mars Financials suffered reputational harm. However, as Thompson and Greene emerged as shining examples of honesty and alertness in the case of a white-collar crime, the company took the initiative to proactively install strict internal controls in an effort to strengthen against future breaches.

In the above case it is very clearly evident that all organizations are prone to white collar crimes and a proper due diligence and audit is required in order to prevent crimes from happening. It has been proven also that preventing a financial crime from happening is better than detection as money once lost is very difficult to recover and takes years in courtroom and legal proceedings. Financial frauds have been happening, but the major recognition came after the Enron case. The Enron case in 2001 opened the eyes of the world and proved to be a watershed moment as when Enron collapsed, it went down with assets exceeding $60 billion, causing one of the largest bankruptcies in the history of the USA. This event led to extensive discussion and led to the enactment of laws targeting malpractices towards accounting standards and practices, which had enduring impacts on the financial industry. The chain of events led to the downfall of Arthur Andersen LLP, one of the biggest auditing and accounting firms in the world, and the bankruptcy of Enron Corporation in 2001.

6.3 BIRTH OF FORENSIC ACCOUNTING AND FRAUD INVESTIGATION

In contemporary business history, the Enron scandal is a glaring example of corporate deception and financial wrongdoing. Enron Corporation, which was once hailed as a symbol of success and innovation in the energy industry, collapsed in 2001, leaving a path of destruction in its wake. Enron used sophisticated financial strategies and aggressive accounting techniques to inflate profits artificially and hide rising debt. The company was led by individuals such as CEO Jeffrey Skilling, founder Kenneth Lay, and CFO Andrew Fastow. Enron's stock price surged until reality could no longer be concealed, despite early warning indications of trouble and doubts about its accounting practices (S.A Rahman Bukhari, 2019). Enron filed for bankruptcy in late 2001, sending shockwaves through the financial community after large losses and secret debts were revealed. Regulatory agencies' subsequent investigations revealed corruption within the corporation, which resulted in the indictment of several important executives on counts ranging from conspiracy to fraud. Thousands of employees lost their jobs because of the fraud, and it was not the only part of the severe consequences; the investors also lost a lot of money. Sarbanes-Oxley Act and other legislative reforms aimed at improving corporate accountability and transparency were ultimately brought about by the Enron scandal, which revealed stark shortcomings in regulatory supervision and corporate governance. It is still a story that acts as a cautioning tale about the value of leadership in the business sector. Enron was the perfect example of ignorance of red flags, the importance of a strong and ethical board of members and a deep thought that it could happen in the future if proper precautions were not taken care ("Twenty Years Later: The Lasting Lessons of Enron," n.d.). The Enron case was the first of its kind to highlight the importance of forensic accounting.

6.4 CORPORATE FRAUDS & FINANCIAL DATA MANIPULATION

Enron was not the first and the last company to indulge in financial data manipulation; in the upcoming years, we would see Bernie Madoff who would indulge in Ponzi schemes; his company was among the top ten companies in the stock exchange, and it was revealed that approximately $19 Billion dollars were swept by his company. The money belonged to investors and citizens who had lost their hard-earned money (Dimmock & Gerken, n.d.). The recent fraud that has shaken the American market is the Theranos case in which Ms. Elizabeth Holmes fooled the investors as her company came up with a unique blood testing kit that would be able to perform multiple tests using a few ml of blood. It eventually turned out to be a hoax as it was just a way to gain investor's trust and money. Around $9 Billion was lost in this scandal (Kandel, 2020).

If we talk about the Indian scenario, the Satyam case is called the Enron of India. The founder, Mr. Ramalinga Raju, indulged in various deceptive schemes, which included fake employees and manipulation of financial statements for the company. It was also involved in manipulation activities for a longer period of time and around 1.5 billion dollars was lost during the entire duration of this scheme (*Bhasin-CAcctingScandalatSatyam-EJBSS-March2013.Pdf*, n.d.). This led to changes in the various compliances and brought many laws that could help in the identification and prevention of such financial frauds.

The manipulation using financial statements is done by companies to show a good image of their organization in front of investors in order to attract more investments. (Beneish, 1999). The liability and assets are manipulated in a way that short-term liability is shown as long-term liability, and the value of assets is inflated to show a surplus in books of accounts.

For detection of such fraud and manipulative practices services of forensic accountants and financial fraud investigators are required.

Forensic accounting is a branch of accounting that has the combination of accounting skills, legal understanding, information technology, behavioral insights, and data analytics for the purpose of investigating and avoiding financial crime. It requires an in-depth understanding of a company's internal controls and management practices, making it an ideal solution for addressing fraudulent activities. (Hamdan, 2019). The forensic investigation is done to investigate the financial, scams which are done by companies or by individuals in order to gain any financial benefits in any way possible.

Forensic accountants use various techniques that can identify hidden patterns, anomalies, and red flags in financial data. The services are not only useful in corporate, but banking sectors also. There have been many studies, which have studied the effectiveness of using data analytics techniques for identifying financial frauds. They also have knowledge of many tools like Ms. Excel, CaseWare IDEA, and Galvanize ACL. They also possess the knowledge of compliance, laws and ethical standards, which are applicable in the organization (Rangoonwala, 2020). The investigators have knowledge of various fraud theories, which are used individually and in groups in order to pinpoint the fraud and areas of red flags, for example, Altman z score, Benish M score and many more.

If we look at the current scenario, then the influence of technology is increasing in various domains of accounting like auditing. There have been recent developments in the field of auditing and accounting as automation is being added in auditing and similarly in forensics also. (Mcbride & Philippou, 2021). Big data is stepping in aggressively into finance as data is increasing day by day and along with its need to be analyzed accurately and efficiently to identify hidden patterns and anomalies in books of finance.

There have been many studies that have identified that data analytics is essential in increasing accuracy and efficiency, and it helps in the decision-making process. (Farooq Aziz, 2023). Companies are also including analytics in their operations, but there are some concerns related to credibility and legitimacy. Companies wish to have a competitive edge as they need to create a strong position in the market by adapting to new technologies and applications. These new skills and capabilities are now essential in order to navigate the strong waters in industry (Kaya & Akbulut, 2018).

Big data analytics is getting very crucial for the accounting and auditing professional as it is transforming the way the accountants and auditors have been doing their work or have been collaborating with their clients. Now, they are using machine learning applications and various visualization software to reshape their work processes. Even now, the auditors are very actively using machine learning tools to analyze their contracts, identify the journal entries and even increase their fraud detection capabilities. (Chu &

Yong, 2021) In a way, it is also possible for the accountants and auditors to use the visualization tools to go for predictive analytics and also to identify the trends in business processes, so it is essential for them to embrace the new technologies and advancements that can help in analysis.

It may not be a novel issue, but if looked closely at the recent financial crisis that has occurred in the last few years, it says that the frequency and intensity of crime have increased to such a degree that there is a need for managers to adopt a range of anti-fraud measures that aid in preserving resources, control cost and also save their respective market positions. It is true that IT systems play a central role in having robust operational environments but with time the volume of processed data increases, and consequently the internally controlled teams and the software are not able to manually scrutinize every transaction that happens to be the need of the hour, therefore, the use of data analytic is gaining more popularity. Such measures are required to be implemented into the system for continuous monitoring and also to maintain a robust fraud prevention mechanism in the company. (Bănărescu, 2015) The continuous monitoring of the data will help the companies to identify the hidden patterns and anomalies that may be present in the transactions. The same analytics can be utilized in order to analyze behavioral patterns. It can also be used by the banks' credit or debit card transaction systems as a risk engine having the capability to identify such behavior. In simpler words, it can be said that identification of the spending pattern of a person can be noted, accordingly, the profile of a person with regards to his/her paying capacity or his/her day-to-day expenditures. If any transaction above the person's daily limit is processed, then the bank can immediately send alert notification to the customer or the organization regarding the risky transactions and it can process the same as per the instruction from the customer or the company thus saving money, especially in the case of the fraud which is happening via sharing of an OTP or password where people fall victim to the social engineering frauds.

There is another aspect of fraud, which is known as "Bankruptcy," and it is defined as the condition of an organization's inability to pay back the loan they took from any banking institution or the money invested by investors. Some companies declare themselves bankrupt, and out of them, a handful of them may be genuine, but even fewer find it an excuse to pay the investor(s) or bank(s) their due finances. Companies try to hide their assets and commit so much as to show their long-term liability as short-term and present a situation where they do not have sufficient funds to run their day-to-day operations or even pay their employees.

The interesting aspect of the given situation is the generation of shell companies, which are made by certain companies to divert their losses and showcase surplus accounts. Shell companies are companies that do not exist in reality but are present on paper and are the front face for other companies to indulge in money laundering and tax fraud.

Money laundering is defined as a centralized system that involves transactions that are complex in nature, and the value associated with that is very high and is executed across numerous foreign countries. It is a highly complicated process thus, poses a challenge to many such countries and investigation agencies involved (Buchanan, 2004). In India, it is known as the "Hawala" system, and it poses a big risk to companies and individuals involved in tax frauds as they try to hide their black money with the help of tax haven nations, consequently causing extreme difficulty in the processes of prosecution and investigation.

6.4.1 Stages in Money Laundering

1. Placement: The placement is the initial stage where the illegally gained funds are being entered into the banking system, they use various services like currency exchange, or they sell their real estate properties or artwork at very high price in order to put money into the banking system.
2. Layering: The layering is the second stage where the web of financial transactions is made so that the money can be transferred between different accounts across different countries and jurisdiction and even, they take use of different financial institutions the reason for creating such a complex web of transaction is to deviate the investigation agencies and make them delay the investigation.
3. Integration: The integration is the last stage in the money laundering process during this process the money is being entered again into the market to buy high value assets or real estate or some costly artworks in order to legitimize the illicit money which has been made and to make the investigation much more difficult for the investigation agencies.

   The fraudsters take advantage of the loopholes, which are available into the banking system, and they exploit the gaps in the regulatory and compliance, also they take advantage of weaknesses in the banks and thus they are able to facilitate their activities. The government deploys various measures and investigation agencies along with law enforcement agencies to detect and stop the money laundering, but it became difficult because of the loopholes which are present in the system. There is another big factor, which is the great amount of pressure from the political side to stop or delay the investigation.

6.5 USE OF DATA ANALYTICS IN IDENTIFICATION OF MONEY TRAIL IN MONEY LAUNDERING

Data analytics play a vital role in identifying money trail(s) in money laundering. One of the biggest contributors in money laundering is cryptocurrencies and using the latest data techniques investigation agencies can identify the wallets in which the cryptocurrencies have been transferred and also help in the identification of the owner(s) of wallet(s) and the intermediaries (if applicable) who are involved in the transaction process (Buchanan, 2004).

Various studies have been conducted in order to understand the efficacy of data analytics techniques for identifying money laundering and monitoring their corresponding transactions (Palshikar et al., 2014). The objective behind the aforementioned studies was to identify the machine algorithms and methods which can be used to detect transactions that fall under the category of suspicious and especially the terminologies (keywords) related to money and the act itself. The same algorithms are applicable in identifying anomalies in the bank transaction system or any other financial institution (Chen et al., 2018).

The Concept of Data Visualization applies to the graphical representation of data after it has been cleaned and analyzed. The data visualization consists of various charts and graphs which plot the status of data and its value. The same concepts can be applied to money laundering, and this has been proven by research (Singh & Best, 2019). The above discussion of money laundering clarifies one point of notice, that is, data analytics has found its way in forensic accounting and fraud investigation and it is very efficient in identifying hidden patterns and anomalies.

6.6 RISK ASSESSMENT AND REAL-TIME MONITORING

One question that arises is whether data-driven forensics can be used in the case of real-time monitoring. The answer to this question is yes because with the rise of AI and ML, the algorithms are getting increasingly intelligent to learn and identify patterns based on the data given, and they are able to perform with good accuracy. There have been many new innovative techniques where the AI-ML has been used in the automation of the audit process. Normally, an audit is performed manually with human intervention, which is a time-consuming process and is prone to errors.

Auditing requires checking of entries and to see if they have been executed as per the accounting standards. The same checks and balances can be added in the algorithm and those algorithms can work at higher speed with even more accuracy. The auditing also requires the hiring of specialized human resources, which is a costly affair and thus costs a fortune from the viewpoint of a company, but the AI-ML can help save the cost, and a minimal amount of human resources will be utilized for the same. The fraud examination can also be done in real life using data analytics as once the algorithms are trained to analyze the data, it will automatically be able to monitor the transactions.

The risk assessment is another segment of fraud investigation as it is part of preventive forensics and essential in order to prevent fraud from occurring. The main issue in forensic investigation is the recovery of lost amounts. To prevent frauds from happening, the organization has to go through continuous fraud risk assessments. This is normally done by Chartered Accountants (CA's) or Certified Public Accountants (CPA's) and a risk assessment matrix is made sometimes to check the possibility of risks and/or leakages. Risk assessments are mandatory procedures for any organization to save itself from the probability of fraud. Data Analytics can help in handling the risk assessment part and it can have all the parameters which are part of the matrix.

6.7 ETHICAL AND LEGAL CONSIDERATIONS IN DATA-DRIVEN FORENSICS

1. Privacy & Prevention of Data
    - Ethical Concern: The customers have a right to privacy, and their personal data should be analyzed using proper mechanisms.
    - Legal Consideration: The guidelines of compliance with laws protecting data such as the (GDPR) General Data Protection Regulation Act in the EU or United States is crucial.
    - Implementation: The data should be anonymized or encrypted whenever possible to protect the identities of people who are involved in financial transactions.
2. Transparency and Accountability
    - The Transparency in the system ensures that end users understand how data is being used and for what purposes.
    - The customers or stakeholders should be informed of in what ways their data is being or will be used.
    - Bank or any other financial institution should preserve thorough records of their data analysis activities and must be prepared to submit compliance verifications with relevant regulations.
3. Fairness of Data and Non-Discrimination
    - Data-driven decisions should be fair and not against any religion or race and should not be used for any illegal activity.
    - The law should be fair and equal to all.
    - The Algorithms and Models should be regularly updated and checked for any biases, thus reducing the possibility of false positives.
    - It should not have any form of bias towards/against any particular group or organization
4. Accuracy and Reliability of Data
    - Reliability and accuracy are essential for any decision. It should be fair, devoid of errors (or with minimum errors).
    - The data entered into the algorithm should be checked properly, else, data validation shall be invoked. If the data changes, then it

creates confusion and creates unnecessary chances of risk. Thus, this represents the significance of Integrity.

5. Consent and Opt-Out
    - The stakeholders and customers should have the right to opt out and also the right to the use and analysis of data.
    - The banking or any other financial institutions should provide clear information about data collection and processing procedures, obtain consent from individuals which are required, and provide rules and guidelines for individuals to opt out of data processing activities.
6. Data Security and Confidentiality
    - Data security is essential to safeguard sensitive information from unauthorized access or disclosure.
    - The organization should inform their customers about the possible breach of data and have a proper grievance mechanism to address it. The authorities should be informed along with proper information.
    - Security measures should be applied to prevent unauthorized access of data from hackers, including encryption, access controls, and regular security audits.
7. Integrity & Professionalism with Responsibility
    - The expert(s) involved in forensic analysis should have high ethical standards and a moral code of conduct.
    - The investigation or any analysis procedure undertaken should follow the laws and prescribed global and national standards.
    - Special training & guidelines should be provided to professionals to ensure ethical behavior and responsibility towards data driven forensics.

6.8 CONCLUSION

Forensic accounting and fraud investigation is a rapidly changing and growing field with a wide range of applications. People commit fraud for three reasons: Pressure, Opportunity, & Rationalization. Most frauds are committed by people who are at high positions who are aware of the loopholes in the system. They have extensive knowledge of the organization and are influential enough to affect decisions or decision-makers. The Enron case is considered as the "mother" of forensic accounting & fraud investigation as this case brought the limelight on the importance of fraud detection and prevention. The loss was one of the biggest in the United States. It underwent repercussions on the economy as thousands of investors lost their hard-earned money. This resulted in the Sarbanes-Oxley Act to prevent fraud. After Enron came Bernie Madoff who used his Ponzi scheme to deprive people of their financial capacity. The Ponzi scheme fooled people to invest their money in his company which eventually resulted in loss of their money. In the discussion, another point of focus is the Thernos company, which was able to fool investors by claiming that multiple tests could be done by using a few mL of Blood. The Kit was later proved to be just a gimmick, and which was marketed which happened to be the only way to attract more investors. In the Indian scenario, the Satyam scam by Mr. Ramalingam Raju is the most prominent. He masqueraded people by inflating his company's financial statements, creating ghost employees, and via other manipulation techniques presented a flowery picture of his company.

A forensic accountant uses various tools like MS excel CaseWare IDEA, Galvanize ACL; these tools are very effective in the identification of financial frauds and help the investigators and auditors in identifying the red flags or the anomalies that are present in the financial data. Apart from these tools accountants and auditors also use the technique of data mining, which is very essential owing to the fact that, with the increase in time, the complexity and size of data are increasing exponentially and the current tools have a limit in terms of analysis of data therefore there was a need for having new technologies that could help the accountants and investigator for investigation of financial fraud. The various techniques that are available for the identification of hidden patterns or to identify anomalies are the Altman Z score, Beneish M score, Benford's law etc. These techniques are mostly based on data analytics, and they use various methods and data mining to identify the manipulations that have been done in the financial records. Data analytics is used in money laundering. It is a centralized system developed by fraudsters to launder money across various jurisdictions and countries. They make complex layers to confuse and delay the investigations so that they can convert their illicit funds into white money. The money laundering has stages like placement, layering and integration.

The data analytics find its application in money laundering. There have been many studies that have used the techniques of data analytics to identify the money trail and monitor the transactions in real time which could help them analyze the flow of money. They were able to identify the individuals who were involved in the criminal act of money laundering. Overall, data analytics proves to be a vital part of forensic accounting and fraud investigation, helping in the identification of fraud, changing the course of regular investigations, and making them much more effective by converting them into an application of data driver forensics, saving time and resulting in more efficiency.

REFERENCES

Aziz, F. (2023). Data analytics impacts in the field of accounting. *World Journal of Advanced Research and Reviews*, *18*(2), 946–951. https://doi.org/10.30574/wjarr.2023.18.2.0863

Bănărescu, A. (2015). Detecting and preventing fraud with data analytics. *Procedia Economics and Finance*, *32*, 1827–1836. https://doi.org/10.1016/S2212-5671(15)01485-9

Beneish, M. D. (1999). The Detection of earnings manipulation. *Financial Analysts Journal*, *55*(5), 24–36. https://doi.org/10.2469/faj.v55.n5.2296

Bhasin-CAcctingScandalatSatyam-EJBSS-March2013.pdf. (n.d.).

Buchanan, B. (2004). Money laundering—A global obstacle. *Research in International Business and Finance*, *18*(1), 115–127. https://doi.org/10.1016/j.ribaf.2004.02.001

Chen, Z., Van Khoa, L. D., Teoh, E. N., Nazir, A., Karuppiah, E. K., & Lam, K. S. (2018). Machine learning techniques for anti-money laundering (AML) solutions in suspicious transaction detection: A review. *Knowledge and Information Systems*, *57*(2), 245–285. https://doi.org/10.1007/s10115-017-1144-z

Chu, M. K., & Yong, K. O. (2021). Big data analytics for business intelligence in accounting and audit. *Open Journal of Social Sciences*, *9*(9), Article 9. https://doi.org/10.4236/jss.2021.99004

Dimmock, S. G., & Gerken, W. C. (n.d.). *Finding Bernie Madoff: Detecting Fraud by Investment Managers*. Asian Bureau of Finance and Economic Research (ABFER).

Gottschalk, P., & Gunnesdal, L. (2018). White-Collar Crime Research. In P. Gottschalk & L. Gunnesdal, (Eds.), *White-Collar Crime in the Shadow Economy* (pp. 1–14). Springer International Publishing. https://doi.org/10.1007/978-3-319-75292-1_1

Hamdan, M. W. (2019). The role of forensic accounting in discovering financial fraud. *International Journal of Accounting Research*. https://doi.org/10.35248/2472-114x.18.6.176

Kandel, D. (2020). *Elizabeth Holmes and the Theranos Scandal*. Working paper in "Professional Issues, Ethics and Computer Law" Module CS5052NI. London Metropolitan University. https://doi.org/10.13140/RG.2.2.29685.81124

Kaya, İ., & Akbulut, D. H. (2018). Big data analytics in financial reporting and accounting. *Press Academia Procedia*, 7(1), Article 1. https://doi.org/10.17261/Pressacademia.2018.892

Mcbride, K., & Philippou, C. (2021). "Big results require big ambitions": Big data, data analytics and accounting in masters courses. *Accounting Research Journal*, *35*(1), 71–100. https://doi.org/10.1108/ARJ-04-2020-0077

Palshikar, G. K., Apte, M., & Baskaran, S. (2014). *Analytics for Detection of Money Laundering*. TCS Technical Architects' Conference 2014. Tata Consultancy Services Limited

Prasmaulida, S. (2016). Financial statement fraud detection using perspective of fraud triangle adopted by SAS no. 99. *Asia Pacific Fraud Journal 1*(2), 317. https://doi.org/10.21532/APFJ.001.16.01.02.24

Rangoonwala, N. (2020). Evaluation of various Bankruptcy Prediction Models. In *An Interdisciplinary Journal of Navrachana University* (Vol. 2). www.nuv.ac.in

Rahman Bukhari, S. A. (2019). *The Enron Case Study: History, Ethics and Governance Failures*. https://doi.org/10.13140/RG.2.2.16562.86723

Schuchter and Levi—2016—The Fraud Triangle revisited.pdf. (n.d.).

Singh, K., & Best, P. (2019). Anti-Money Laundering: Using data visualization to identify suspicious activity. *International Journal of Accounting Information Systems*, *34*, 100418. https://doi.org/10.1016/j.accinf.2019.06.001

Twenty Years Later: The Lasting Lessons of Enron. (n.d.). *Twenty Years Later: The Lasting Lessons of Enron*. https://corpgov.law.harvard.edu/2021/04/05/twenty-years-later-the-lasting-lessons-of-enron/

What is Fraud. (n.d.). www.acfe.com/fraud-resources/fraud-101-what-is-fraud

Chapter 7

Unmasking the Threat

A Viewpoint on AI-Based Deepfake Financial Crimes

Beemamol M

7.1 INTRODUCTION

One day, person X received a video call from his friend. The friend seemed so upset and panicked, and it naturally got concerning for the person on the other end. Then he tells his six-year-old kid was hit by a car and admitted to the hospital, and he is in the Intensive Care Unit (ICU) now. He also goes on to say that he did not get enough money to pay for the surgery. Now, he is crying and asking person X if he could lend him some money to save his son.

> Of course, I will give him the money to save the boy. He's my friend, and he needs my help.

This is just a specimen of the dime-a-dozen frauds happening these days. The person one sees in "flesh and blood" may not be who one thinks he is. Despite the fact that "known friend" was speaking on FaceTime (China Business Now, 2023).

According to the World Economic Forum (2023), cybersecurity ranks among the top ten global risks now and in the near future. Cybersecurity Ventures predicts cyber crime costs will reach $10.5 trillion by 2025. Gartner experts project that supply chain vulnerabilities will impact 45% of global organizations in the next two years (Ene, 2023). Only 4% of organizations feel confident protecting linked devices and associated technologies from cyberattacks. Such vulnerabilities can lead to significant operational, financial, legal, and reputational losses for businesses (Ene, 2023).

The widespread use of deepfake technology driven by artificial intelligence has resulted in a surge in financial offenses and mounting financial damages. Such crimes are observed across diverse demographics and countries, shifting the pattern from traditional to AI-based methods. Corporations are growing more apprehensive about the peril presented by deepfake video and voice deception. Regular report 2023 reveals that over 50% of citizens in the United Arab Emirates (UAE) and the United States (US) have fallen victim to deepfake voice fraud, impacting 37% of businesses, higher than

DOI: 10.1201/9781003471103-7

the global average. Even small and medium-sized businesses face challenges, with 46% affected by synthetic identity theft and 28% by deepfake video fraud. Identity theft costs businesses over $300,000, with the banking industry experiencing an average loss of $310,000, while 31% of financial institutions endure costs nearing half a million dollars (Regula, 2023).

Pavel Goldman-Kalaydin, Head of AI & Machine Learning (ML) at Sumsub (a global Anti-fraud company), said,

> *Deepfakes have become easier to make and, consequently, their quantity has multiplied, as is also evident from the statistics. To create a deepfake, a fraudster uses a real person's document, takes a photo of it and turns it into a 3D persona. Anti-fraud and verification providers who do not work constantly to update deepfake detection technologies are lagging behind and putting both businesses and users at risk. Upgrading deepfake detection technology is an essential part of modern effective verification and anti-fraud systems.*
>
> (Business Wire, 2023)

7.2 DEFINING DEEPFAKE TECHNOLOGY

Deepfakes is an AI and deep learning-based human imitation made using cutting-edge technology. It might be an artificially created picture or video of someone's expression, a sound file or voice-mimicking filter, or anything else that makes use of ML to seem human (Rana et al., 2022; Shen et al., 2018; Uddin Mahmud & Sharmin, 2020; Westerlund, 2019). Image and sound manipulation have been practiced for a very long time. For instance, movies have employed graphic editing techniques to correct visual imperfections, while individuals have been employing photo editing tools to create memes since the inception of the internet (Kietzmann et al., 2020; Uddin Mahmud & Sharmin, 2020). Deepfakes are hyper-realistic digital manipulations that combine "deep learning" with "fake" to show humans talking and acting in ways that have never really occurred (Rana et al., 2022; Shen et al., 2018; Uddin Mahmud & Sharmin, 2020; Westerlund, 2019). Deepfakes utilize neural networks to examine extensive data samples in order to replicate a person's facial expressions, mannerisms, speech, and inflections (Westerlund, 2019). The accessible method to build deepfakes is provided by Generative Adversarial Networks (GANs) (Shen et al., 2018). Rapid advancement in the capacity to produce convincing artificial deepfake material is primarily attributable to GANs (Caldwell et al., 2020).

Late in 2017, a Reddit user quoted the phrase "deepfake" for the first time (Somers, 2020). On the news content and aggregation website, this user set up a section where they posted pornographic movies using face-swapping software that was available for free (Rana et al., 2022). Deepfakes exploit social media sites where rumors, conspiracy theories, and false information may spread quickly since users often follow the herd (Uddin Mahmud & Sharmin, 2020; Westerlund, 2019). Meanwhile, a persistent "infopocalypse[1]" encourages individuals to believe that their trust must be pinned to only those pieces of information that are from their trusted social networks, such as family, close friends, or relatives, and confirms their beliefs (Westerlund, 2019). However, it becomes difficult for individuals to tell the difference when they encounter hyper-realistic deepfake images or videos of close people, which drives them to believe it. Detecting deepfakes is challenging due to their use of genuine footage, convincing audio, and their optimization for rapid dissemination on social media. Consequently, many viewers are misdirected into believing that the videos they encounter are authentic (Westerlund, 2019). The availability of an increasing amount of open-source software further contributes to the creation of realistic and high-quality deepfakes, allowing individuals with minimal technical knowledge and no creative expertise to manipulate videos, swap faces, alter emotions, and synthesize speech with remarkable precision (Westerlund, 2019).

To create a deepfake video (as shown in Figure 7.1), a deep neural network undergoes "training" where it learns specific patterns and characteristics of a person by analyzing extensive hours of genuine video footage, ultimately leading to the generation of a convincing deepfake video (Maras & Alexandrou, 2019; Westerlund, 2019). This is done to provide a realistic representation of how that individual could appear from various perspectives for the algorithms. The next stage is to combine the trained learning algorithms with computer graphics capabilities to add the AI-generated face and voice characteristics over the live video of a person. These patterns are formed from neural network input (Chiradeep, 2022).

7.3 TYPES OF DEEPFAKES

7.3.1 Textual Deepfakes

It was formerly thought that a computer could not do creative jobs such as writing or drawing during the beginning of the development of ML and Natural Language Processing (NLP) (Chiradeep, 2022). Textual deepfakes refer to the use of AI and NLP methods to produce very convincing and cohesive content that looks to have been authored by a certain person or in a certain writing pattern (Kowalczyk et al., 2022; Chiradeep, 2022; O'Neill et al., 2021). Such language models are created to emulate the style, linguistic idiosyncrasies, and writing patterns of a particular source, whether it is a well-known author, a person from history, or an individual (O'Neill et al., 2021). Advanced language models, like OpenAI's Generative Pre-Trained Transformer (GPT) series, which are trained on massive quantities of text data from the internet, are often used to construct textual deepfakes

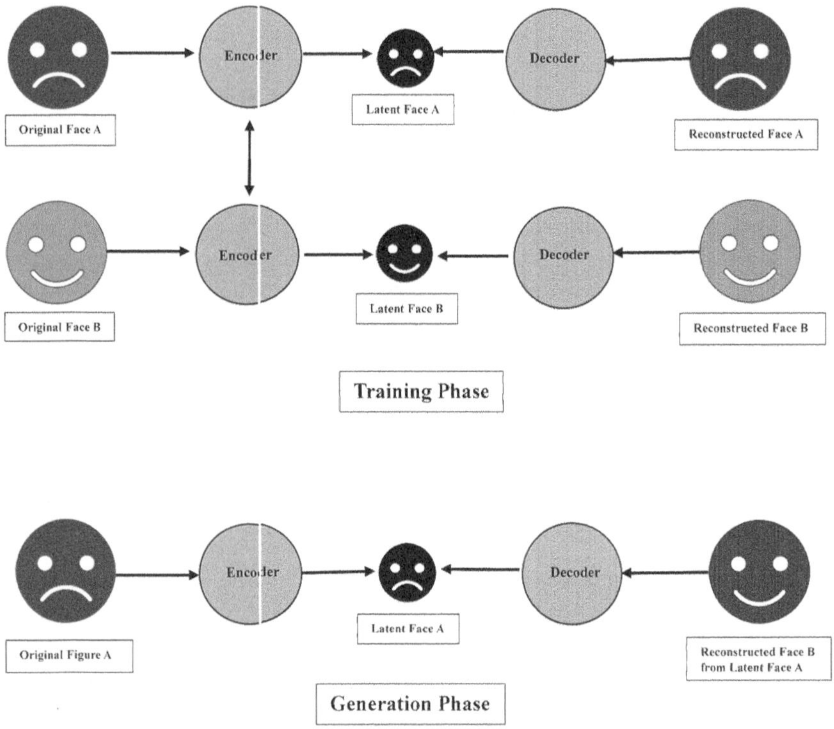

Figure 7.1 Deepfake Video Creation Process.

(Kowalczyk et al., 2022). There are several uses for textual deepfakes, including translation, creative writing, chatbots, and virtual assistants (Sison et al., 2023). Nevertheless, the utilization of textual deepfakes also raises concerns of disinformation, plagiarism, and manipulation (Sison et al., 2023).

7.3.2 Deepfake Video

It is the most common sort of deepfake since it is easier for people to understand happenings and tales via videos and photographs than text and is always present in social media environments (Maras & Alexandrou, 2019). Modern video-generating AI is more capable and potentially dangerous than natural language AI. In 2020, MarioNETte is a tool that lets users make deep-fake videos of famous individuals, historical figures, and leaders (Mirsky & Lee, 2021). Another person imitates the facial motions of the desired personality and then applies them to the deepfake of the intended personality to achieve this (Chiradeep, 2022). Deepfake videos can be created for various purposes, including entertainment, visual effects in movies (Kietzmann et al., 2020), and research. However, their potential misuse raises serious concerns, such as misinformation, reputation damage (Kwok & Koh, 2021), manipulation and political manipulation (Yadlin-Segal & Oppenheim, 2021).

7.3.3 Deepfake Audio

Deepfake audio, often referred to as synthetic audio or voice cloning, is the process of creating misleading audio recordings of someone else's voice using AI and deep learning methods to make it seem as if they are expressing things or phrases, they have never spoken (Hamza et al., 2022; Chiradeep, 2022). Commercial software, including Lyrebird and Deep Voice, has recently been released (Hamza et al., 2022). But it only takes a few words for the computer to become used to your voice and accent (Chiradeep, 2022). The program can duplicate your voice as soon as you put sufficient recordings of yourself. You may pronounce a word or a phrase after uploading a sample of your voice recordings, and the deepfake program will describe the text in your accent (Chiradeep, 2022). Deepfake audio can be created for various purposes, including voiceovers in movies, audiobooks, and voice assistants. However, it also poses significant risks and challenges: voice phishing (vishing), social engineering (Bateman, 2020), fraudulent calls and disinformation and manipulation (Yadlin-Segal & Oppenheim, 2021).

7.3.4 Deepfakes on Social Media

Social media sites have emerged as a prevalent channel for disseminating deepfakes, mostly because of their extensive audience and convenient content-sharing capabilities. Here are some critical aspects of deepfakes on social media: misinformation and disinformation, political manipulation (Yadlin-Segal & Oppenheim, 2021), character assassination, fake celebrity endorsements, the spread of hate speech (Sayers et al., 2021) and harassment (Yadlin-Segal & Oppenheim, 2021), social engineering and phishing and manipulated audio chats (Firc et al., 2023).

7.4 REAL-TIME OR LIVE DEEPFAKES

Unbelievably sophisticated deepfake technology enables businesses to make advertising clones, governments to impersonate political rivals, and hackers to replicate user voices to bypass voice-based verification (Chiradeep, 2022). YouTubers are already utilizing cutting-edge deepfake technology to change their appearance in real time (Samoilenko & Suvorova, 2023). For instance, the open-source AI program DeepFaceLive can use video conferences and streaming networks to change your face into someone else's (Samoilenko &

Suvorova, 2023). Real-time deepfakes have various applications, including entertainment, gaming, voice assistants, and chatbots (Wu et al., 2023). However, real-time deepfakes also raise significant ethical and security concerns. The ability to create dynamic and convincing content during live streams can be exploited for misinformation, impersonation, or fraud (Mirsky & Lee, 2021).

7.5 CONVENTIONAL TO AI-BASED FINANCIAL CRIMES

Financial crime refers to a range of illicit behaviors that specifically aim to unlawfully appropriate another person's assets for personal benefit. (Gottschalk, 2010). (Pickett & Pickett, 2002) define financial crime as "deceptive actions undertaken for unlawful profit, often breaching trust and concealing the true nature of the activities." This category of criminal activity encompasses several forms of fraudulent behavior, such as check fraud, mortgage fraud, medical fraud, corporate fraud, bank account fraud, payment fraud, currency fraud, health care fraud, as well as insider trading, tax violations, kickbacks, embezzlement, identity theft, and money laundering. (Gottschalk, 2010).

With the rapid advancement of technology and increasing global interconnectedness, a new type of crime has emerged worldwide, driven by the growth and prevalence of data communication and control (Okutan & Çebi, 2019). Cyber crime, which uses computers as tools to commit illegal acts like fraud, pornography, trafficking in stolen intellectual property, identity theft, and privacy violations, is the most rapidly expanding type of criminal activity (Jain & Gupta, 2020). Cyber crimes encompass a wide range of activities, including malware, phishing, "Man in the Middle" (MitM) attacks, trojans, Denial of Service attacks or Distributed Denial of Service Attacks (DDos), cyberterrorism, cyberstalking, child pornography, cyber fraud, keyloggers, screen loggers, evil twins, botnets, social engineering, worms, sniffers, cyber laundering, and cyberbullying (Okutan & Çebi, 2019). Given the constantly changing nature of cyber crime, undertaking risk analysis has become exceedingly difficult, needing constant monitoring and adaptation to successfully battle this growing threat.

Traditional investigative techniques frequently fail to detect and stop these illegal actions. However, AI has become a potent weapon in this war, allowing for a more effective and efficient method of conducting financial crime investigations (Guest, 2023). It encompasses a broader range of techniques that go beyond biological observation in understanding and simulating intelligence in computers (Mccarthy, 2007). Massive volumes of data may be quickly analyzed by ML algorithms, revealing worrisome patterns and abnormalities that could often go undetected. The data these algorithms process allows them to continuously learn, which improves their capacity to recognize novel or evolving criminal tactics (Guest, 2023).

Conversely, the criminals employed AI-driven deepfake technology to commit financial offenses. The advent of deepfake technology has created fresh opportunities for criminals to abuse the susceptibilities of individuals, organizations, and financial institutions (Bateman, 2020). Deepfake financial crimes can be defined as "criminal activities carried out by individuals or organizations through AI-based deepfake technology to get financial gain." Deepfake financial crimes refer to illicit activities in which criminals use deepfake technology to create manipulated audio, video, or images to deceive individuals, organizations, or financial institutions for financial gain or to cause harm (Bateman, 2020). Deepfakes are AI-generated content that appears remarkably authentic, making it difficult to distinguish from genuine recordings. This paper examines the five cases of financial crimes perpetrated with deepfake technology.

7.6 DEEPFAKE TECHNOLOGY AIDING FINANCIAL CRIMES

7.6.1 Deepfake Social Media Financial Crime

7.6.1.1 Case 1: India

In this case, a resident of Kozhikode, Kerala, India, received an unsolicited video call on WhatsApp from an unknown number. To his surprise, he recognized the caller as one of his former colleagues from Andhra Pradesh. The caller mentioned the names of their common acquaintances to gain the victim's trust, and the victim, believing it to be a genuine call, engaged in the conversation. During the conversation, the caller deceitfully claimed that a relative was in urgent need of medical support and requested ₹ 40,000 (approximately $ 490). The victim, wanting to help his friend, willingly transferred the money online. However, the caller then asked for an additional ₹ 35,000 (approximately $430), which raised suspicions in the victim's mind. To verify the authenticity of the situation, the victim contacted his old friend and learned that the call was indeed a scam. Realizing he had been deceived, the victim promptly reported the scam to the police to prevent others from falling victim to the same fraud (Bhati, 2023).

> The victim said to the media, "*I had no reason in the world to think that it was a scam. I have known him for more than 40 years. I even saw his face on my phone's screen, and I thought it was him,*" (Sankar, 2023)

7.6.1.2 Case 2: China

On April 20, at approximately 11:40 a.m., Mr. Guo received an unexpected video call from his friend on the messaging app WeChat. During the call, his friend informed him about a situation where another acquaintance was participating in a project bid in a different city. The acquaintance required a bid bond of ¥ 4.3 million (approximately $622,000), and they sought to use Mr. Guo's company's bank account for the transaction. The friend asked for Mr. Guo's bank account number, claiming to have transferred the money. To establish trust, the friend even sent a screenshot of the supposed bank transfer receipt through WeChat. Relying on the video chat and without verifying the receipt's authenticity, Mr. Guo believed his friend and did not check if the money had been deposited into his account. Consequently, at 11:49 a.m., he transferred ¥ 4.3 million in two transactions to the other party's account. After the transfer, Mr. Guo sent a message on WeChat to inform his friend that the matter had been dealt with. However, to his surprise, the friend responded with a question mark, indicating confusion. Upon calling his friend, who claimed to have no knowledge of the money transfer, Mr. Guo realized that he had become a victim of an elaborate scam (Davis, 2023; Today Online, 2023; Zekun, 2023).

> "*At the time, I verified the face and voice of the person video-calling me, so I let down my guard*," the article quoted Mr. Guo saying.
>
> (Today Online, 2023)

7.6.2 Deepfake Video Financial Crime

7.6.2.1 *Case 1: Canada*

A woman from Ontario fell to a devastating investment scam, losing $750,000 in the process. In January of that year, she came across a video online where Elon Musk seemingly endorsed an investment opportunity, offering shares at $250 each through a website.

> "*I thought Elon Musk offering his shares for $250 would be nice to own*," the victim said.

Enticed by the prospect, she entered her personal details, including email and phone number, into the website. Soon after, she began receiving numerous calls from various individuals around the world. One of these callers, claiming to be a family man with a surname resembling one of her relatives, convinced her that he could immediately assist her with investments. He referred to the Elon Musk video and offered to help her with the investment process.

To gain control over her computer and purportedly help her invest, the scammer advised her to download a remote access tool called AnyDesk. With this tool installed, the scammer could take complete control of her computer remotely. He displayed internet records that falsely suggested her investments were flourishing, leading her to believe her money was safe.

> *"Next thing I know, he was taking $20,000 there and $10,000 there. He made me believe 100 percent that I was making money,"* said the victim.

Subsequently, she uncovered the fact that none of her financial resources had been allocated for investment purposes and that the entire scenario was a fraudulent scheme. Her hard-earned money had been stolen, leaving her devastated and defrauded (Foran, 2022).

7.6.3 Deepfake Audio Financial Crime

7.6.3.1 Case 1: Hongkong

A Japanese corporation's branch manager in Hong Kong got a call from a person whose voice he recognized as the director of his parent company. The director brought wonderful news: the business was going to be acquired; thus, he had to approve certain trades for $35 million. A lawyer had been recruited to oversee the proceedings, and emails from the director and lawyer clarifying where the money needed to go were visible in the branch manager's inbox. The manager made transactions since he thought everything looked genuine (Brewster, 2021).

7.6.3.2 Case 2: UK

The Chief Executive Officer (CEO) of a United Kingdom (UK)-based energy company had a phone conversation, believing it was with his superior. However, it turned out to be the boss of the German parent company who requested a transfer of €220,000 (approximately $243,000) to the bank account of a Hungarian supplier. Fraud specialist Euler Hermes Group provided the case information.

> He added that the CEO recognised "*the subtle German accent in his boss's voice – and, moreover, that it carried the man's 'melody'.*"

The fraud expert claims that the fraudster, who has not yet been identified, contacted the business three times: first to start the transfer, the second time by pretending to have received reimbursement, and a third time by requesting a follow-up payment. The victim became doubtful at this point since he could see that the alleged compensation had not been processed; moreover, he discovered that the call originated from an Austrian number rather than a German one (Imossi, 2019; Sorvino, 2023).

The individual victim cases highlight the universality of deepfake technology as a tool for committing financial crimes. It transcends geographical boundaries and affects individuals across different developing countries.

Perpetrators use social media platforms, such as WhatsApp and WeChat, to establish connections with their victims and exploit the victims' trust by using deepfake technology to impersonate someone familiar to the victims. In the case of deepfake video financial crime (case 3), the perpetrator used the identity of Elon Musk, the well-known entrepreneur and public figure to gain the trust of the victim and defraud. In the organizational victim cases, deepfake audio is used for perpetrating financial crimes. Scammers deceived victims by impersonating individuals through voice calls to facilitate money transfers. Multiple countries were involved in the execution of these financial crimes. The scammers used international transactions and various accounts, complicating the tracing and recovery of stolen funds. Exploiting pre-existing relationships and victim trust, their convincing impersonations create a new layer of deception challenging traditional cybersecurity measures. The perpetrators capitalize on emotions like trust and urgency to manipulate victims successfully. The most immediate and apparent consequence of deepfake financial crimes is the loss of money. Fraudsters trick people into sending money under false pretenses, and once the money is transferred, it is difficult to get it back. The victims could lose faith and confidence in digital communication networks, financial institutions, and even in their relationships with friends and colleagues. Feelings of vulnerability and anxiety may result from the trust violation (Westerlund, 2019).

These incidents serve as prime examples of the cognitive dissonance that deepfake financial fraud victims go through. When people have two opposing views or concepts, it causes cognitive dissonance, which makes them uncomfortable psychologically and makes them want to change one of their beliefs to make the contradiction go away (Chang & Chong, 2010). Victims of deepfake financial crimes go through two distinct stages of cognitive dissonance. During the initial phase, perpetrators deceive victims by creating an illusion of reality. In some cases, victims may believe the source because the deepfake seems so realistic, but they may also be suspicious of something not quite right. Their judgment may be hampered by the dissonance this internal struggle produces. This means that instead of acting on their initial caution or skepticism, victims may decide to act on the false information provided by the deepfake. They could have another episode of cognitive dissonance in the second phase after becoming victims. This happens when victims start to suspect or figure out that the transaction was a scam. Some victims may justify their conduct even in the face of proof of deceit because they find it emotionally difficult to acknowledge they were duped. The victims may endure psychological and emotional anguish throughout this process as they grapple with the challenge of acknowledging that they have been duped. (Chang & Chong, 2010).

Significant psychological suffering may result from deepfake deception, particularly when victims think they were duped with the identity of a familiar person and may feel humiliation, shame, anger, betrayal, powerlessness, fear of future attacks, frustration, and anxiety (Chang & Chong, 2010). Furthermore, victims of deepfake financial crimes suffered enormous financial losses as a consequence of the fraudsters' convincing them to transfer large quantities of money based on false promises, which caused both psychological and emotional harm in addition to major monetary damages. Deepfake financial crimes not only exploit victims' trust and judgment but also subject them to cognitive dissonance, which can have long-lasting psychological and emotional consequences. Personal and professional relationships can be damaged, eroding trust and impacting credit and reputation (Kwok & Koh, 2021).

Organizations may suffer from serious negative consequences as a result of deep fake financial crimes. Organizations might experience significant financial losses due to unauthorized financial transfers, false investment claims, or other misleading business dealings orchestrated through deepfake technology. These losses may have a negative impact on the company's financial health and bottom line. Deepfake financial crimes may seriously damage an organization's image (Mustak et al., 2023). Customers' confidence and investor support may decline as a result of the public and stakeholders losing faith in the company's capacity to protect their money and private information (Mustak et al., 2023). It also may result in legal and regulatory ramifications for organizations. This can include inquiries, penalties, or legal action, particularly if neglect or insufficient security measures are used to prevent the crimes. Business activities may be hampered when recovering from the occurrence of deepfake financial crime. The company must devote resources to investigating the incident, bolstering security procedures, and rebuilding client confidence, which will take time away from essential business operations.

Deepfake financial crimes pose a risk to organizations' competitive edge. Businesses may exploit such situations to attract clients and investors away from affected companies. Robust security measures are necessary to combat deepfake threats, including specialized technology, training, and authentication mechanisms, leading to increased security expenses and potential budgetary constraints. Shareholders and investors may suffer financial losses, leading to a decline in trust and shareholder resentment. Cyber insurance costs may rise due to heightened risks from deepfake threats. Employees may feel vulnerable, impacting morale and productivity. Customers may discontinue business with affected companies, resulting in decreased sales and consumer churn.

7.7 DETERRENCE OF DEEPFAKE FINANCIAL CRIMES

The application of deterrence theory may successfully address the prevention of financial crimes via deepfakes. There is no text provided. Essentially, this theory has evolved over time and provides a structure for understanding how individuals form judgments regarding participating in unlawful activities. It was first proposed by pioneering criminologists Cesare Beccaria and Jeremy Bentham. With this view, people make logical calculations, balancing the costs and advantages of their decisions (Erickson et al., 1977). The prospect of punishment is emphasized as a key deterrent element in classical deterrence theory. By enforcing harsh punishments on individuals found guilty, the legal system may effectively deter prospective criminals in the field of deepfake financial crimes. Repercussions like jail time, heavy fines, or asset confiscation may serve as powerful deterrents, preventing people from committing deepfake financial fraud.

General deterrence theory, which builds on the classical approach, emphasizes the significance of public knowledge of the repercussions of illegal behavior. Educating people about the seriousness of the sanctions and the risk associated with deepfake financial crimes is essential. Campaigns for public education and media relations may be effective means of educating people about the legal repercussions of participating in such fraudulent activity (Quackenbush, 2010). The idea that engaging in such illegal behavior is not worth the risk is reinforced when the public observes people incurring serious legal repercussions for their acts. These incidents may serve as warning stories, deterring others from trying to commit the same fraud. Additionally, the goal of specific deterrence, which is an expansion of classical deterrence theory, is to prevent individual criminals from committing the same crimes again (Quackenbush, 2010). When it comes to deepfake financial crimes, the legal system may work to make sure that the penalties meted out to offenders are harsh enough to discourage them from committing the same crimes in the future. This might include limiting their access to financial or technological systems in addition to enforcing legal sanctions. Although prevention relies heavily on deterrence, it also has to address the underlying reasons for financial crimes with deepfakes.

7.8 CURRENT LEGAL AND REGULATORY MEASURES

US President Joe Biden issued a comprehensive executive order in October 2023 to address dangers related to AI, including privacy and national security. As a result of legislation that was enacted in numerous US states, including Texas and California, making it illegal to publish and distribute deepfake films that might influence elections, the Department of Commerce was given the responsibility of creating guidelines for labeling AI-generated material. Legislation in Virginia penalizes the dissemination of deepfake, nonconsensual pornography. Congress has presented the DEEP FAKES Accountability Bill, 2023, which requires internet platforms to designate deepfakes and imposes criminal penalties for noncompliance (Sumeda, 2023).

China's Cyberspace Administration released new rules in January that limit the use of deep synthesis technology and suppress misinformation. These guidelines mandate that information be clearly labeled using technology, that it be traceable back to its original source, and that it be compliant with local laws, ethical standards, and the right political and public opinion movements (Chatterjee, 2022). The European Union (EU) has strengthened its Disinformation Code of Practice, which now requires major social media platforms such as Twitter, Meta, and Google to identify and disclose deepfake content, or else face substantial financial penalties. The Digital Services Act now supports the Code, which was first launched in 2018 as a voluntary self-regulatory tool to strengthen digital platform monitoring and prevent different types of abuse. Furthermore, deepfake providers would have to comply with disclosure and openness criteria under the proposed EU AI Act.

While India does not have particular legislation addressing deepfake technology, there are other legal avenues available to prosecute those involved in related offenses. The Information Technology Act of 2000 has measures with jail sentences and fines in Section 66E for privacy protection and Section 66D for situations with harmful intent. The deletion of altered and impersonating photographs from social media is prohibited by IT Rules. Deepfake-related cyber crimes are covered by sections of the Indian Penal Code. Deepfakes that utilize copyrighted content without authorization may be subject to the Copyright Act of 1957. In December 2023, the government proposed rules to enhance accountability, as experts highlighted the need for a more comprehensive legal framework to manage new AI technology and their potential downsides (Bhaumik, 2023).

7.9 LEGAL AND REGULATORY CHALLENGES

The execution of current laws and regulations is one of the main legal and regulatory difficulties mentioned by (Van der Sloot & Wagensveld, 2022). Even while defamation, fraud, and other types of damage linked to deepfakes are prohibited by law in many places, it may be difficult to track down and punish people who create and distribute deepfake information. The regulatory challenges noted by (Van der Sloot & Wagensveld, 2022) are, in the near future, experts believe that manipulation will be present in most internet information. This covers more malevolent deepfakes to inflict damage or disseminate false information, as well as more subtle manipulations like changing the skin tone during video chats. Effective monitoring and enforcement of rules are hampered by the widespread usage of deepfakes. Over time, deepfake technology is anticipated to grow more affordable, quicker, and more lifelike. Deepfake detection using automated techniques becomes harder and harder as technology advances. It is anticipated that detection rates will drop, making the task of removing hazardous information more difficult.

When deepfakes use someone else's likeness without permission, it might violate their privacy. These concerns could not be sufficiently addressed by current privacy rules, and striking the right balance between the protection of private rights and the right to free speech is a difficult regulatory task. It is possible that enforcement organizations such as law enforcement and Data Protection Authorities don't have the tools and knowledge needed to adequately handle the deepfake issue as it grows. Deepfake case investigation and prosecution may be expensive and time-consuming. There are concerns about inhibiting technological progress and restricting artistic freedom when deepfake technology is outright banned. One of the biggest challenges is finding the ideal balance between innovation and regulation. Deepfake technology presents regulatory problems that need a multifaceted strategy including legislative frameworks, technical advancements, public awareness campaigns, and international collaboration. It is a difficult and continuous challenge for legislators and society at large to strike the correct balance between preserving freedom of speech and innovation and safeguarding people and society from the negative effects of deepfakes (Van der Sloot & Wagensveld, 2022).

7.10 TIPS FOR RECOGNIZING DEEPFAKES

Although stringent rules and regulations can discourage criminal behavior, it is equally crucial to provide public education and support to prevent individuals from being victims of deepfake financial crimes. A few crucial signs may be used to help recognize these deceptive videos. Look out for variations in body parts and skin texture, since deepfakes often have trouble recreating these subtleties. Some telltale indicators of a deepfake include shadows around the eyes, abnormal blinking patterns, or an abnormal glare on spectacles. Keep a tight eye on lip motions since an inaccurate lip sync might reveal the lie. Other telltale signs include variations in the person's lip color or the existence of facial hair that deviates from their typical look. Finding phony facial imperfections or moles might help identify a deepfake even more. Even while certain classic markers have become less trustworthy due to advancements in technology, irregularities in lighting and shading may still be helpful in identifying these bogus videos (Lawton, 2023).

Along with these regulatory and legal initiatives and tips to identify the deepfakes that can deter them, it is important to incorporate advanced technological strategies.

7.10.1 Double Check Strategy and Zero-Trust Model

Implementing supplementary authentication measures to verify the legitimacy of data, communications, and transactions is a strategy aimed at mitigating the risks connected with social engineering and deepfake technology.

(Babbs, 2021). The Zero Trust paradigm entails a change in security mindset from the conventional "trust but verify" to "never trust, always verify" in order to prevent deepfake financial crimes and social engineering attacks. The zero-trust security model's main principles are "never trust, always verify," "implement least privilege," and "always assume breach" (NSA-USA, 2021).

It is crucial to impose Multi-Factor Authentication (MFA) on all users gaining access to critical systems and data, in accordance with the double-check method. This makes it such that, even in the case that a deepfake social engineering attack succeeds in getting a user's credentials, the attackers will still have to go past extra authentication barriers, need more than simply a password; for really sensitive tasks, requires biometric verification or a one-time passcode created by an authentication app or transmitted by SMS. The core tenet of Zero Trust is continuous verification is essential for spotting and reducing risks associated with deepfakes. It is important to constantly check all data and communication channels, including audio and video, for irregularities or indications of manipulation. Apply the principle of least-privileged access to media content as well as data and systems.

Before acting, be sure that every piece of media content, particularly those pertaining to sensitive or financial discussions, has been expressly checked for legitimacy. Make it more difficult for malicious people to insert deepfakes into financial communications by using cryptographic methods or digital signatures to confirm the authenticity and integrity of media material. Be prepared for the possibility that attackers would try to trick workers or breach financial systems using deepfake technology. Put in place strict security procedures to identify and stop any efforts of this kind. Employees should get regular training on how to spot possible deepfakes and report them right away. Investigate the use of behavioral biometrics and biometric authentication techniques that are more resilient to impersonation and deepfake attacks, such as speech recognition patterns that can distinguish artificial sounds. In close collaboration with banks and other financial institutions, add further layers of verification to transactions that are flagged as high risk, maybe due to social engineering or deepfake attacks.

In the rapidly evolving technological landscape, adopting a proactive approach is crucial. Real-time surveillance enables swift response to deepfake financial crimes (Bank of America, 2022). AI can identify abnormal patterns and behaviors in transactions and communications, raising red flags for investigation. Voice biometrics powered by AI enhance identity verification, making impersonations more challenging for deepfake performers (Mascellino, 2023). Using blockchain technology to provide an unchangeable and transparent record of activity may increase confidence in financial transactions. Blockchain may assist in validating the veracity of messages and guard against manipulation or tampering (Helo & Hao, 2019). In order to identify suspicious behaviors suggestive of deepfake financial crimes, ML models powered by AI can understand user behavior and transaction patterns. To improve the precision of deepfake detection, AI may do multi-modal analysis, merging data from many sources, such as video, audio, and textual material. It is possible to create cooperative AI networks across financial institutions, social media sites, and technological firms to exchange knowledge on new deepfake risks and bolster defenses.

7.11 CONCLUSION

This article examines the alarming rise of AI-based deepfake financial crimes. This study examines financial crimes committed in multiple countries using deepfake audio, video, and social media. Results show that deepfake financial crimes require a proactive approach. Businesses handling sensitive financial information must use a "double-check strategy" and a "zero-trust approach" due to the rise of deepfakes. Training and awareness campaigns are necessary to prepare people for deepfake attacks. To avoid an "infopocalypse" and vulnerability exploitation, keep up with financial crime developments.

Deepfake financial criminals use technology to deceive victims and steal money, posing a major threat to banks and financial institutions. Regulators must update laws and regulations to enforce digital due diligence and protect consumers and businesses from this threat. The study emphasizes the importance of using blockchain and AI to fight financial crime. Blockchain's immutability and AI's advanced detection can reduce deepfake risks. This paper builds on the limited knowledge of deepfake technology-based financial crimes to support future empirical research. Future research can conduct extensive empirical investigations to gather primary data from victims, organizations, and financial institutions affected by deepfake financial crimes, providing a deeper understanding of the impacts on various stakeholders. Global analysis of deepfake financial crimes can reveal geographical variations, trends, and jurisdictional challenges. Exploring AI-generated deepfakes in specific financial contexts like investment fraud and market manipulation can offer insights. Studying psychological and behavioral aspects related to deepfake vulnerability can inform targeted awareness campaigns. Research can focus on cutting-edge technology solutions, such as blockchain integration and AI-based deepfake detection tools, to strengthen financial systems' resilience against threats. Collaboration, awareness, and technological advancements will be needed to stay ahead of those who exploit individuals' and organizations' vulnerabilities in a world of sophisticated synthetic media.

Note

1 Information Apocalypse (infopocalypse) - when individuals become afraid that much information, especially videos, cannot be trusted as a consequence of repeated exposure to false information, such phenomenon is known as the "information apocalypse."

REFERENCES

Babbs, A. (2021, December 14). Double-checking your cybersecurity. *CPO Magazine.* www.cpomagazine.com/cyber-security/double-checking-your-cybersecurity/

Bank of America. (2022). How to protect your business from deepfakes. *Cyber Security Journal*, 7, 1–6.

Bateman, J. (2020). *Deepfakes and synthetic media in the financial system: Assessing threat scenarios*. Carnegie Endowment for International Peace. Available from: https://carnegieendowment.org/research/2020/07/deepfakes-and-synthetic-media-in-the-financial-system-assessing-threat-scenarios?lang=en.

Bhati, D. (2023, July 17). Kerala man loses Rs 40,000 to AI-based deepfake WhatsApp fraud, all about the new scam. *India Today*. www.indiatoday.in/technology/news/story/kerala-man-loses-rs-40000-in-ai-based-deepfake-whatsapp-fraud-all-about-the-new-scam-2407555-2023-07-17

Bhaumik, A. (2023, December 4). Regulating deepfakes and generative AI in India. *The Hindu*. www.thehindu.com/news/national/regulating-deepfakes-generative-ai-in-india-explained/article67591640.ece

Brewster, T. (2021, October 14). Fraudsters cloned company director's voice in $35 million heist, police find. *Forbes*. www.forbes.com/sites/thomasbrewster/2021/10/14/huge-bank-fraud-uses-deep-fake-voice-tech-to-steal-millions/?sh=4484f5b17559

Business Wire. (2023, May 30). New digital fraud statistics: Forced verification and deepfake cases multiply at alarming rates in the UK and continental Europe. *Business Wire*. www.businesswire.com/news/home/20230530005196/en/New-digital-fraud-statistics-forced-verification-and-deepfake-cases-multiply-at-alarming-rates-in-the-UK-and-continental-Europe

Caldwell, M., Andrews, J. T. A., Tanay, T., & Griffin, L. D. (2020). AI-enabled future crime. *Crime Science*, 9(1), 1–13. https://doi.org/10.1186/s40163-020-00123-8

Chang, J. J. S., & Chong, M. D. (2010). Psychological influences in e-mail fraud. *Journal of Financial Crime*, 17(3), 337–350. https://doi.org/10.1108/13590791011056309

Chatterjee, A. (2022, December 25). Deepfake technology: how and why China is planning to regulate it. *The Hindu*. www.thehindu.com/sci-tech/technology/deepfake-technology-how-and-why-china-is-planning-to-regulate-it/article66277740.ece

China Business Now. (2023, May 26). 4.3 million yuan "Deepfake" scam sparks AI-powered crime fears in China. *China Business Now*. https://m.21jingji.com/article/20230526/herald/e42029b882e3b6b1905dd083a16141f2.html

Chiradeep, B. M. (2022, May 23). Deepfake types, examples, prevention. *Spiceworks*. www.spiceworks.com/it-security/cyber-risk-management/articles/what-is-deepfake/

Davis, M. (2023, May 29). AI scams in China: The new face of fraud. *Nspirement*. www.nspirement.com/2023/05/29/ai-scams-in-china-the-new-fraud.html

Ene, C. (2023, February 22). 10.5 trillion reasons why we need a united response to cyber risk. *Forbes Technology Council*. www.forbes.com/sites/forbestechcouncil/2023/02/22/105-trillion-reasons-why-we-need-a-united-response-to-cyber-risk/?sh=12d471393b0c

Erickson, M. L., Gibbs, J. P., & Jensen, G. F. (1977). The Deterrence Doctrine and the Perceived Certainty of Legal Punishments. In *Review* (Vol. 42, Issue 2).

Firc, A., Malinka, K., & Hanáček, P. (2023). Deepfakes as a threat to a speaker and facial recognition: An overview of tools and attack vectors. *Heliyon*, *9*(4). https://doi.org/10.1016/j.heliyon.2023.e15090

Foran, P. (2022, September 20). Ontario woman lost $750,000 in Elon Musk deep fake scam. *CTV News*. https://toronto.ctvnews.ca/this-is-how-an-ontario-woman-lost-750-000-in-an-elon-musk-deep-fake-scam-1.6074849

Gottschalk, P. (2010). Categories of financial crime. *Journal of Financial Crime*, *17*(4), 441–458. https://doi.org/10.1108/13590791011082797

Guest. (2023, April 16). The use of Artificial Intelligence in combatting financial crimes. *Financial Express*. www.financialexpress.com/market/cafeinvest/the-use-of-artificial-intelligence-in-combatting-financial-crimes/3049056/

Hamza, A., Javed, A. R., Iqbal, F., Kryvinska, N., Almadhor, A. S., Jalil, Z., & Borghol, R. (2022). Deepfake audio detection via MFCC features using Machine Learning. *IEEE Access*, *10*, 134018–134028. https://doi.org/10.1109/ACCESS.2022.3231480

Helo, P., & Hao, Y. (2019). Blockchains in operations and supply chains: A model and reference implementation. *Computers and Industrial Engineering*, *136*, 242–251. https://doi.org/10.1016/j.cie.2019.07.023

Imossi, T. (2019, October 7). UK energy boss conned out of £200,000 in 'deep fake' fraud. *ABI*. www.theabi.org.uk/news/uk-energy-boss-conned-out-of-200000-in-deep-fake-fraud

Jain, A., & Gupta, N. (2020). Cyber crime. *National Conference on Industry 4.0*, 152–158.

Kietzmann, J., Lee, L. W., McCarthy, I. P., & Kietzmann, T. C. (2020). Deepfakes: Trick or treat? *Business Horizons*, *63*(2), 135–146. https://doi.org/10.1016/j.bushor.2019.11.006

Kowalczyk, P., Röder, M., Dürr, A., & Thiesse, F. (2022). Detecting and understanding textual deepfakes in online reviews. *Proceedings of the 55th Hawaii International Conference on System Sciences*, 1480–1489. https://hdl.handle.net/10125/79516

Kwok, A. O. J., & Koh, S. G. M. (2021). Deepfake: a social construction of technology perspective. *Current Issues in Tourism*, *24*(13), 1798–1802. https://doi.org/10.1080/13683500.2020.1738357

Lawton, G. (2023, April 12). How to prevent deepfakes in the era of generative AI. www.techtarget.com/searchsecurity/tip/How-to-prevent-deepfakes-in-the-era-of-generative-AI

Maras, M. H., & Alexandrou, A. (2019). Determining authenticity of video evidence in the age of Artificial Intelligence and in the wake of deepfake videos. *International Journal of Evidence and Proof*, *23*(3), 255–262. https://doi.org/10.1177/1365712718807226

Mascellino, A. (2023, February 1). Voice deepfakes on the rise; biometrics can help. *Biometric Update.* www.biometricupdate.com/202302/voice-deepfakes-on-the-rise-biometrics-can-help

Mccarthy, J. (2007). *What is Artificial Intelligence?* (pp. 1–15). Standford University. www-formal.stanford.edu/jmc/

Mirsky, Y., & Lee, W. (2021). The creation and detection of deepfakes. *ACM Computing Surveys*, *54*(1), 1–44. https://doi.org/10.1145/3425780

Mitra, A., Mohanty, S. P., Corcoran, P., & Kougianos, E. (2021). A Machine Learning based approach for deepfake detection in social media through key video frame extraction. *SN Computer Science*, *2*(2). https://doi.org/10.1007/s42979-021-00495-x

Mustak, M., Salminen, J., Mäntymäki, M., Rahman, A., & Dwivedi, Y. K. (2023). Deepfakes: Deceptions, mitigations, and opportunities. *Journal of Business Research*, *154*, 1–33. https://doi.org/10.1016/j.jbusres.2022.113368

NSA-USA. (2021). *Embracing a Zero Trust Security Model.* National Security Agency. https://media.defense.gov/2021/Feb/25/2002588479/-1/-1/0/CSI_EMBRACING_ZT_SECURITY_MODEL_UOO115131-21.PDF.

Okutan, A., & Çebi, Y. (2019). A framework for cyber crime investigation. *Procedia Computer Science*, *158*, 287–294. https://doi.org/10.1016/j.procs.2019.09.054

O'Neill, L., Anantharama, N., Buntine, W., & Angus, S. D. (2021). Quantitative discourse analysis at scale-AI, NLP and the transformer revolution. http://soda-wps.s3-website-ap-southeast-2.amazonaws.com/RePEc/ajr/sodwps/2021-12.pdfPUBLISHEDONLINE

Pickett, S. K. H., & Pickett, J. M. (2002). Financial crime investigation and control. In *Wiley* (Vol. 1). Wiley. www.wiley.com/en-ca/Financial+Crime+Investigation+and+Control-p-9780471203353

Quackenbush, S. L. (2010). General deterrence and international conflict: Testing perfect deterrence theory. *International Interactions*, *36*(1), 60–85. https://doi.org/10.1080/03050620903554069

Rana, M. S., Nobi, M. N., Murali, B., & Sung, A. H. (2022). Deepfake detection: A systematic literature review. *IEEE Access*, *10*, 25494–25513. https://doi.org/10.1109/ACCESS.2022.3154404

Regula. (2023). *Identity verification investment: A study on its business impact.* Regula Forensics. Available from: https://static-content.regulaforensics.com/Landing_pages/the-state-of-identity-verification-2023-report/Identity%20Verification%20Investment-A%20Study%20on%20Its%20Business%20Impact.pdf.

Samoilenko, S. A., & Suvorova, I. (2023). Artificial Intelligence and deepfakes in strategic deception campaigns: The U.S. and Russian experiences. In E. Pashentsev (Ed.), *The Palgrave Handbook of Malicious Use of AI and Psychological Security* (pp. 507–529). Springer International Publishing. https://doi.org/10.1007/978-3-031-22552-9_19

Sankar, A. (2023, July 10). Deepfake video call said to be from Dubai used to swindle Kerala man out of thousands. *N UAE*. www.thenationalnews.com/uae/2023/07/19/deepfake-video-call-pretending-to-be-dubai-friend-used-to-swindle-man-out-of-thousands/

Sayers, D., Sousa-Silva, R., Höhn, S., Ahmedi, L., Allkivi-Metsoja, K., Anastasiou, D., Beňuš, Š., Bowker, L., Bytyçi, E., Catala, A., & Çepani A. (2021). The dawn of the human-machine era: A forecast of new and emerging language technologies. https://hal.science/hal-03230287

Shen, T., Liu, R., Bai, J., & Li, Z. (2018). "Deep Fakes" using Generative Adversarial Networks (GAN). http://noiselab.ucsd.edu/ECE228_2018/Reports/Report16.pdf

Sison, A. J. G., Daza, M. T., Gozalo-Brizuela, R., & Garrido-Merchán, E. C. (2023). ChatGPT: More than a "weapon of mass deception" ethical challenges and responses from the Human-Centered Artificial Intelligence (HCAI) perspective. *International Journal of Human–Computer Interaction*, 1–20. https://doi.org/10.1080/10447318.2023.2225931

Somers, M. (2020, July 21). Deepfakes, explained | MIT Sloan. *MIT Management, Sloan School*. https://mitsloan.mit.edu/ideas-made-to-matter/deepfakes-explained

Sorvino, C. (2023, July 21). How butcherbox is killing It with free bacon for life while rivals like blue apron unraveled. *Forbes*. www.forbes.com/sites/chloesorvino/2023/07/21/how-butcherbox-is-killing-it-with-free-bacon-for-life-while-rivals-like-blue-apron-unraveled/?sh=31f6740645cc

Sumeda. (2023, November 15). What is Biden's executive order on AI and what it means. *The Hindu*. www.thehindu.com/sci-tech/artificial-intelligence-executive-order-joe-biden-explainer-reaction-highlights/article67518709.ece

Today Online. (2023, May 24). China scammer uses AI to pose as man's friend, steal millions. *Today Online*. www.todayonline.com/world/china-scammer-uses-ai-pose-mans-friend-steal-millions-2177761

Uddin Mahmud, B., & Sharmin, A. (2020). Deep insights of deepfake technology: A review. *Journal of Applied Science and Technology (DUJASE)*, *5*((1 & 2)), 13–23.

Van der Sloot, B., & Wagensveld, Y. (2022). Deepfakes: regulatory challenges for the synthetic society. *Computer Law and Security Review*, *46*. https://doi.org/10.1016/j.clsr.2022.105716

Westerlund, M. (2019). The emergence of deepfake technology: A review. *Technology Innovation Management Review*, *9*(11), 39–52.

World Economic Forum. (2023). The Global Risks Report 2023. https://www3.weforum.org/docs/WEF_Global_Risks_Report_2023.pdf

Wu, H., Hui, P., & Zhou, P. (2023). Deepfake in the metaverse: An outlook survey. *IEEE Computer Society*. http://arxiv.org/abs/2306.07011

Yadlin-Segal, A., & Oppenheim, Y. (2021). Whose dystopia is it anyway? Deepfakes and social media regulation. *Convergence*, *27*(1), 36–51. https://doi.org/10.1177/1354856520923963

Zekun, Y. (2023, May 22). Police warn of AI fraud after man duped by "friend." *China Daily*. www.chinadaily.com.cn/a/202305/22/WS646b4fd3a310b6054fad4731.html

Chapter 8

Machine Learning and AI in Cyber Crime Detection

Chitrak Chakraborty and Sakalya Mitra

8.1 INTRODUCTION

8.1.1 Defining Cyber Crime

The landscape of cyber crime is both extensive and constantly evolving, presenting a multifaceted challenge in the vast and interconnected realm of digital networks. Cyber crime encompasses a diverse array of illicit activities that exploit vulnerabilities in the digital ecosystem. From the more traditional forms of hacking and identity theft to the sophisticated methods of phishing and ransomware attacks, the definition of cyber crime remains fluid and dynamic, adapting and expanding in tandem with technological advancements.

The advent of technology has not only facilitated the digitization of various aspects of our lives but has also provided new avenues for criminal activities to manifest. As individuals, organizations, and governments increasingly rely on digital platforms for communication, transactions, and data storage, the attack surface for cyber criminals has expanded exponentially. Consequently, the scope and complexity of cyber crimes have grown, necessitating a deeper understanding of the nuances of these digital transgressions.

To comprehend the gravity of the situation, it is crucial to recognize that cyber criminals are not confined by geographical boundaries or traditional constraints. They operate in a borderless and fluid environment, utilizing sophisticated tools and techniques to exploit vulnerabilities in the digital infrastructure. The evolving nature of technology serves as a catalyst for innovation among cyber criminals, pushing them to develop new and more intricate methods of infiltrating systems and compromising sensitive information.

In this context, understanding the intricacies of cyber crime becomes paramount. It involves dissecting the modus operandi of cyber criminals,

DOI: 10.1201/9781003471103-8

deciphering their tactics, techniques, and procedures (TTPs), and staying abreast of emerging trends. This knowledge is fundamental for devising effective strategies to detect, prevent, and respond to cyber threats.

8.1.2 Growing Threat Landscape

Given how quickly cyberthreats are developing, the contemporary era stands witness to an unparalleled surge in both the frequency and sophistication of malicious activities. Several interconnected factors contribute to this unprecedented rise, making it more important than ever to dig deeper into the dynamics of the current scenario of cyber threats.

Increased Connectivity

The pervasive integration of digital technologies into every facet of modern life has led to unprecedented levels of connectivity. While this connectivity brings about numerous advantages, such as seamless communication and enhanced efficiency, it also widens the attack surface for cyber criminals. The intricate web of interconnected devices, systems, and networks creates a multitude of entry points for potential cyber threats. As the Internet of Things (IoT) takes over and smart devices become one of the most common digital entities, the attack surface expands exponentially, necessitating heightened vigilance and security measures.

Advanced Hacking Techniques. Cybercriminals are always improving their strategies and methods, leveraging the latest advancements in technology to orchestrate increasingly sophisticated attacks. Advanced hacking techniques include zero-day exploits, polymorphic malware, and escape strategies that are able to get past conventional security systems.

Lucrative Nature of Illicit Digital Activities

The financial incentives associated with cyber crime contribute significantly to the surge in cyber threats. Illicit digital activities, such as ransomware attacks, data breaches, and identity theft, can yield substantial financial gains for cyber criminals. The anonymity provided by the digital realm, coupled with the potential for large-scale financial rewards, attracts a diverse range of actors, from individual hackers to organized cyber crime syndicates. The financial motivation not only fuels the frequency of attacks but also drives cyber criminals to invest in developing more advanced and persistent threats.

This dynamic and expansive cyber threat landscape necessitates an urgent and comprehensive response. Traditional security approaches, often reliant on static and rule-based systems, struggle to keep pace with the evolving tactics of cyber criminals. Hence, the search for innovative solutions has reached above the threshold of urgency.

Evolving Attack Vectors

Beyond traditional forms of cyber threats, the attack vectors themselves are evolving. Cybercriminals are increasingly utilizing the capabilities of sophisticated techniques such as supply chain attacks, where malicious actors infiltrate trusted vendors or service providers to compromise downstream targets. The rise of fileless malware, which operates in-memory and leaves minimal traces, poses a significant challenge to conventional detection methods. The need for a comprehensive cybersecurity strategy that is capable of catering to both internal system vulnerabilities and external threats is highlighted by these dynamic attack vectors.

Nation-State Actors and Cyber Warfare

The involvement of nation-state actors in cyber warfare introduces a geopolitical dimension to the cyber threat landscape. State-sponsored attacks, often characterized by their advanced capabilities and strategic objectives, pose unique challenges to global cybersecurity. The theft of intellectual property, disruption of critical infrastructure, and influence campaigns are some manifestations of state-sponsored cyber activities.

Rise of Insider Threats

While external threats garner significant attention, the risk of insider threats is on the rise. Insiders, whether intentional or unwitting, can pose a substantial risk to organizations. Disgruntled employees, negligent actions, or unintentional sharing of sensitive information can lead to data breaches and compromises.

Human-Centric Cyber Threats

Social engineering attacks, which manipulate human psychology to exploit individuals or gain unauthorized access, continue to be a prevalent and evolving threat. Phishing, pretexting, and other forms of social engineering prey on human vulnerabilities, making them challenging to prevent solely through technical measures. In essence, addressing the contemporary surge in cyber threats requires a nuanced understanding of the interconnected factors driving this escalation. The perpetual evolution of cyber threats directs the need for an adaptive security posture, with machine learning and AI playing a pivotal role in shaping the future of cybersecurity.

8.1.3 Need for Advanced Detection Mechanism

Dynamic Nature of Threats

The rapid evolution of cyber threats requires a departure from static detection systems that rely on predefined signatures. Traditional methods, based on known patterns or signatures of malicious activity, face limitations in identifying novel and complex threats. Cybercriminals continually adapt and modify their tactics, rendering signature-based systems less effective against emerging threats. Advanced detection mechanisms must possess the agility to recognize and respond to previously unseen attack vectors, emphasizing the need for dynamic and proactive approaches.

For instance, study-based ensemble techniques (SVM, ANN, KNN, LR, DT, RF) proved highly fruitful in raising the security of Intrusion Detection Systems (or IDS). A remarkable conclusion was the ability recognized in averting serious breaches in the Internet of Things infrastructure, it may provide profound insights that might lead to the creation of an almost impenetrable intrusion detection system in the future.

Zero-Day Vulnerabilities

The prevalence of zero-day vulnerabilities, undisclosed and unpatched by software vendors, poses a significant challenge to conventional security measures. Cybercriminals exploit these vulnerabilities to launch attacks before security patches are developed and deployed. Traditional signature-based systems struggle to detect and mitigate zero-day exploits due to their reliance on known patterns. Advanced detection mechanisms, particularly those driven by machine learning and AI, excel in identifying anomalous behavior and patterns, offering a proactive defense against zero-day vulnerabilities.

A recent study showcased the innovation brought out by the use of ensemble machine learning techniques for zero-day malware classification, specifically, the Random Forest Algorithm proved a noteworthy delivery of precision. The result also yielded 95% accuracy and 3.8% error rate.

Behavioral Anomalies

Machine learning and AI introduce a behavioral analysis paradigm that goes beyond static signatures. By learning from historical data, these technologies can discern normal patterns of behavior within a system or network. Deviations from these established baselines trigger alerts, enabling the detection of anomalies that may indicate a potential security threat. This behavioral approach is particularly effective in identifying subtle and nuanced attack patterns that might go unnoticed by traditional signature-based systems.

It was established by a 2024 study that enhancing the network defense capabilities, particularly in the case of IoT, ML algorithms' characteristics have been thoroughly examined, and the results show that they can improve danger perception, response, and adaptability.

Adaptive and Self-Learning Systems

The adaptive nature of machine learning and AI enables security systems to evolve alongside the evolving threat landscape. Unlike static systems that require constant updates to incorporate new signatures, machine learning algorithms can autonomously adapt to emerging threats. These self-learning systems continually refine their models based on new data, enhancing their ability to detect and respond to novel cyber threats without manual intervention. This adaptability is crucial in a cyber landscape where the only constant is change.

New insights were drawn by a study that aimed at securing cyber-physical systems (or CPS) using Federated Machine Learning Technology. It was shown that CPS may become self-adaptive without jeopardizing the privacy and security of sensitive data by using a federated method. This design provided a viable route for the creation of safe and self-adjusting CPS.

8.2 OVERVIEW OF CYBER CRIME DETECTION

8.2.1 Traditional Approaches to Cyber Crime Detection

Cyber crime detection, in its early stages, heavily leaned on traditional approaches, primarily anchored by signature-based methods. These methods, rooted in the identification of known malicious patterns, have been foundational to the cybersecurity landscape. The two mainstays of traditional cyber crime detection are signature-based detection and rule-based systems.

Signature-Based Detection

Signature-based detection relies on predefined signatures or patterns associated with known cyber threats. These signatures are akin to digital fingerprints of malicious code or activities that have been previously identified and cataloged. When a security system encounters a file or behavior matching one of these signatures, it raises an alert or takes predefined actions, such as blocking the potential threat. While effective against known threats, signature-based detection systems struggle when confronted with new or evolving variants of malicious code.

Rule-Based Systems

Rule-based systems, another traditional approach, employ predefined rules or criteria to identify suspicious behavior within a network or system. These rules are typically crafted based on anticipated patterns of malicious activity. For example, a rule may specify that a certain number of failed login attempts within a specific time frame triggers an alert. While rule-based systems provide a level of customization and flexibility, they are inherently limited by their static nature. Adapting to emerging threats or unforeseen attack vectors requires manual intervention to update and create new rules, making them less effective in dynamic cyber environments.

Limitations of Traditional Approaches

Cyber crime detection has historically relied on traditional approaches, predominantly characterized by signature-based methods. Signature-based detection involves the use of predefined patterns or signatures to identify known malicious code or activities. Additionally, rule-based systems are employed to set criteria for identifying suspicious behavior. While these methods have been the cornerstone of cybersecurity for years, the evolving nature of cyber threats necessitates a re-evaluation of these traditional approaches.

Struggle to Keep Pace with Rapid Evolution

The struggle of signature-based systems to keep pace with the rapid evolution of cyber threats is a fundamental challenge in contemporary cybersecurity. This section delves deeper into the dynamics of this struggle, emphasizing the inherent limitations of relying on predefined patterns or signatures of known malicious code.

a. Dynamic Tactics of Cyber Criminals: Cybercriminals operate in an environment characterized by constant innovation and adaptation. They employ dynamic tactics, swiftly adjusting their strategies to exploit vulnerabilities and evade detection. As a result, new variants of malware can emerge rapidly, each with unique characteristics designed to bypass traditional security measures.
b. Identification and Cataloging Process: The process of identifying, cataloging, and disseminating signatures for each new threat is a time-consuming endeavor. Security experts must analyze the characteristics of the new malware, extract its unique signature, and then disseminate this information to security systems across the network. This manual or semi-manual process introduces a considerable

time lag between the identification of a new threat and the deployment of updated signatures to detect it.

c. Inherent Lag and Vulnerability Window: The inherent lag in updating signatures creates a vulnerability window during which systems remain exposed to new and emerging threats. Cybercriminals capitalize on this delay, taking advantage of the time it takes for security systems to catch up with their latest tactics. This exploitation window provides cyber adversaries with an opportunity to launch successful attacks before security defenses can adapt to the evolving threat landscape.

Vulnerability to Polymorphic Malware

The vulnerability of signature-based systems to polymorphic malware highlights a significant weakness in traditional cybersecurity approaches. Polymorphic malware, characterized by its ability to dynamically alter its code, poses a formidable challenge that traditional signature-based systems struggle to effectively address.

a. Dynamic Code Alteration: Polymorphic malware possesses the capability to dynamically change its code while retaining its malicious functionality. This dynamic alteration occurs each time the malware replicates or moves to a new system, resulting in a diverse set of code variants. As a result, each instance of polymorphic malware may appear different, making it challenging for signature-based systems to recognize and categorize these constantly evolving iterations.
b. Evading Signature Recognition: Traditional signature-based systems rely on recognizing specific patterns or signatures associated with known threats. However, the ever-changing nature of polymorphic malware ensures that each variant possesses a unique signature. As a consequence, the static nature of signature-based detection becomes a vulnerability, as it cannot adapt quickly enough to identify and catalog the myriad variations produced by polymorphic malware.
c. Continuous Adaptation by Cybercriminals: Cybercriminals leverage polymorphic malware precisely because of its ability to thwart traditional signature-based defenses. By continuously modifying the code structure, cyber adversaries can create an almost infinite number of variations, each capable of evading detection by signature-based systems. This adaptability empowers cybercriminals to stay ahead in the arms race against cybersecurity measures, perpetuating a constant challenge for defenders.

Susceptibility to Zero-Day Vulnerabilities

The susceptibility of traditional cyber crime detection systems to zero-day vulnerabilities underscores a critical weakness in their ability to protect against emerging threats. Zero-day vulnerabilities representing exploits for which no known signature or rule exists, pose a significant challenge for signature-based systems.

a. Definition of Zero-Day Vulnerabilities: Zero-day vulnerabilities are flaws or weaknesses in software, hardware, or applications that are unknown to the vendor or developers. The term "zero-day" indicates that the vulnerability is exploited by cybercriminals on the same day it is discovered, providing no opportunity for the development and distribution of patches or updates.
b. Inability to Recognize Unseen Threats: Signature-based systems rely on predefined patterns or signatures to identify known malicious code. However, when confronted with zero-day vulnerabilities, where there is no prior knowledge or signature available, these systems are rendered ineffective. Since they cannot recognize previously unseen threats, zero-day exploits can bypass traditional detection measures without triggering alerts.
c. Exploitation of the Detection Gap: Cybercriminals are well aware of the detection gap presented by zero-day vulnerabilities. They actively exploit this window of opportunity to launch sophisticated and often devastating attacks. By leveraging unknown vulnerabilities, attackers can infiltrate systems, compromise data, and execute malicious activities without fear of immediate detection by signature-based systems.

8.2.2 Introduction to Machine Learning and AI in Cyber Crime Detection

Traditional cyber security measures, reliant on static signature-based detection systems, face significant challenges in addressing the dynamic nature of modern cyber threats. This section underscores the limitations of conventional approaches and introduces the transformative potential of machine learning (ML) and artificial intelligence (AI) in revolutionizing cyber crime detection mechanisms.

The Transformative Role of Machine Learning

Machine learning, a subset of artificial intelligence, empowers systems to learn from data, recognize patterns, and make predictions or decisions without explicit programming. In the context of cyber crime detection, ML algorithms can analyze vast datasets, identify anomalies, and continuously evolve to recognize new and emerging threats.

Machine learning algorithms prove their worth, especially in the context of the detection of patterns that are often not apparent through traditional rule-based systems. By analyzing historical and real-time data, ML models can discern normal behavior from potential threats, enhancing the ability to detect anomalies indicative of cyberattacks.

Leveraging Artificial Intelligence for Adaptive Defense

Artificial intelligence, encompassing machine learning, and other advanced techniques offers a paradigm shift in cyber crime detection. AI systems can go beyond rule-based approaches, dynamically adapting to evolving cyber threats by learning from the ever-changing digital landscape.

AI-driven cyber defense systems leverage advanced analytics, anomaly detection, and predictive modeling to identify and mitigate threats in real time. These systems are always picking up new information, which helps them become more adept at detecting threats and providing a proactive defense against new ones.

Enhancing Threat Intelligence with Machine Learning

Machine learning enhances threat intelligence by automating the analysis of massive datasets, extracting relevant patterns, and predicting potential threats. By integrating ML into threat intelligence platforms, organizations can gain actionable insights and early warnings about evolving cyber threats.

Machine learning algorithms excel at processing and analyzing large volumes of data, enabling the identification of subtle patterns indicative of malicious activities. This capability enhances the effectiveness of threat intelligence, allowing organizations to respond swiftly to emerging threats and vulnerabilities.

Real-Time Detection and Response

One of the key advantages of machine learning and artificial intelligence in cyber crime detection is their ability to operate in real time. These technologies enable the immediate identification of anomalies, rapid threat assessment, and automated response mechanisms, reducing the time window for potential cyberattacks.

8.3 TYPES OF CYBER CRIME

Cyber crime manifests in various forms, targeting individuals, organizations, governments, and societal structures. This chapter provides an in-depth

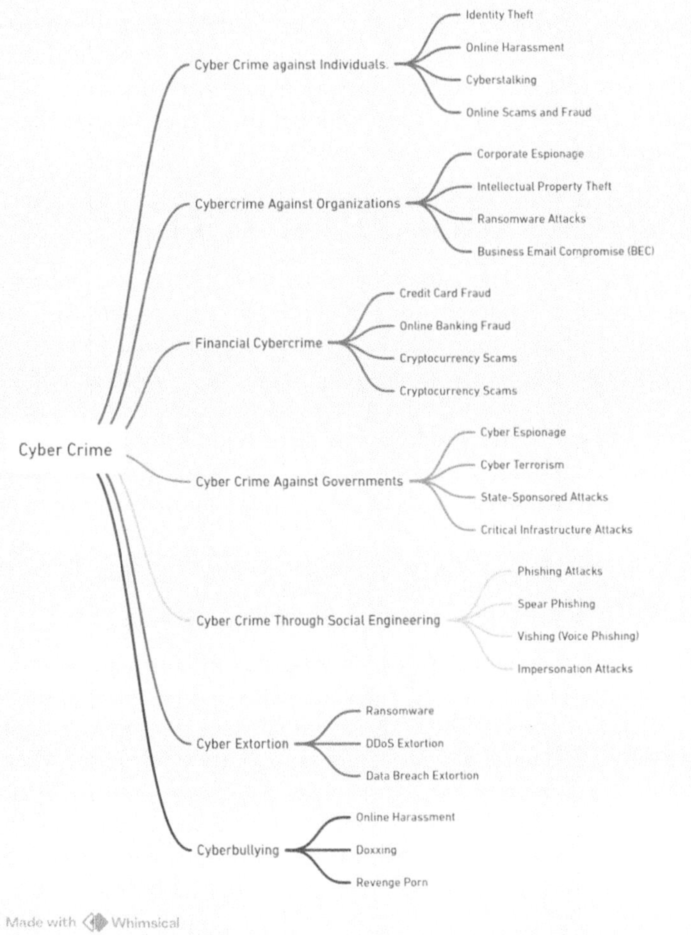

Figure 8.1 Types of Cyber Crime.

exploration of diverse cybercriminal activities, categorizing them based on their primary targets and methodologies (see Figure 8.1).

8.3.1 Cyber Crime Against Individuals

Cyber crime against individuals refers to illegal activities carried out in the digital realm with the specific intent of targeting and causing harm to individual people.

Identity Theft

Identity theft occurs when cybercriminals gain unauthorized access to personal information, such as social security numbers, credit card details, or bank account information, with the intent to commit fraudulent activities.

- Methods:
  - Phishing: Cybercriminals may fool people into sending sensitive information by sending them misleading emails or texts.
  - Data Breaches: Hackers target organizations to obtain large datasets containing personal information.
- Consequences:
  - Financial Loss: Stolen information can be used to make unauthorized transactions or open fraudulent accounts.
  - Emotional Distress: Victims may experience anxiety, fear, and frustration due to the violation of their privacy.

Online Harassment

Online harassment involves the use of digital platforms to intimidate, bully, or threaten individuals, causing emotional distress.

- Forms:
  - Cyberbullying: Harassment, often repetitive, through various online channels.
  - Hate Speech: Targeted abusive language based on factors like race, gender, or religion.
- Consequences:
  - Psychological Impact: Victims may suffer from anxiety, depression, or other mental health issues.
  - Social Isolation: Harassment can lead individuals to withdraw from online and offline social activities.

Cyberstalking

Cyberstalking is the persistent and unwanted online pursuit or monitoring of an individual, causing fear or distress.

- Methods:
  - Monitoring Online Activities: Stalkers may track an individual's online presence, including social media, emails, and location data.
  - Anonymous Threats: Stalkers may use digital platforms to send threats or intimidating messages.

Consequences:
- Fear and Anxiety: Victims may live in constant fear due to the invasion of their privacy.
- Impact on Daily Life: Cyberstalking can disrupt daily routines and cause emotional turmoil.

Online Scams and Fraud

Online scams and fraud involve deceiving individuals through various schemes to extract sensitive information or financial assets.

Examples:
- Phishing Scams: Fake emails or websites mimic legitimate entities to trick individuals into revealing personal information.
- Fake Online Sales: Fraudulent websites offering products or services with the intention of stealing payment information.

Consequences:
- Financial Loss: Individuals may lose money through unauthorized transactions or by purchasing non-existent goods/services.
- Trust Erosion: Victims may become skeptical of online transactions, impacting their confidence in digital platforms.

8.3.2 Cyber Crime Against Organizations

Organizations are prime targets for cybercriminals seeking to exploit vulnerabilities in digital infrastructure, compromise sensitive information, and disrupt operations. The following subsections provide a more in-depth look at different types of cyber crimes against organizations:

Corporate Espionage

Corporate espionage involves clandestine activities aimed at acquiring confidential information, trade secrets, or intellectual property from a targeted organization. This form of cyber crime is often driven by economic motives, with competitors or foreign entities seeking a competitive advantage.

Methods:
- Insider Threats: Employees, contractors, or associates with access to sensitive information may betray the organization.
- Hacking and Infiltration: External actors may employ advanced cyber techniques to infiltrate organizational networks and systems.

Consequences:
- Loss of Competitive Edge: Stolen information can be used by competitors, eroding the victim organization's market position.

Financial Impact: The organization may face financial repercussions due to the compromise of valuable business strategies or proprietary data.

Intellectual Property Theft

Intellectual property theft involves the unauthorized acquisition and use of an organization's proprietary information, inventions, or creative works. This cyber crime poses a severe threat to an organization's innovation, competitiveness, and market standing.

Methods:
- Cyber Intrusions: Hackers may breach organizational systems to access and steal intellectual property.
- Insider Collaboration: Employees or contractors may collude with external entities to exploit intellectual property.

Consequences:
- Market Devaluation: Stolen intellectual property flooding the market can devalue the original creator's innovations.
- Innovation Setbacks: Organizations may experience setbacks in research and development efforts.

Ransomware Attacks

Ransomware attacks are a pervasive form of cyber crime where malicious actors encrypt an organization's data and demand payment (usually in cryptocurrency) for its release. These attacks pose a significant threat to data integrity, operational continuity, and financial stability.

Methods:
- Phishing: Employees may unknowingly download malware through deceptive emails or messages.
- Exploiting Vulnerabilities: Hackers may exploit weaknesses in software or network security to deploy ransomware.

Consequences:
- Data Loss: Organizations may lose access to critical data, impacting daily operations.
- Financial Extortion: Paying the ransom does not guarantee data recovery, and organizations may incur financial losses.

Business Email Compromise (BEC)

Business Email Compromise involves unauthorized access to and manipulation of email accounts within an organization. Cybercriminals exploit compromised accounts for fraudulent activities, often involving financial transactions or deceptive communication.

Methods:
Phishing and Social Engineering: Perpetrators trick employees into revealing login credentials through deceptive tactics.
Email Spoofing: Manipulating email headers to make messages appear legitimate.
Consequences:
Financial Fraud: Compromised email accounts can lead to unauthorized fund transfers or other fraudulent financial activities.
Reputation Damage: Misuse of email accounts for deceptive communication can harm the organization's reputation.
Mitigation Strategies:
Cybersecurity Awareness Training: Educate employees on recognizing and avoiding cyber threats.
Regular System Updates: Keep software and security systems up to date to address vulnerabilities.
Multi-Factor Authentication (MFA): Implement MFA to enhance access security.
Incident Response Plans: Develop and regularly test plans to respond effectively to cyber incidents.
Collaboration with Cybersecurity Experts: Work with professionals to assess and improve organizational cybersecurity measures.

8.3.3 Financial Cyber Crime

Financial cyber crime involves illicit activities targeting digital financial systems with the primary aim of monetary gains. Here are specific forms of financial cyber crime:

Credit Card Fraud

Credit card fraud occurs when unauthorized transactions are made using stolen credit card information, leading to financial losses for individuals and financial institutions.

Methods:
Skimming: Malicious devices capture card information during legitimate transactions.
Phishing: Fraudsters trick individuals into revealing credit card details through deceptive means.
Consequences:
Financial Loss: Individuals and banks may suffer monetary losses.

Identity Theft: Stolen credit card information may lead to broader identity theft issues.

Online Banking Fraud

Online banking fraud targets individuals and organizations, exploiting vulnerabilities in digital banking systems to gain unauthorized access or conduct fraudulent transactions.

Methods:
- Phishing: Cybercriminals use deceptive emails or websites to obtain login credentials.
- Malware Attacks: Malicious software may compromise devices, enabling unauthorized access to online banking.

Consequences:
- Unauthorized Transactions: Illicit access can lead to unauthorized fund transfers or other financial activities.
- Loss of Trust: Individuals and organizations may lose trust in digital banking systems.

Cryptocurrency Scams

Cryptocurrency scams exploit the decentralized and pseudonymous nature of cryptocurrencies for fraudulent schemes, misleading investors or stealing digital assets.

Methods:
- Ponzi Schemes: Fraudulent investment schemes promise high returns but are unsustainable.
- Phishing: Cybercriminals use fake websites or emails to trick users into revealing private keys.

Consequences:
- Financial Loss: Investors may lose funds invested in fraudulent schemes.
- Market Manipulation: Scams can lead to market volatility and impact the reputation of cryptocurrencies.

8.3.4 Cyber Crime Against Governments

Governments face unique cyber threats that can compromise national security and critical infrastructure. Here are various forms of cyber crime against governments:

Cyber Espionage

Cyber espionage involves the covert gathering of classified or sensitive information for political, military, or economic purposes. State and non-state actors engage in espionage activities.

- Methods:
  - Malware Attacks: Cyber spies may use sophisticated malware to infiltrate government networks.
  - Social Engineering: Deceptive tactics target individuals with access to sensitive information.
- Consequences:
  - National Security Threat: Stolen information can compromise strategic interests.
  - Diplomatic Tensions: Espionage activities can strain international relations.

Cyber Terrorism

Cyber terrorism employs digital attacks to create fear, disrupt essential services, or advance ideological goals. These attacks pose a direct threat to national security.

- Methods:
  - Denial of Service (DoS) Attacks: Overloading systems to disrupt services.
  - Critical Infrastructure Targeting: Attacks on power grids, communication networks, or transportation systems.
- Consequences:
  - Fear and Panic: Cyber terrorism aims to create public fear and panic.
  - Disruption of Services: Attacks can lead to significant disruptions in essential services.

State-Sponsored Attacks

State-sponsored attacks are orchestrated by governments to compromise the information systems of other nations, often for political, economic, or military reasons.

- Methods:
  - Advanced Persistent Threats (APTs): Long-term, targeted attacks to gain unauthorized access.
  - Propaganda and Disinformation: Spreading false information to manipulate public opinion.

Consequences:

International Tensions: State-sponsored attacks can lead to diplomatic and geopolitical tensions.

Economic Espionage: Stolen economic or trade-related information can impact nations' economies.

Critical Infrastructure Attacks

Critical infrastructure attacks target essential systems, such as power grids or transportation networks, posing significant risks to national security and public safety.

Methods:

SCADA System Exploitation: Manipulating Supervisory Control and Data Acquisition systems.

Physical and Cyber Hybrid Attacks: Combining cyberattacks with physical damage.

Consequences:

Public Safety Risk: Disruption to critical infrastructure can pose direct risks to public safety.

Economic Impact: Attacks on critical systems can have severe economic consequences.

8.3.5 Cyber Crime Through Social Engineering

Social engineering exploits human psychology to manipulate individuals into divulging confidential information.

Phishing Attacks

Phishing attacks deceive people into divulging important information by using phony emails, texts, or websites.

Spear Phishing

Spear phishing is a targeted form of phishing, tailored for specific individuals or organizations, often using personalized information to enhance credibility.

Vishing (Voice Phishing)

Vishing involves using voice communication, typically over phone calls, to deceive individuals into providing sensitive information.

Impersonation Attacks

Impersonation attacks involve the fraudulent posing as a trustworthy entity to deceive individuals into taking harmful actions or divulging information.

8.3.6 Cyber Extortion

Cyber extortion involves coercive tactics to extract money or assets through digital means.

Ransomware

Cyber extortion in the form of ransomware encrypts data and demands money to unlock it, presenting a serious risk to both people and organizations.

DDoS Extortion

DDoS extortion involves threatening to launch a distributed denial of service (DDoS) attack unless a ransom is paid, disrupting online services.

Data Breach Extortion

Data breach extortion involves threatening to expose or sell stolen sensitive data unless a ransom is paid, exploiting the fear of reputational damage.

8.3.7 Cyberbullying

Cyberbullying leverages digital platforms to harass or intimidate individuals.

Online Harassment

Online harassment, a subset of cyberbullying, involves persistent and harmful behavior intended to distress or harm individuals through digital channels.

Doxxing

Doxxing is the malicious act of publicly revealing private or personal information about an individual, often with the intent to harass or cause harm.

Revenge Porn

Revenge porn involves the non-consensual sharing of intimate or explicit images with the intent to harm, embarrass, or coerce individuals.

8.4 MACHINE LEARNING MODELS IN CYBER CRIME DETECTION

Cyber crime encompasses a broad spectrum of illicit activities, including but not limited to data breaches, malware attacks, identity theft, and financial fraud. Traditional rule-based systems and signature-based detection methods have proven inadequate in dealing with the dynamic and polymorphic nature of contemporary cyber threats. ML has become a cornerstone in the development of intelligent systems capable of learning from data and making informed decisions.

8.4.1 Supervised Learning in Cyber Crime Detection

Supervised learning forms the backbone of many machine learning applications, including those in cybersecurity. The essence of supervised learning lies in training models on labeled datasets, where each input is associated with a corresponding output. In the context of cyber crime detection, this means exposing the model to instances of both normal and malicious behavior, allowing it to learn the characteristics that distinguish between the two.

Support Vector Machines for Anomaly Detection

Support Vector Machines (SVMs) have emerged as a popular choice for anomaly detection in cybersecurity. Anomaly detection involves identifying patterns or instances that deviate significantly from the norm, which is crucial for detecting novel cyber threats. SVMs excel in this task by constructing hyperplanes that maximize the margin between different classes, effectively separating normal behavior from anomalies.

Decision Trees for Malware Classification

Decision Trees offer another powerful approach within the supervised learning framework, with applications in the classification of malware. Malware, encompassing a diverse array of malicious software, poses a significant threat to cybersecurity. Detecting and classifying malware is a complex task, often requiring the analysis of various features and behaviors exhibited by the software.

Applications of Supervised Learning in Cybersecurity

Intrusion Detection Systems (IDS). Supervised learning models, including SVMs and Decision Trees, find extensive applications in Intrusion Detection Systems (IDS). These systems monitor network traffic, user activities, and system logs to identify anomalous patterns that may indicate unauthorized access or potential cyber threats. The ability of supervised learning models to discern normal behavior from anomalies enhances the efficiency of IDS, providing a proactive defense against cyber intrusions.

Phishing Detection. Phishing attacks, where adversaries attempt to deceive individuals into divulging sensitive information, are prevalent in the cyber landscape. Supervised learning models can be trained to recognize patterns associated with phishing emails or websites. By learning from labeled datasets that distinguish between legitimate and phishing communication, these models contribute to the identification and mitigation of phishing threats.

Behavioral Analysis. Supervised learning is instrumental in behavioral analysis, where the focus is on understanding patterns of user behavior. By training models on labeled datasets that include both normal and potentially malicious activities, cybersecurity professionals can develop models capable of detecting deviations from established behavioral norms. This is particularly valuable for identifying insider threats and detecting unauthorized access to sensitive information.

Challenges and Considerations

While supervised learning has proven to be a potent tool in cyber crime detection, it is not without its challenges. The effectiveness of supervised learning models heavily relies on the quality and representativeness of the labeled datasets. As cyber threats continue to evolve, maintaining up-to-date and diverse datasets becomes crucial for ensuring the adaptability of these models.

Additionally, the interpretability of models, especially in the case of complex algorithms like SVMs or deep learning models, poses a challenge. Understanding how a model arrives at a particular decision is critical for cybersecurity professionals to trust and act upon its predictions. Striking a balance between model complexity and interpretability is an ongoing consideration in the deployment of supervised learning for cyber crime detection.

8.4.2 Unsupervised Learning in Cyber Crime Detection

The escalating sophistication of cyber threats necessitates innovative approaches to detection and mitigation. Unsupervised learning, a paradigm within machine learning, offers a promising avenue in cyber crime detection by allowing systems to discern patterns and anomalies without relying on labeled datasets. Unsupervised learning involves training models on unlabeled datasets, aiming to discover inherent patterns, structures, or relationships within the data. In the context of cybersecurity, where the landscape is dynamic and new threats constantly emerge, unsupervised learning provides a flexible and adaptive approach to anomaly detection and threat identification.

Clustering Algorithms in Cyber Crime Detection

One prominent application of unsupervised learning in cybersecurity is through clustering algorithms. Clustering groups together similar data points based on inherent similarities without prior knowledge of the classes or labels. K-means clustering, hierarchical clustering, and DBSCAN (Density-Based Spatial Clustering of Applications with Noise) are widely utilized in cyber threat analysis.

Dimensionality Reduction Techniques

Unsupervised learning also leverages dimensionality reduction techniques to uncover hidden structures in high-dimensional data, a common characteristic in cybersecurity datasets. Principal Component Analysis and t-SNE are some popular techniques.

Challenges in Unsupervised Learning for Cyber Crime Detection:

Ambiguity and Interpretability. Unsupervised learning models may produce clusters or patterns that are quite complicated to interpret. Understanding the meaning and implications of these patterns requires domain expertise, and the ambiguity of results can hinder decision-making in real-time cyber threat scenarios.

Noise and False Positives. Unsupervised learning models may be sensitive to noise or outliers in the data, leading to false positives. Discriminating between genuine anomalies and noise is a constant challenge, and refining models to reduce false positives is an ongoing area of research.

Scalability and Resource Intensity. Some unsupervised learning algorithms, especially those involving clustering or dimensionality reduction, may be computationally intensive. Ensuring scalability and efficiency in processing large volumes of data in real time is a critical consideration for the deployment of unsupervised learning in cybersecurity systems.

8.4.3 Deep Learning in Cyber Crime Detection

Cyber crime has become an escalating global concern, necessitating innovative and advanced technologies to bolster cybersecurity defenses. Deep learning, a subset of machine learning (ML), has emerged as a transformative force in the field of cyber crime detection. This essay delves into the realm of deep learning, exploring its applications, strengths, and challenges in the context of identifying and mitigating cyber threats.

Convolutional Neural Networks (CNNs) in Image-Based Threat Detection

One notable application of deep learning in cybersecurity is the use of Convolutional Neural Networks (CNNs) for image-based threat detection. As cyber threats increasingly involve visual elements, such as phishing attacks embedded in images, CNNs excel at automatically learning relevant features.

Recurrent Neural Networks (RNNs) for Malware Analysis

Malware, a persistent and diverse cyber threat, requires sophisticated analysis techniques. Recurrent Neural Networks (RNNs) are well-suited for this task due to their ability to capture sequential dependencies in data. In the context of malware analysis, RNNs can analyze code sequences, system call patterns, or network traffic flows to identify malicious behavior.

Natural Language Processing (NLP) in Cyber Threat Intelligence

Sifting through massive volumes of textual data, including security reports, blogs, and forums, is a common task for cyber threat intelligence. Deep learning models have been shown to be effective at removing relevant information from unstructured text, especially when they use natural language processing (NLP) approaches. Tasks such as topic modeling, entity identification, and sentiment analysis are mastered by NLP-driven deep-learning models.

Challenges and Considerations

While deep learning holds immense promise in cyber crime detection, it is not without challenges. The following considerations shed light on some of the hurdles that researchers and cybersecurity professionals face in deploying and optimizing deep learning models:

Data Privacy and Ethical Concerns. Models for deep learning, especially those developed on big datasets, may inadvertently capture sensitive information. Striking a balance between effective cyber crime detection and respecting data privacy is crucial. Ethical considerations surrounding the use of deep learning in cybersecurity, especially in handling personally identifiable information, must be addressed to ensure responsible and transparent practices.

Interpretable Models. The interpretability of deep neural networks is often compromised by their inherent complexity, which makes it difficult to comprehend the reasoning behind a model's decision. Interpretability is crucial for cybersecurity because it helps people trust the system and recognize signs of compromise. This problem is being addressed by efforts to create explainable AI (XAI) techniques.

Adversarial Attacks. Adversarial attacks involve manipulating input data to deceive the model into making incorrect predictions. Deep learning models, including CNNs and RNNs, can be susceptible to such attacks. Cyber adversaries may exploit vulnerabilities in the model's architecture to evade detection. Developing robust models that are resilient to adversarial attacks is an ongoing area of research in deep learning for cybersecurity.

8.5 FEATURE ENGINEERING AND DATA PREPROCESSING

As discussed in the above section, ML models play a crucial role in cyber crime detection and prevention. But the effectiveness of these models depends not only on the choice of algorithms but also on the quality of the input data. Feature engineering, data preprocessing, and handling imbalanced datasets are critical aspects of preparing data for machine learning applications in cyber crime detection. Studying the importance of feature selection, strategies for handling imbalanced datasets, and techniques for data augmentation, with a focus on enhancing the performance of machine learning models in the domain of cyber crime detection, is crucial to developing state-of-the-art algorithms and systems that can tackle a wide variety of cyber crimes.

8.5.1 Importance of Feature Selection

Feature selection is a crucial step in the process of building machine learning models for cyber crime detection. In this context, features refer to the attributes or variables that the model uses to make predictions. The goal of feature selection is to identify and retain the most relevant features while discarding irrelevant or redundant ones. This process serves several purposes, including improving model interpretability, reducing computational complexity, and enhancing the model's generalization performance.

Lyu et al. (2023), in their paper on surveying the various feature selection techniques for modeling ML algorithms for cyber crime detection, state that there are various techniques that are widely used, but broadly they can be classified as Filter-based, Wrapper based, Embedded and some hybrid techniques combining the benefits of all these methodologies.

8.5.2 Handling Imbalanced Datasets

Imbalanced datasets, where one class significantly outnumbers the others, pose a common challenge in cyber crime detection. Models trained on such data may exhibit a bias towards the majority class, leading to suboptimal performance in detecting instances of the minority class (typically representing cyberattacks). Addressing this issue requires specialized techniques to balance the class distribution and ensure that the model learns from both the majority and minority classes.

One approach to handling imbalanced datasets is through resampling techniques. These techniques involve either oversampling the minority class, undersampling the majority class, or a combination of both. Oversampling methods, such as Synthetic Minority Over-sampling Technique (SMOTE), generate synthetic instances of the minority class to balance the class distribution. Under-sampling, on the other hand, involves removing instances from the majority class to achieve a balanced dataset.

8.5.3 Data Augmentation Techniques

Data augmentation is a technique commonly employed to enhance the diversity of the training dataset by artificially creating variations of existing data. In the context of cyber crime detection, data augmentation can be particularly valuable, as it helps the model generalize better to unseen instances and increases its robustness to different attack scenarios.

For cyber crime datasets, data augmentation may involve introducing variations in network traffic patterns, altering timestamps, or injecting synthetic instances of known attack patterns. This not only helps in creating a more comprehensive training set but also aids the model in learning the underlying patterns of cyberattacks.

Techniques such as rotation, flipping, and zooming, commonly used in image data augmentation, can be adapted to non-image datasets. Additionally, temporal data in cyber crime detection, such as the sequence of network events, can benefit from time-based augmentations, like time warping or time series synthesis.

MacDermott et al. (2022) stated that their work on Detection social media trolls used analysis of social media dataset and textual data. So advance Natural language Processing (NLP) techniques were employed. In order to better enhance the dataset and increase the number of training samples, word embeddings using standard GloVe technique improved the data and led to better performance of models.

8.6 CHALLENGES IN CYBER CRIME DETECTION WITH ML

In the digital era, the expertise of cybercriminals rises in tandem with technological advancements. Strong cyber crime detection systems are thus becoming more and more important. While machine learning (ML) has become an effective technique for detecting and averting cyberattacks, using ML for the detection of cyber crimes presents a unique set of difficulties. Understanding and mitigating the challenges remains an area of concern for employing ML based methodologies for the purpose of cyber crime detection.

8.6.1 Adversarial Attacks

Adversarial attacks pose a serious threat to the effectiveness of machine learning models used in cyber crime detection. These attacks involve manipulating input data to deceive the model, causing it to misclassify or make incorrect predictions. In the context of cyber crime detection, adversaries may craft malicious data specifically designed to bypass ML-based security systems.

One of the primary reasons adversarial attacks are a challenge in cyber crime detection is that the attackers often have knowledge of the ML algorithms and can exploit vulnerabilities in the models. For example, in a phishing detection system, an attacker might subtly alter the features of a phishing email to make it appear benign to the ML model, leading to a false negative.

Mitigating adversarial attacks in cyber crime detection requires constant monitoring and adaptation of ML models. This includes incorporating adversarial training techniques, which involve training models on both clean and adversarial data to enhance their robustness. Regular updates to the models based on new attack patterns are also essential to stay ahead of evolving threats.

8.6.2 Interpretability and Explainability

Interpretability and explainability are critical aspects of deploying ML models in any application, and they become even more significant in the context of cyber crime detection. Understanding the decision-making process of an ML model is essential for gaining trust from users, stakeholders, and regulatory bodies.

To address this challenge, researchers and practitioners are working on developing more interpretable ML models and explaining the decisions made by complex models. Techniques such as LIME (Local Interpretable Model-agnostic Explanations) and SHAP (SHapley Additive exPlanations) aim to provide insights into model predictions. Incorporating these techniques helps security analysts understand why a particular instance is flagged as potentially malicious, improving the overall trustworthiness of the system.

Scalability and Real-Time Processing

Scalability and real-time processing are crucial considerations in the deployment of ML models for cyber crime detection, given the dynamic and rapidly evolving nature of cyber threats. Traditional ML models may struggle to handle large volumes of data in real-time, resulting in delays in identifying and responding to cyberattacks.

Addressing scalability and real-time processing challenges involves the development of efficient algorithms, optimized hardware, and distributed computing solutions. Techniques like stream processing, where data is processed in real-time as it is generated, can enhance the speed of cyber crime detection systems. Additionally, cloud-based solutions and parallel processing can contribute to scalability by distributing computational tasks across multiple nodes.

8.7 CASE STUDIES AND APPLICATIONS

8.7.1 Microsoft's Azure Sentinel

Microsoft's Azure Sentinel is a cloud-native security information and event management (SIEM) system that utilizes machine learning to analyze vast amounts of data in real time (see Figure 8.2). It helps organizations detect and respond to cyber threats more efficiently by leveraging ML algorithms to identify anomalous patterns and behaviors. Yelevin (2023) explains how Sentinel uses various different technologies to tackle cyber crime and

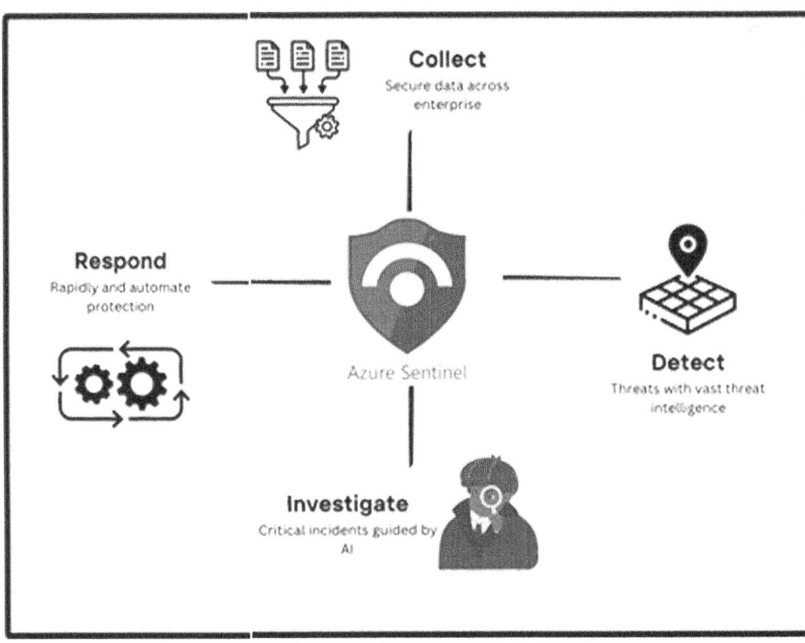

Figure 8.2 The Various Functionalities of Microsoft Azure Sentinel.

the various technological research going for further development of this sophisticated system.

Anomaly Detection. Azure Sentinel employs ML algorithms for anomaly detection, which involves identifying patterns or behaviors that deviate from the norm. By analyzing large datasets of security events and user behavior, the system can establish a baseline of normal activities. Any deviations from this baseline can be flagged as potential security incidents. This helps in the early detection of unusual or suspicious activities that might indicate a cyber threat.

User and Entity Behavior Analytics (UEBA). UEBA is a critical component of Azure Sentinel's ML capabilities. By applying ML algorithms to user and entity behavior data, the platform can identify abnormal patterns associated with user accounts or devices. For example, if a user suddenly accesses sensitive information outside of their usual working hours or from an unusual location, the system might flag this behavior for investigation.

Threat Intelligence Integration. Azure Sentinel integrates threat intelligence feeds and uses ML to analyze this information continuously. ML algorithms can identify emerging threat patterns, understand the context of threats, and provide security teams with relevant insights. This proactive approach helps organizations stay ahead of evolving cyber threats by incorporating the latest threat intelligence into their defense strategies.

Automated Threat Response. ML in Azure Sentinel supports automated threat response by enabling the creation of playbooks and workflows. When potential threats are identified, predefined automated responses can be triggered based on ML-driven decision-making. This may lessen the effect of a cyberattack and shorten the time it takes to react to occurrences.

Incident Prioritization. Azure Sentinel uses ML algorithms to prioritize security incidents based on their severity and potential impact. This helps security analysts focus on the most critical issues first, optimizing their time and resources. ML-driven incident prioritization ensures that high-priority incidents are addressed promptly, enhancing the overall efficiency of the security operations team.

Behavioral Analysis. ML models in Azure Sentinel analyze historical and real-time data to develop behavioral profiles for entities, including users and devices. This behavioral analysis enables the system to identify subtle changes or anomalies that may indicate a security threat. For instance, if a device starts communicating with an unusual set of IP addresses or exhibits unexpected network behaviors, it could be a sign of compromise.

Continuous Learning. Azure Sentinel's machine learning capabilities are based on ongoing learning from fresh data and changing threat environments. Over time, the system adjusts to environmental changes by learning from false positives and negatives and increasing its accuracy. By using an iterative learning process, the machine learning models are guaranteed to continue identifying new and complex threats.

8.7.2 Darktrace's Autonomous Response

Darktrace is a cybersecurity company that employs ML for autonomous response to cyber threats (see Figure 8.3). Its technology is designed to understand "normal" behavior within a network and autonomously respond to deviations that could signal a potential security threat. Organizations are able to quickly combat cyber threats because to this proactive strategy.

According to Darkreading (2023), Darktrace stopped a cyberattack at a global finance firm. With operations spanning many countries and total assets over $5 billion, the company use Darktrace's Self-Learning AI to quickly identify and address cyber-threats throughout the digital landscape. The AI was able to recognize the early warning indicators of new threats and automatically halt attacks that are already underway since it is continuously refining its understanding of the business's "normal" processes. As published by Pr Newswire (2020), Darktrace also won the best AI award in 2022 for its exceptional blend of AI and cyber crime detection facilities. Darktrace comes with various unique integrations that led to a sophisticated product as a culmination of emerging ML based techniques tackling cyber crimes.

Unsupervised Machine Learning. Unsupervised machine learning (ML) is used in Darktrace's system, which implies that instead of manually training

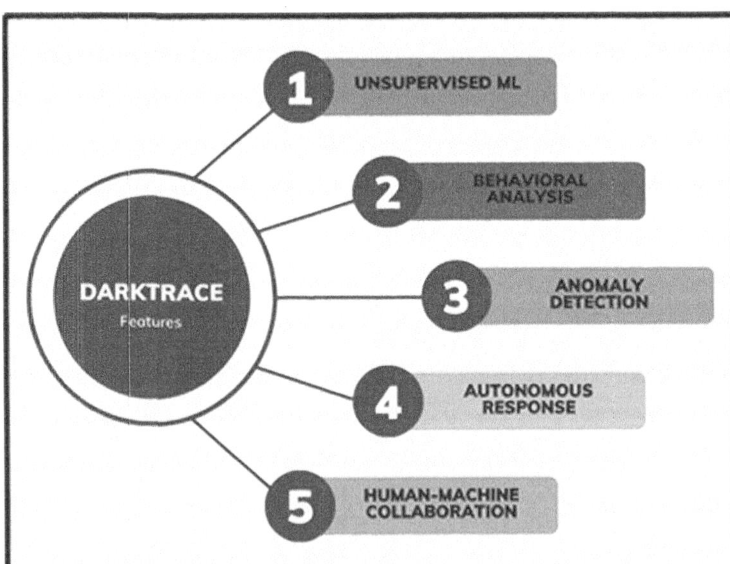

Figure 8.3 The Various Functionalities of Darktrace.

the algorithms on labeled datasets, they learn from the data itself. Unlike supervised learning, where the model is trained on historical data with labeled examples of normal and malicious behavior, unsupervised learning is more flexible and can adapt to previously unseen threats.

Behavioral Analysis. Darktrace focuses on understanding the normal behavior of entities within a network, including devices, users, and applications. It creates a baseline of what is considered "normal" for each entity based on historical data. This baseline is dynamic and continuously updated as the network environment evolves.

Anomaly Detection. The ML algorithms continuously monitor network traffic and behavior in real time. They analyze patterns and deviations from the established baseline, identifying anomalies that may indicate potential security threats. Anomalies could include unusual patterns of data access, network traffic, or deviations from typical user behavior.

Autonomous Response. One of the distinctive features of Darktrace is its Autonomous Response capability. Once a potential threat or anomaly is detected, the system can take autonomous actions to mitigate or contain the risk. These actions can include isolating compromised devices, limiting access, or even blocking certain types of traffic.

Human-Machine Collaboration. While Darktrace's Autonomous Response system can take autonomous actions, it also emphasizes collaboration with human security analysts. The system provides detailed insights and visualizations of detected threats, enabling security teams to investigate and respond effectively. Human expertise is still a crucial component in the decision-making process.

8.7.3 IBM Watson for Cyber Security

IBM Watson for Cyber Security is an AI-powered platform that leverages machine learning to analyze vast amounts of security data (see Figure 8.4). It helps security analysts identify threats, investigate incidents, and respond to cyberattacks more efficiently. The platform aims to augment human capabilities in dealing with the complexity and volume of cybersecurity data. Providing advanced features such as Threat Intelligence Integration, NLP, Anomaly Detection and many more, this is one of the promising applications of leveraging ML for cyber crime detection.

8.8 FUTURE TRENDS AND TECHNOLOGIES

As cyber threats continue to evolve in complexity and sophistication, the role of Machine Learning (ML) and Artificial Intelligence (AI) in cyber crime detection is becoming increasingly pivotal. The future scope of emerging technologies like ML in the ever-growing domain of cyber crime will be enormous.

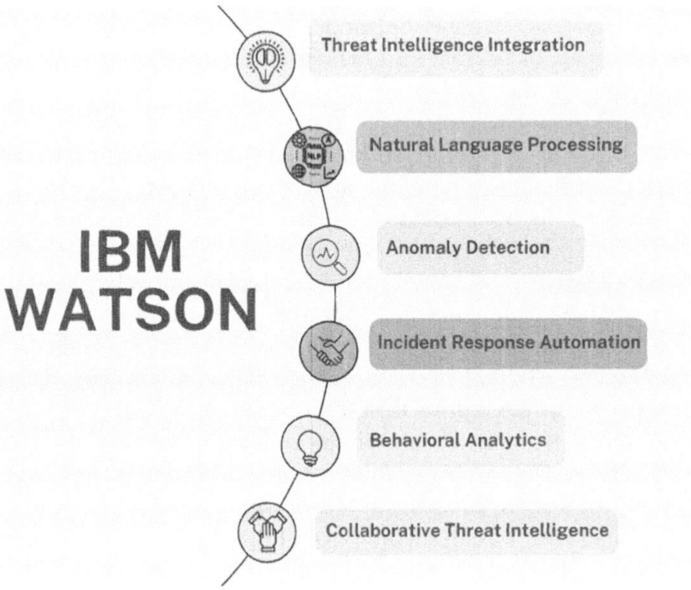

Figure 8.4 The Various Functionalities of IBM Watson.

One of the critical challenges in the adoption of AI for cybersecurity has been the lack of transparency in decision-making processes. Explainable AI (XAI) addresses this concern by enhancing the interpretability of AI models. In the future, cyber crime detection systems are likely to incorporate XAI techniques, allowing security professionals to understand how AI models arrive at specific conclusions. This transparency not only builds trust but also facilitates better collaboration between human analysts and AI systems. Sindiramutty et al. (2024) in their chapter states the need for elimination of black box AI models and need for transparency and explainability in modeling ML solutions for the purpose of cyber crime detection. Sharma et al. (2022) explains, by giving end users more faith that AI will make the best choice, XAI can enhance the user experience for services or products.

Cyber crime detection systems powered by AI and machine learning in the future will depend more and more on improved threat intelligence integration. Adaptive security measures may be greatly enhanced by using reinforcement learning, a subset of machine learning where algorithms learn by doing trial and error. Federated Learning is a decentralized machine learning technique that does not involve sharing raw data across devices or servers when models are trained on them. Federated learning may let organizations work together to enhance ML models in the context of cyber crime detection while maintaining the confidentiality and privacy of their unique datasets.

8.9 CONCLUSION

The use of artificial intelligence (AI) and machine learning (ML) in detection systems is a promising development in the continuous fight against complex threats in the ever-changing world of cyber crime. This chapter has traversed the realms of cyber crime definitions, the expanding threat landscape, and the imperative for advanced detection mechanisms. By examining traditional approaches and their limitations, we highlighted the pivotal role ML and AI play in reshaping the cybersecurity paradigm.

The taxonomy of cyber crime against individuals, organizations, governments, and through social engineering elucidates the multifaceted nature of digital threats. From identity theft to state-sponsored attacks, understanding these diverse challenges becomes imperative for crafting effective defense strategies.

Moving into the realm of ML models, this chapter delved into supervised, unsupervised, and deep learning techniques tailored for cyber crime detection. From Support Vector Machines to Convolutional Neural Networks, these models showcase the versatility of ML and AI in identifying anomalies, classifying malware, and deciphering complex patterns within vast datasets.

Feature engineering and data preprocessing emerged as crucial steps in enhancing model performance. Addressing challenges such as imbalanced datasets and leveraging data augmentation techniques underscored the importance of meticulous preparation in constructing robust cyber defense systems.

Yet, challenges persist. Adversarial attacks, interpretability concerns, and the need for real-time scalability pose hurdles in the pursuit of an infallible cyber defense. As ML models advance, so do the tactics of adversaries, necessitating continuous innovation and adaptation.

Real-world applications and case studies provided tangible insights into the efficacy of ML and AI in combating cyber threats. However, ethical considerations and privacy concerns cast a shadow on the path forward. Striking a delicate balance between security imperatives and individual privacy rights is a challenge that must be met with ethical guidelines and legal frameworks.

As we peer into the future, the chapter explores emerging trends and technologies, offering glimpses of what lies ahead in the dynamic field of cyber crime detection. The conclusion drawn is clear: collaboration, innovation, and ethical considerations will shape the trajectory of cyber security. In this complex, interconnected digital realm, the amalgamation of human intelligence with the power of machine learning and artificial intelligence provides a formidable defense against the ever-evolving landscape of cyber threats.

In closing, the integration of ML and AI in cyber crime detection not only offers a technological evolution but also prompts a paradigm shift